Crafting Writers
K–6

Crafting Writers
K–6

Elizabeth Hale

Stenhouse Publishers
Portland, Maine

KH

Stenhouse Publishers
www.stenhouse.com

Library of Congress Cataloging-in-Publication Data
Hale, Elizabeth, 1971–
    Crafting writers, K–6 / Elizabeth Hale.
    p. cm.
    Includes bibliographical references and index.
    ISBN 978-1-57110-739-8 (alk. paper)
    1. English language—Composition and exercises—Study and teaching (Elementary)—United States. I. Title.
LB1576.H215 2008
372.62'3—dc22

                  2007041422

Cover, interior design, and typesetting by Martha Drury

Manufactured in the United States of America on acid-free, recycled paper
14 13 12 11 10 09 08   9 8 7 6 5 4 3 2 1

8/25/08

To
Lucy McCormick Calkins
who planted the seed

and to

Cheryl Watson-Harris
who helped it grow

Contents

Acknowledgments

To Lucy Calkins: Even though it has been years since I was your student, my appreciation for your instruction has never faded. You were the first to show me how my two passions of writing and teaching could come together in such a meaningful way. And to Cheryl Watson-Harris: Your leadership has been an inspiration to me since my very first year in Boston. You believed in me from the start and created opportunities that allowed me to grow professionally. Thank you for all that you have done for me and for the children of Boston.

To my two other principals, Suzanne Federspiel and Rosemary Harmon: I am so lucky to work with principals I respect immensely and whose company I enjoy so much. Your vision for children is inspiring and your support and trust in my work, so appreciated. To Ann Deveney, who hired me to give my first district-wide workshop in Boston: Thank you for that first opportunity to work with teachers outside my school and for all your support thereafter. Thank you also to all the teachers in the Boston Public Schools who have taken my Introduction to Writing Workshop course: Your questions and conversations helped shape my thinking and my ability to better communicate the skills behind effective writing instruction and conferring.

Thank you to the Boston Athenaeum and the Calderwood Writing Initiative, whose generosity and support of teachers gave me a forum in which to begin this work in earnest. To the Calderwood family of teachers and writers, led by Judith Goldman: I can't think of a more positive, supportive, and enjoyable environment to make public the words and thoughts that would eventually become this book.

Annette Stavros and Sally Dias, thank you for being such advocates for me in the academic world and welcoming me into the Emmanuel College community. To my Literacy and Literacy Methods classes: I am so lucky to have such incredible students. Thank you for all your enthusiasm, and I look forward to hearing about your teaching careers.

Thank you to the teachers at the Tobin K–8, Farragut, and Thomas Kenny schools in Boston and Our Lady's School in Waltham who allowed me to use their students' writing in this book and whose teaching has been an integral part of my own growth: Eleanor Auerbach, Marian Bailey, Jessica Barry, Caitlin Gaffney, Michelle Gann, Vanessa Hargrove, Patricia Keyo, Iris Escoto, Maria Duarte, Judy Norton, Marilyn Pastor, Anna Rosa, and Rosa Verdu. A special thanks to Michelle Gulla: Collaborating with you these last few years has been such a pleasure and an asset to my own growth. I also give a special thank-you to Eli Jeremie: You are such a wonderful teacher and person, and your never-ending support for me has been irreplaceable. To Dee Watson and Helen Cooper, thank you for all your support during my first year of teaching in Boston. Your advice and encouragement that helped me get to my second year has not been forgotten.

Thank you to Thomas Payzant, former superintendent of Boston Public Schools, for your dedication to the district, both in years and quality of work. I am particularly appreciative that your support of writing workshop and its ability to affect students' enthusiasm for writing has never wavered. Thank you also to Mayor Thomas Menino for your many years of service and your dedication to the Boston schools.

To my editor, Bill Varner: I honestly can't imagine having a better experience writing a first book. Working with you has been a true pleasure, and I am grateful for all your advice that helped shape this book. I am also grateful to the wonderful team at Stenhouse, including Erin Trainer, Jay Kilburn, and Doug Kolmar, who supported this book from different angles. To Beth Lothrop and Peggy Sherman: You were both key in moving the process of this book along in the beginning, and I am grateful for your assistance.

Jacquelyn Judge, you have supported me so much from the very start, when this book was just a proposal. I'm grateful for your time, your laughter, and your friendship. To Connie Jacquays and Dyan Smiley: Your friendship, both in and out of the literacy world, has been an important part of my life in Boston. To Jean Marie Liggio, who has seen me through the highs and lows of life, and has been there for me no matter what: Your friendship is a blessing.

To Xavier Rozas: I don't think this book would have been nearly as enjoyable to write without you in my life. Hours of writing always seemed easier when I knew you were at the end of my day.

To Olivia and Joseph Landino: You have been such a gift to our family. I can't wait to see what you will write some day. To Tony Landino: It's been such a pleasure to welcome you into our family. And to Chrissy, my twin sister, my best friend: Thank you for a lifetime of friendship in which mutual admiration and laughter just seems to keep growing. Your unwavering support and love bigger than life means everything to me.

To my mom and dad, Sandy and Stan Hale: I'm not sure if "thank you" quite covers what a parent can make possible for their children, but thank you for everything. For the childhood that really was, for the opportunities in my life that are not always givens, and for the encouragement of my happiness, regardless of what avenues in life I chose to pursue.

1

Introduction

At a recent birthday dinner, I realized I had two types of friends. Six of us had met at a new restaurant and we all ordered the special appetizer—butternut squash soup. This soup was so good that, after only a few spoonfuls, we started talking about making it ourselves. Dara doubted that the restaurant would give us the recipe. Tim shook his head and said there was no need for that. He then proceeded to list off the possible ingredients—onion, chicken stock, butternut squash, apples, nutmeg, cinnamon—and, after a few minutes of puzzlement, Tim and I both realized the secret ingredient might be orange juice or perhaps orange zest. As I looked at the faces around the table of six, I realized that three of us were nodding in agreement with each ingredient he listed. The other three looked at us with something between confusion and amazement. "How do you know that?" Dara asked.

"I'm not sure," Tim replied with a shrug. "I guess I can just tell."

As a literacy staff developer in Boston, I have seen an important connection between what I saw at dinner that night and the teaching of writing. Just as all six of us could recognize that the soup was "delicious" and "flavorful," most people can recognize when writing has "voice" and "lots of details." Only some of us, however, can look at a page of writing with the same degree of confidence and identify the craft an author has used to give the writing voice or lots of detail. It might be no surprise that Tim and I love to cook, whereas some of my friends at the table rely more on takeout and restaurants for dinner. It is not that Tim could "just tell" as if by magic. He had experience putting different, specific ingredients together in order to create "flavorful" soups.

Both cooking and writing are considered to be an art and a science. There are basic rules to each but also a tremendous amount of room for individual choices. When I cook, sometimes I am more scientific, like when I follow a recipe from a cookbook for the first time. At other times I don't measure anything and decide what ingredients to add as I go along, pulling from dishes I've learned from my mother, dishes I've eaten at restaurants, and the more inexplicable facet of intuition. The writing process is also full of countless choices, which leads to products unique as the person creating them. And we wouldn't want it any other way. Imagine going to bookstores where the books have different jackets and plots but are all written in the same style. That's like going to different restaurants, ordering chocolate cake for dessert, and even though it might be served in different shapes, having it taste exactly the same. The artistic side of both cooking and writing is integral to our enjoyment of them.

In schools, however, writing is also an academic subject, a long-standing member of the three Rs—reading, writing, and arithmetic. Until recently, the presence of writing in schools has far out-favored the more scientific side of this art and science. Spelling, grammar, punctuation, sentence diagramming, handwriting, and all the predictable rules of the English language have tended to be the major emphasis of writing instruction and assessments. And, until recently, not knowing a lot about the craft of writing has not been all that problematic. It certainly does not affect how much we can enjoy literature, whether we are teachers or not, and it has never stopped society from producing prolific writers whose books line the shelves of bookstores and libraries.

But now, many teachers at the elementary and middle school levels are being expected to teach the craft of writing—the more artistic side of this art and science. Although this is absolutely a positive shift in education, it has also been challenging for many teachers. This transition seems to have been less of a challenge in the primary grades simply because primary students are learning to craft writing in more scientific ways. Even though there is room for individual expression through both word choice and drawing, a good deal of instruction falls under the rules of writing: letter formation, spacing, making a sentence, letter to sound relationships, and inventive spelling as well as conventional spelling of irregular words. As students need less instruction on *how* to write, there is more room for instruction on how to write *well*. Fortunately, educators recently started to validate the fact that if effective writing is about the words that are used and the way they are put together, then we need to move beyond just teaching the rules of grammar and the rules of mechanics.

Most people would agree with the notion that writing on your own outside of class time, even if it's once in a while, will greatly benefit your own instruction. Writing can be a powerful way to process ideas, reflections, and thoughts, whether one teaches others or not. Teachers who don't see themselves writing at home can still create a writer's notebook with a few entries from each genre to use for instruction. Having a notebook makes a public statement that writing is something adults do on their own: it's not just something done in school. It also makes a tremendous difference to students, whether they say so or not, that we are willing to put parts of our own lives on paper just as we are asking them to do.

While I support the concept that writing outside of class time is desirable, I also believe it is not necessary to write on a consistent basis in order to teach it well. Nor is it realistic or even fair to expect that all teachers, especially elementary school teachers who are responsible for teaching at least three or four other subjects besides writing, should have to write in their spare time. What I do believe is that if the expectation of what we teach students about writing is changing, then so should our preparation. If we are to teach the craft of writing to students, and not just mechanics and spelling, most of us cannot rely solely on our own histories of writing instruction.

Teachers have a valid reason, of course, for not automatically having a ready knowledge of craft. Very rarely, if ever, did we receive instruction in writing. Most of us just got writing assignments and handed them in. We might have received a grade or a smiley face. We even might have received feedback on our mechanics and grammar or comments such as "very nice" or "vague" scribbled in the margin. But when did we ever get actual instruction, either in whole-class lessons or individually, on how to improve the craft and style of our writing? In addition, anyone who went on to become a teacher and study pedagogy did not receive much support about the teaching of writing. Most teacher preparation programs, whether at the undergraduate or graduate level, have been rife with instruction about reading acquisition and how to teach reading. Most programs also address how to teach writing in the primary grades—how to support letter and word development as well as sentence structure through interactive and shared writing. But it seems that very few teacher preparation programs have offered as much guidance on how to teach children in the upper elementary grades to write well.

The fact that I came from a writing background, combined with the fact that I studied under Lucy Calkins, who did focus on upper elementary writing as much as primary writing, meant I had an advantage going into my first teaching job. There were other subject matters I struggled with that first year, but writing was not one of them. This didn't mean I was very good at that point—I still had a lot of growing to do—but because of my previous experiences, I started with a solid foundation and, perhaps more importantly, I was comfortable teaching writing. At the time, I probably couldn't explain very well what made me good at teaching writing, but it didn't really matter. My job was to teach my twenty-eight students, and that's what I did.

When I became a staff developer, however, the nature of my job changed. My job no longer was to help students write well but to help teachers find ways to refine and improve their writing instruction. When I started to teach district-wide workshops on writing workshop in Boston, the same expectations held true. It didn't matter how good or comfortable I personally felt when I conferred with students or planned and taught lessons for writing workshop. What mattered now was how I could help others become more comfortable and independent with teaching writing. This independence is particularly needed for conferring, where the very nature of on-the-spot assessment directly followed by teaching excludes the immediate use of support materials. Teachers can use professional literature to plan lessons and learn more about conferring, but once the conference starts, teachers have to rely on themselves and what they know about writing in that moment. In my workshops, I could show teachers a video of a great conference or describe successful conferences I've had and show samples of improved student writing, but I kept hearing the same question from teachers: "This all makes sense, but when I go back to my classroom, how do I know what to teach?"

I realized I was giving teachers a lot of information about how to go about *doing* a conference, but somehow that wasn't enough. So, rather than spend time primarily on the structure of a conference, I shifted and tried to share the skills behind conferring. I tried to figure out what went on in my mind that helped me notice craft in many different levels of writing and how I made the more craft-like aspects of writing, such as description and sentence fluency, more tangible for students. Although conversation with students was and is part of my research during a conference, this is not where I dug deeper. I was probably not much better than a lot of other teachers when it came to talking with students about their writing. I knew it was what I could see in the writing itself that made me feel more comfortable in conferences, especially with students who were writing below grade level.

As the goal of my instruction shifted, so did the content of my workshops for teachers. I no longer jumped into the stages of a conference or the structure of a mini-lesson. Before we got to the teaching of craft, teachers spent time looking at and studying writing in a step-by-step process. I emphasized getting to know specific craft, not just general concepts, that support the ability to write well. Teachers could then go back to their classrooms and give students tangible, attainable craft lessons to help them reach the larger goals of voice and descriptive writing. Our study of writing also gave teachers a concrete process for noticing craft so they could continue to notice and gather ideas for craft lessons on their own. I wasn't asking teachers in these workshops to become writers or to develop an expertise in writing, but I was asking them to take time to become more familiar with the smaller craft skills behind writing.

For this reason, *Crafting Writers* begins by looking at the art of writing itself. Chapters 2 and 3 introduce readers to specific craft and a process for noticing craft in writing. Chapters 4, 5, and 6 offer many specific writing techniques that relate to different categories of craft such as word choice and sentence variety.

Chapter 7 moves from the art of writing to the teaching of writing and offers strategies for teaching craft in whole-class lessons. Chapters 8, 9, and 10 look at teaching craft in one-on-one conferences and demonstrate how knowing many specific craft techniques can help teachers see strengths and possible next steps in all levels of writing.

The last two chapters look at aspects of writing workshop that support overall instruction: the management of conferences, group conferences, and using rubrics to assess writing.

Specific Craft

One of my first lessons about teaching was not in a classroom but a pool. I worked as a lifeguard on the weekends the summer after my junior year in college. The Columbia University pool is in an immense room, several floors below the main entrance, without a single window. Because I was there to make sure no one drowned, I wasn't allowed to read or do homework while on duty. It might be no surprise that I spent most of my time watching people swim. It was easy to recognize the good swimmers and notice how smoothly they moved through the water. I didn't grow up as a swimmer myself, but watching some of the more experienced swimmers, with their amazing combination of power and grace, made me want to get better at this sport. Just watching them, of course, would only get me so far. I knew I needed help.

Luckily, my friend Chris Tessin was on the Columbia swim team and agreed to give me lessons over the summer.

From the first day of these informal lessons, Chris always taught me specific techniques. After watching me swim a few laps, he told me that the first thing I needed to work on was breathing on both sides when I swam. I also had to work on keeping my head lower in the water. After I got better at those skills, Chris taught me specific techniques to help me improve my arm stroke. First I had to roll my shoulders more. Then Chris taught me how to keep my elbows higher, and later on in the summer, he taught me how to keep my arm movements symmetrical. Whether he was teaching me about my breathing, my arms, or my kicking, he always gave me specific teaching points.

In order for me to improve, it was essential that Chris's suggestions were specific. I would not get very far with Chris just telling me, "Make your arm stroke smoother," even if that was my eventual goal. In order to make significant improvement, I needed someone to name the small skills that would *add up* to a smooth arm stroke. The same is true in writing. Teachers can tell students as many times as they want that their writing needs more voice or description. But these are not next steps. Much like "swimming smoothly" is an overall description of the desired final product, so are "writing with details" and "writing with voice," descriptions we hope will define our students' writing.

Another reason it was so important that Chris gave me specific teaching points is that it kept me accountable for practicing what he taught me. Any technique he introduced was specific enough that I could work on it when I swam by myself. I could make myself accountable for rolling my shoulder or keeping my elbow up. But if he had told me to practice making my arm stroke smoother, how would I hold myself accountable for that? He even could have modeled it for me, but the fact is, I couldn't just leap from swimming my way to swimming like him. There were too many small skills that went into the final product.

As long as we give students general next steps in writing, they will have a hard time holding themselves accountable when they go back to their desks and write on their own. Even though "adding more details" may be an accurate assessment of a student's writing needs and describes what we want him or her to do, it is not a next step.

This is not to say that discussing the concept of voice or helping students recognize descriptive details is not helpful or important. We want students to be aware of their goal, and any exposure to or conversation about good writing is beneficial. But instruction that supports recognition of descriptive writing should be purposefully different from instruction that helps students write descriptively themselves.

Let's first look at some common ways teachers try to help students write with more description.

Teaching Voice

Voice has become the pinnacle of good writing in schools. Just about every rubric has a section for voice, and teachers know that if writing has voice, it's good. When I was taking creative writing courses in college, *voice* meant a unique style: you can almost tell who wrote it. Hemingway has a unique voice, as does James Joyce. In elementary and middle school, voice is also about having a style to your writing, but it is more about hearing the individual in the writing. According to several different elementary writing rubrics I gathered from various sources—districts, teachers, and literacy coaches—a student would receive a top score in voice if the writing met the following descriptors:

> As individual as fingerprints
> Begs to be read out loud—you cannot wait to share it
> Passionate, compelling—but never overdone
> Uses tone, flavor as a tool to enhance meaning
> Tough to put down—holds readers enrapt

Most teachers do not find it difficult to assign a number to a piece of writing based on these criteria. As stated before, *recognizing* good writing has never been problematic. One of the best aspects of these types of rubrics is that they help teachers look through various lenses, rather than only one, to judge and score student writing. And the above descriptions of voice certainly support students' understanding of what it means to have voice. But by offering students only a description of where we want to them to be, we are giving them an expectation without guidance on how to get there.

So often I hear the question: "How do you teach voice?" My response is: "You don't." For some students, the voice in their writing is a result of several years of independent reading and taking in the different rhythms texts can offer. This doesn't mean we can't have instruction that supports writing with voice. Rather than trying to teach voice directly, however, it is more effective to focus on giving students next steps that will eventually help them *reach* voice. We need to show students many specific craft techniques they can choose from that will *add up* to voice and descriptive writing. Writing with voice, unless students do it naturally, is a gradual process. It does not happen all at once, especially not in any one grade. In his book *Writing Tools* (2006), esteemed journalist and teacher of writing, Roy Peter Clark offers his favorite definition of voice, written by his colleague Don Fry: "Voice is the sum of all the strategies used by the author to create the illusion that the writer is speaking directly to the reader from the page" (112). Even writing instruction at the adult level respects the fact that voice is not something that is easily taught and learned. It comes from each individual being exposed to, learning, and experimenting with written language over a period of time.

Adding Details to a Piece of Writing

Another common way to teach descriptive writing in lessons is to display a piece of writing on chart paper or on the overhead that is "not very interesting." This kind of lesson usually falls under the heading "Adding details to make our writing more interesting." The idea is that students offer suggestions of words or phrases that could make the writing more descriptive. And, with the help of students, teachers usually do end up with a sentence or two that is far better than the original. Students' ability to do this activity well, however, can be deceiving and sometimes frustrating for teachers. If students can help create interesting, descriptive sentences when they are on the rug, why can't they do it in their own writing when they go back to their seats? The same students who were offering wonderful adjectives and exciting verbs are the same students going back to their desks and writing run-on sentences and "It was fun."

Think back to my swim lessons with Chris. The equivalent to the "Adding details" activity would have been for me to watch an unskilled swimmer and suggest how she could be better. I would have lots to offer: "Her head should be in the water! She needs to splash less! Her legs are too far under the water!" It's easy to give advice objectively to someone else when I am not involved in the process of making it happen. I'm not the one balancing all those skills. Would giving advice to someone else help me with my swimming? It would probably help somewhat. It might strengthen the part of my mind that critiques my own swimming. It might even make me feel a little more confident about my swimming since I could offer suggestions. But when I go back to my own swimming, I have to think about and control all the different movements that make up swimming. When watching a beginning swimmer, I can notice, with focused attention, the way she kicks, and then I can look for something else to notice about her swimming. When I am the one swimming, I don't have the luxury of focusing my attention on one skill at a time. I could, but I would probably sink.

Just like swimming, the act of writing entails using dozens of skills at one time. When elementary students write in their own notebooks, they are juggling what they know about mechanics, craft, sentence structure, spelling, and dialogue all while thinking about what they actually want to say. For English language learners who are still developing English vocabulary and the syntax of our not-so-predictable language, there can be the added skill of translating words in their minds. Unless writing instruction is isolated and specific, it can very easily get lost when students write on their own. So, while exposing students to the concept of adding different types of details to writing can be beneficial, it is not fair to expect that it will necessarily lead to student ownership. Not only is *offering suggestions* for details that could be added to someone else's writing a different skill from actually *writing* with detail, but *squeezing in* details is also a different skill from using details *as* you write. We want students to get better at using details as they write, not adding them in after the fact.

Asking Questions to Bring Out Details

In a writing conference, a common tactic to get students to add more detail is to ask questions: What did the birthday cake look like? What sounds could you hear? How did you feel? Most often this strategy has effective results—chances are the students' answers can become written details that enhance their writing. Lucy Calkins (1994) reminds us that, when it comes to conferring, "We need to give the writer something that will help not only today, with this piece of writing, but also tomorrow, with other pieces of writing" (228). Asking questions absolutely can be effective, and I do ask questions in my conferences, but I use them as a *vehicle* for my teaching. Unless this type of questioning is followed by a specific teaching point, it benefits mostly the writing rather than the writer. Asking questions to stimulate writing does offer some good exposure to the thinking process behind adding details, but at least in a conference, the goal is to leave students with a skill they can use in the writing they do tomorrow and the next day.

What Do I Mean by Specific Craft?

Specific craft techniques are what I consider to be the small building blocks of different aspects of good writing, such as description, voice, and sentence fluency. Teaching specific craft, whether it is through whole-class lessons or conferences, shows students one particular way to write at a time so that each one is small enough to hold in their hands and own.

There is one example of specific craft that most teachers already know very well: similes.

EXAMPLE SENTENCE	SPECIFIC CRAFT
Olivia's hands were as sticky as glue.	A simile using *as*

One reason a simile is a specific craft technique is that it has an accompanying definition: a comparison using *like* or *as*. This specificity not only lets you

Table 2.1 Ways to Describe by Comparing	
VARIATIONS OF A SIMILE	**SPECIFIC CRAFT**
Olivia's hands were stickier than glue.	"One upping" a simile
Olivia's hands were sticky as if she had just washed them in honey.	Using *as if* to give a description
Olivia's hands were so sticky that her hand almost stuck to the doorknob.	Using *so . . . that* to give a description

use similes easily when writing, but it also makes them recognizable in student writing. Most adults, whether they are teachers or not, can read student writing and notice similes just as easily as they can notice mechanics. In fact, I could probably write a simile about any topic at all, and teachers would recognize my use of this craft technique. Students also easily understand similes and can hold on to them after the lesson is over. Similes are one example of specific craft, but when teaching writing, you want to give students *many* different and specific ways to bring description into their writing. There are other ways to compare that can be just as specific and just as descriptive as similes.

Table 2.1 shows some examples of other ways to describe by comparing. In the second column of this table, I attempt to name the craft behind the writing, a skill that will be explored further in the next chapter. I purposefully use the word *attempt* because there aren't given definitions of these other craft techniques that were handed down to me when I was in school in the way a comparison using *like* or *as* was.

The second column in Table 2.1 is important because naming is what turns a descriptive phrase into a specific craft technique. When you figure out the formula behind the writing, you can use it again in other writing. Naming also makes more atypical craft recognizable in student writing. I did not commit the above ways of comparing to memory, but once I named these specific alternatives, they started to pop out at me when I read student writing just as similes do.

And when it comes to teaching comparisons for descriptive writing, I no longer rely only on similes. This is not to say similes are not a good craft technique to teach. But we often overemphasize similes—not just in one grade, but in several—because they are specific, effective, and familiar. Not surprisingly, this overemphasis can lead to overuse in student writing. An integral part of voice and effective description is writing with variety. When I have several different ways to teach students how to write descriptively by comparing, I can offer students more choices as they write.

So, where are all these specific craft techniques?

Table 2.2 Writing with the Sense of Sound	
EXAMPLE SENTENCE	**BASIC CRAFT**
I heard seagulls.	Including sound in writing
EXAMPLE SENTENCE	**SPECIFIC CRAFT**
I could hear seagulls.	Writing *I could hear* (instead of *I heard*)
I heard seagulls squawking.	Using an *ing* verb to describe the sound
In the air seagulls were squawking.	Writing a sound without the words *I heard*
Seagulls squawked above us as we walked onto the beach.	Giving the reader a sound and a visual using *as*
The seagulls above us were squawking like an unrehearsed chorus.	Describing a sound using a simile

Under the Umbrella

Many craft skills taught in elementary grades are what I sometimes call "umbrella" concepts. One example is teaching a lesson on the five senses. Although using the five senses is not too large a concept for students to understand, it is often too large a teaching point to translate into lasting student use. A natural next step toward more specific instruction would be to have separate lessons on the different senses. A third-grade teacher, for example, could focus on the sense of sound during a unit of study rather than all the five senses at once.

Teaching only sound may not seem groundbreaking and is probably something a lot of teachers already do. In terms of teaching specific craft, however, I would argue that even a concept like describing with the sense of sound is an umbrella under which are craft techniques that are even more specific. There are many different ways to use sound in writing. Table 2.2 gives some examples of specific craft that could fall under the umbrella of *writing with sound*.

Noticing and gathering specific craft techniques benefits instruction in several ways.

You Can Teach Several Mini-Lessons on a Particular Type of Craft

When a craft skill is taught in a mini-lesson—sound, for example—very often it is tempting to teach this same skill again the next day. After all, writing with sound is such a wonderful way to add description, it is understandable that teachers would want to spend more than one day on it. As a result, we sometimes only remind and review over several days of mini-lessons rather than teach one new skill each day. With specific craft, you can offer a class of students several different and very specific ways to use sound. Instead of reviewing the *concept* of including sound in writing, teachers can expand students' repertoire of how to include sounds in their writing.

You Can Recognize Strengths More Easily in Below-Level Writing

Looking under the umbrella helps you notice specific ways of using craft from the most basic to the more advanced, which legitimizes even the most simple craft technique. This means you can start to see craft in all levels of student writing. I no longer have to wait for "wonderful, descriptive" writing to see and comment on craft in student writing.

You Have Specific Teaching Points for Students in Your Class Who Write Well

Very often, teachers are unsure about how they can help students who are already writing well, whose writing is full of description and voice in addition to having volume and proper punctuation. Conferring was never meant to be only about fixing writing that needs help. Although students who write well may be more apt to help direct their own conferences, teachers can still help these students improve as writers in ways the students themselves may not see. When I confer with a fifth grader who is writing well and I see him or her using a simile, for example, I can teach this student one of the variations of comparing. My goal is not to necessarily show the student a better way to compare, just a different way, so that he or she now has more choices as a writer.

✿ ✿ ✿

It's important to point out that most of the craft discussed in this book focuses on a particular aspect of craft: craft that relates to word choice and is at the sentence level. We can also study text for its larger structures—its beginning and ending or how the story moves in time, for example. The way text is structured is also part of crafting a piece of writing, but a good deal of professional literature already explores the structure of writing in this way. In addition, although the overall structure of a piece of writing can greatly support the development and organization of a piece as well as provide fertile ground for description, it's often the words and punctuation that students use as they write their sentences that will lead them to write with "voice" and "lots of detail."

Any specific craft I have mentioned so far came from looking at and studying writing, both formally and informally. Although one intention of this book is to share with you many ready-to-teach craft techniques, it is essential that I also share a process for looking at writing so that you can accumulate specific craft points on your own. The next chapter takes a closer look at this process of gathering craft.

3

Gathering Craft

The year after I graduated from college, I lived in Italy for nine months. At first, having never formally studied Italian, I could only appreciate the sound of their incredibly lyrical language. As I began to speak Italian myself, I learned not only the meaning of words but also the Italian way of putting words together. I was crafting sentences in ways that were both similar to and different from the way I spoke in English. See if you can name any kind of writing skill—craft or mechanics—in the following Italian sentences:

> *Il sole rosso sorgeva sull'oceano mentre Luigi stava camminando verso la spiaggia di sabbia bianca. Quindi disse: "Questo piacerebbe moltissimo a Matilde. Penso che andró a svegliarla."*

If you speak and read Italian, you might point out the use of *while* (*mentre*) to combine two actions in one sentence. Or you might have noticed the colors used to describe the sun and the sand (*rosso* and *bianca*). But even if you don't speak a word of Italian, there are still writing skills you could name—the quotation marks, the colon, and the periods. Most skills that fall under mechanics, such as punctuation use and paragraph indents, are instantly recognizable, even when you can't read the words on the page. So, it's no wonder that mechanics skills are the first things a teacher might notice about student writing. They are physical marks completely separate from letters and words. Craft, on the other hand, is all words. It's not separate from writing; it's embedded in writing. I say this in part to validate why some teachers find it more challenging to plan craft lessons, as opposed to mechanics lessons, based on their students' writing. I also say this to validate that noticing craft in writing is something that has to be developed; it doesn't just happen all by itself.

A good deal of professional literature offers ideas for craft lessons. I do believe, however, that after teachers have their feet on the ground in terms of the structure of writing workshop and have experienced teaching craft, there should be an intentional development toward independence in planning craft lessons. This is not to say teachers should stop consulting professional literature or other support materials. But ideally, the primary resource of each teacher's planning is the student writing in his or her own classroom.

When researching student writing for the purpose of instruction, the goal is to be able to see specific craft that *is* there and craft that *could be* there—similar to that way we see both the presence and lack of punctuation. This ability to notice craft is nowhere more important than in conferring. Unlike preparing for mini-lessons, when you can at least use professional literature at home the night before as you plan, there is no guide to turn to during your conferences. When you are sitting next to Shane, for example, no book will tell you what to teach him—what unique strengths and needs he shows in his writing. There certainly are books that can support your *conversations* with students, the *structure* of your conferences, and what you *might* teach in conferences. But deciding what to teach each student in a conference is something you have to do on your own. The best way to get better at conferring is to get better at noticing craft skills yourself.

Reading Like a Writer: The Process and the Products

Many writing workshop authors refer to the skill of noticing craft in writing as "reading like a writer." I have found that there are two different but related benefits to reading text like a writer. The first benefit has to do with the process itself. As I mentioned before, seeing craft is not something you just read about then suddenly start doing really well. It's more like starting a new sport and using muscles you haven't really used before. The only way the muscles are going to get stronger is through use. This is the very reason that the early chapters in *Crafting Writers* focus on writing and the later chapters focus on teaching. Being familiar and comfortable with the content you are teaching matters. Trying to get better at noticing craft in writing only during your conferences, when it counts, when a student is looking at you wondering what you will say, is like trying to learn how to play guitar while on stage. Pressure is just not conducive to learning. Any investment of time practicing a skill "behind the scenes" will benefit both your ability and your comfort level when it comes to actual conferences.

The second benefit of reading text like a writer has to do with the actual products that come out of the process. "Gathering Craft," the title of this chapter, refers to the fact that when you read like a writer, you ideally "hang on" to what you see. Many, if not most, craft techniques are not out there on the surface for the taking. Reading like a writer, whether you're reading literature or student writing, can help excavate the craft that is embedded in writing.

The best place to start developing this skill of reading like a writer is not with student writing, but with children's literature. Very often, when reading student writing, our minds tend to notice what is lacking. This is a natural teacher reaction, because in theory, our job is to support the forward development of our students' writing skills. Starting with children's literature instead of student writing makes it easier to focus only on noticing and learning about craft; there's not much room to get distracted by judging how good the writing is or how it could be better.

Here is how I describe my process for gathering craft:

1. Recognizing the small parts of good writing
2. Naming the specific craft
3. Answering the question, Why is it good?

You can apply this process to different types of books, depending on the genre you want to teach. For personal narrative, I particularly like using books by Patricia Polacco because her writing is not overly poetic or symbolic. It's important to notice not only "artful" craft, but also craft that makes up more ordinary sentences.

Recognizing the Small Parts of Good Writing

As I mentioned before, most adults can recognize when writing is "good." When reading published literature or student writing, it is not too difficult to notice sentences you simply like. There is something about the sound of the words or the images they produce that is appealing. The good news is that the process for gathering craft begins with this type of recognition. Rather than start right off looking for the hidden craft in text, you can start with recognizing when you simply like the writing.

Below is an excerpt from Patricia Polacco's book *Chicken Sunday* (1992). If you haven't read this book, it might be a good idea to first read the paragraph normally, then reread it with more of a "writer's eye." As you read, try to notice what phrases or sentences you like. You can underline them in pencil or just make a mental note as you read.

> *Stewart reached into the hole in the trunk of our "wish tree" in the backyard. He pulled out a rusty Band-Aid tin. The three of us held our breath as we counted the money inside that we had been saving for weeks.*
>
> *"If we are going to get that hat for Miss Eula in time for Easter, we are going to need a lot more than this," I announced.*
>
> *"Maybe we should ask Mr. Kodinski if we could sweep up his shop or something to earn the rest of the money," Stewart said.*
>
> *"I don't know," Winnie said fearfully. "He's such a strange old man. He never smiles at anyone. He always looks so mean!" We all agreed it was worth a try anyway.*
>
> *The next day we took a shortcut down the alley in the back of the hat shop. Bigger boys were there. They were yelling. Eggs flew past us and pelted Mr. Kodinski's back door.*
>
> *Just as the boys ran away the door flew open. Mr. Kodinski glared straight at us! "You there," he yelled. "Why do you kids do things like this?". . .*
>
> *"All I want to do is live my life in peace. I'm calling your grandmother," he shouted as he wagged his finger in Stewart's face.*

One sentence that many people tend to like, including myself, is the following:

> *The three of us held our breath as we counted the money inside that we had been saving for weeks.*

There is something about this sentence that is appealing. In order to gather actual craft techniques, however, it is important to narrow down, as specifically as possible, what part of the writing is "good." We need to keep putting sentences we like through a sieve until we can pinpoint the effective writing. Oftentimes these are phrases, not entire sentences. In the sentence above, for example, one phrase that stands out for me is "held our breath."

Another sentence I like a lot is this one:

> *"I'm calling your grandmother," he shouted as he wagged his finger in Stewart's face.*

Very often when you start looking carefully at good sentences, you will find more than one small part that seems craft-like. In the sentence above, I like "shouted" and "as he wagged his finger."

Looking back at the entire excerpt, I also like "Bigger boys were there," which is a short enough sentence to be a small part on its own. This sentence doesn't start with the typical "There were. . . ." There is also something about the brevity of this sentence that is appealing. Other small parts I like include "rusty Band-Aid tin," "glared straight at us," "Eggs flew," "said fearfully," and "pelted."

Studying craft in literature in this way doesn't mean you are supposed to notice something craftlike in every single sentence you read. The following sentence is an example of this:

The next day we took a shortcut down the alley in the back of the hat shop.

This is a perfectly fine sentence. Upon reading it, however, I would not say there is anything that pops out at me. It is always worth rereading what might seem like an ordinary sentence. Many people are used to bypassing sentences that are not overflowing with poetic phrases and similes. But if a sentence like this still doesn't do much for you, there's nothing wrong with moving right along to the next sentence.

One phrase a lot of people like in the Polacco excerpt is "'wish tree.'" Just for now, we're going to put on hold craft that involves punctuation—in this case the quotation marks. This is not meant to devalue mechanics in any way. On the contrary, punctuation can greatly enhance craft, bringing a complexity and rhythm to sentences that words on their own can't do. I find it helpful, however, to look at craft that involves punctuation separately, and we'll do this in Chapter 5.

Naming the Specific Craft

The "small parts" that we have identified so far in this chapter now have the potential to be teachable craft techniques. In order to turn the feeling of "I really like that phrase" into a teachable craft technique, however, we have to name it. It might be tempting to name words and phrases in general ways, ways you might already be familiar with, such as "using stronger words," "giving the reader a mind movie," or "show not tell." Although you may be accurate in these assessments, this kind of naming captures only *generally* what an author is doing, not *specifically* what an author is doing.

When I learned about naming craft from Katie Wood Ray, both from her workshops and her book *Wondrous Words* (1999), I realized how much naming lets us harness good writing. Reading like a writer helps me discover new craft techniques. But it is naming the craft that lets me hold on to those discoveries and put them in my pocket to take with me. I might use them myself when I write, perhaps at first with some awareness and then later with less intention. But more importantly, as a teacher of writing, I can take this craft out of my pocket to teach in whole-class lessons and conferences. And, because I am familiar with these craft techniques that are in my pocket, I can also recognize them when they are embedded in students' writing.

So How Do We Name Specific Craft?

Very often, we can name a craft technique by looking at the structure of a phrase. The definition of a simile is an example of this type of naming. In every simile there are two things or concepts connected with either *as* or *like*—it's almost like a formula, which is why similes can be recognized so easily in text and so easily composed when writing about different topics.

Similes already have a name and definition handed down to us from a previous generation, but clearly not all craft techniques do. As mentioned in the previous chapter, naming is not about figuring out the "right" name. What you actually end up calling the craft doesn't really matter, as long as it makes sense. There are several different aspects of craft, however, that can be helpful to notice in order to do the naming.

❀   Parts of speech
❀   Variations of words
❀   Combinations

After I explain each of these in more detail, I'll demonstrate how I might name the craft that has been gathered so far in this chapter. Remember, it's not that I am telling you *the* names for craft techniques as if the names have been hidden from you all these years; I'm just sharing how I would name them. You might name each technique something else, which is fine, as long as it makes sense.

Parts of Speech

Katie Wood Ray helped me understand that I didn't have to wait for some outside authority to go ahead and name craft. Parts of speech help define structure behind craft. After noticing effective phrases in writing, I could "use my knowledge of parts of speech to first realize and then explain . . . what made these phrases stand out" (1999, 22). You can certainly start with the basic terms: *adjective, adverb,* or *pronoun,* for example. But in order to use parts of speech to name craft as effectively as possible, sometimes you have to go beyond basic naming. You have to be open to playing with the terms, adding to them or embellishing them, in order to mirror what is happening in the writing.

In *Wondrous Words* (1999), for example, Katie presents a craft technique called *out-of-place adjectives*. She gives the examples "drink lemonade cold" and "hot tea spiced" from *My Mama Had a Dancing Heart* by Libba Moore Gray (1995). Katie Wood Ray did not come up with the idea of out-of-place adjectives and then say "Hmmm, let's see if I can find a book that matches that technique." It was the other way around: she learned the technique from reading and analyzing published writing. Then, noticing there was something appealing about those phrases, she looked at the structure and tried to think of a name that would reflect what was going on in that phrase.

One of the first craft points I gathered from literature was when I was reading *Cherries and Cherry Pits* by Vera B. Williams (1991) and read the following sentence: "On her feet are old, old shoes." She repeated the same adjective, which emphasizes the oldness of the shoes. This could simply be called *repeating adjectives*.

We could apply this kind of naming with the phrase "said fearfully" from *Chicken Sunday*. If you look at this phrase objectively, from a grammar perspective, it could be called *said with an adverb*. This now becomes a very specific craft technique that can be used in many different contexts:

Said wishfully   Said anxiously
Said hopefully   Said angrily

Notice that when naming the specific craft used in this phrase, I only labeled a portion of it with a part of speech. The reason is that you need a specific word to make it useful. I could have named "said fearfully" by saying it's *a verb with an adverb*. But that gives us nothing to hold on to: it goes back to the rule of adverbs going with verbs, which applies to every adverb in the English language.

Anchoring craft techniques with a particular word or a particular context takes advantage of what tends to be most dominant in students' minds as they write—the content of their stories. Writing is a multi-task activity. Very often children, and even adults, aren't aware of the mechanics and craft they actually use as they write. Sometimes it "just comes out." I know when I'm writing I don't think in terms of nouns and adverbs, so children probably don't either. But you can pretty much assume that if their pencils are moving, students are at least aware of the story they want to tell and the words they choose to write down.

If I taught a mini-lesson on using *said with an adverb* as a way to make dialogue more descriptive, I could model how using an adverb with *said* can show an emotion, sometimes even conveying what someone's expression might look like. A week later, a student might be writing about the time she made her sister late for school and write, "'Come on Vanessa, you can make your sandwich faster than that,' my sister said." Writing the word *said* along with the image she is probably picturing in her mind (her sister looking annoyed) might bring from the back of her mind, whether on a conscious or subconscious level, my instruction about *said with an adverb*. She then might go on to write, "my sister said impatiently" or "my sister said angrily" depending on her vocabulary development at that time.

Looking again at the phrases I liked in the *Chicken Sunday* passage, I would probably name "Bigger boys were there" with parts of speech as well. Although nouns exist in almost every sentence, there is something unusual about this sentence starting with a noun. Most students, and perhaps even most adults, might write it as, "There were bigger boys there," so I might just call this *starting a sentence with a noun*. Even though this particular craft technique might fall under a category that has to do with word order or sentence variety, naming it with a part of speech, with the place in the sentence as the anchor, helps to make this kind of sentence more tangible to recognize and to try out in writing.

Variations of Words

Many times, the terms *exciting words* or *strong verbs* are used when teachers talk about vocabulary that goes beyond basic words: *shouted* instead of *said*, *peered* instead of *looked*, *shuffled* instead of *walked*. Although it may be true that these words are strong, this kind of naming doesn't really capture any type of technique or concept that can be easily repeated by students.

What I have noticed about these "exciting" words is that they often fall along a continuum. For example, there are many ways to *say* something. If we were to chart variations of the word *said* from quietest to loudest, it might look something like this:

*whispered   murmured   mentioned   commented   **said**   declared   barked   exclaimed   shouted   screeched   hollered   screamed*

It's not that writers at some point in time were looking for different ways to write the word *said*. Words are invented out of the need to express what already exists in life. As humans, the ways we say things run a range both in volume and emotion. The variation in words available reflects these variations that exist in life.

Variations are not just about volume, of course. The variations for *look* might run the gamut from *glanced* all the way to *glare*, with *peer* being somewhere in the middle. *Shuffled* would certainly fall at one end of the range for how a person can move. Words from the *Chicken Sunday* list that could be part of a variation include *flew* and *pelted*.

There are still benefits to teaching the concept of exciting words or word choice, especially because this gives students a language for describing good writing. Students can certainly recognize and talk about exciting words. But because the concept of exciting words relates to literally all topics students could possibly write about, there is not much to hold on to in terms of taking away a specific technique. And of course what we ultimately want students to get better at is using a variety of interesting words themselves, not recognizing them. By teaching the concept that there is a range of words we can use within a particular context—the way one might walk, look at, or say something—the basic word itself becomes the trigger for choosing an alternative word. Students are more apt to remember the range of words that are available to use when they are about to write "she *said*" or "my aunt *looked*," than to remember to use "exciting words" when they write . . . anything.

Combinations

Combinations have to do with a topic that is already familiar to most teachers—the five senses: sight, sound, smell, touch, and taste. The five senses are taught frequently, either as a set or individually, for a reason. We experience the world through each of these five senses. The more senses a writer uses throughout a piece of personal narrative writing, the more he or she can bring that memory alive for the reader. And when writing fiction, writers use the five senses to bring scenes and characters alive as if they were real. Combining two senses in a sentence provides a more concentrated, multidimensional image for the reader. Consider the following sentence, which I identified earlier in this chapter.

> *"I'm calling your grandmother," he shouted as he wagged his finger in Stewart's face.*

In this example, the author includes a sound ("shouted") and a visual ("wagged his finger") all in one sentence. We might call this craft technique *sound with a visual* or, more precisely, *dialogue with a visual*.

When you show students that the word *as* allows you to join a sound with a visual in the same sentence, you provide them with a concrete word to use for this particular technique. Similar to teaching variations of words in a particular context, showing students a particular word or phrase at the center of a craft technique gives students something to hold on to long after a lesson or conference is over. Sometimes these combinations need commas and sometimes they don't. Both types of combinations will be explored in the following chapters.

The craft that writers use is far too vast to always be easily named. And I wouldn't disagree with anyone who says that not all craft can or should be named. After all, writing is still an art form, and not every part of it should be scientifically broken down. But remember, the goal of all this naming is not to identify and label every single phrase in a book, but to gather craft techniques that can be used for instruction.

Answering the Question, Why Is It Good?

After naming craft, the next step in the process is to think about "the Why"— why is a certain craft technique good? How does it affect the reader? I demonstrated this briefly when I introduced the use of repeating an adjective with "old, old shoes." Vera B. Williams could have just written "old shoes." When I slowed down my reaction to the way she described the shoes, repeating an adjective rather than just writing it once, I realized it produced an exaggerated picture in my mind. I saw, not just old shoes, but *really* old shoes with the soles coming apart and maybe a hole at the toe. Vera B. Williams could have written "Her shoes were very old" or "Her shoes were really old." Repeating the adjective *old* is not only more descriptive, but the repetition of words gives the sentence a slightly different rhythm than a basic sentence.

Going beyond naming craft to considering how a craft technique affects the reader helps to solidify understanding of craft by students, and so it should be part of teachers' preparation for teaching craft. After I made the Why a standard part of my practice while gathering craft or teaching it, I realized that any learning is more powerful when we are given the Why: its benefits are not isolated to the teaching of writing.

Although I didn't realize it at the time, Chris used the Why to help me better understand what he taught in our swim lessons. Like many noncompetitive swimmers, I had always kept my arms fairly straight under water during my freestyle stroke. Swimming this way had always felt just fine to me. Chris told me several times during my lessons to bend my arm underwater and make an S-curve. But whenever I tried moving my arms that way, it felt unnatural. Later in the week, when I swam on my own, I would inevitably go back to my straight arms.

Finally, one day during a lesson, Chris told me to get out of the water. While I stood there dripping on the pool deck, slightly confused, he had me hold one arm straight out in the air. Then he told me to push down his hand with my straight arm. When I tried, he resisted. It was difficult to push down. Then Chris told me to try it again, but this time I was allowed to bend my arm. With my elbow up high, it was easy to push his hand far down, even when he resisted. "All right, so *that's* why you do the S-curve," Chris said, slightly exasperated. "Trying to push water with a straight arm takes a lot more energy. If you bend your arm, you can push the water with less effort." Suddenly it made sense. I understood the Why behind the direction he had been giving me for weeks.

The next few times I went swimming by myself, I had a different motivation. I understood how this S-curve would affect my swimming; it was no longer just something I was told to do. Even though it was still awkward to make the S-curve under water, I continued to do it on my own. Eventually this small technique that Chris taught me became a natural part of my stroke.

The Why lets instruction go beyond following rules to true learning and understanding, even when it comes to informal learning. My sister Chrissy, for example, had been telling me for years not to let my car's gas tank get below one-quarter full. I knew she was right, but I never seemed to do it. After all— why stop and pay money earlier than you have to? It was not until I took an introductory mechanics class that I learned you shouldn't let the gas get too low because it puts more pressure on the fuel pump and, in the winter, a very low gas tank leaves more room for any moisture to freeze. Once I understood why I should fill up my tank earlier, I actually owned the motivation to follow the rule my sister had been telling me for years.

Just as the Why helped to turn directions into understanding in these experiences, so is offering the Why in our conferences and mini-lessons more powerful and productive than merely telling students what they can do to improve in their writing. The Why shifts the emphasis from the teacher-student relationship ("because my teacher told me to") to the relationship between student and writing ("because this is how it will affect my writing").

It has become second nature for me to articulate the Why, both during instruction and when I am gathering craft from writing. But when I first tried to make it a habit, it didn't always come naturally. After all, writing instruction for most of us when we were students had to do with following rules, not understanding the reasons behind the rules. So sometimes, especially at first, it might take a little time to think about why we use certain craft or mechanics skills. But there is always a reason.

The Why Behind Descriptive Writing

The reason most descriptive writing is effective is because it makes a memory or story come alive for the reader. This makes sense since we usually write in order for someone else to understand our thoughts or see what we see in our minds. But it is important to continue the emphasis on specificity. Saying a craft technique makes the writing more descriptive or that it makes a mind movie is not quite good enough. We need to try and answer the question, How *exactly* does a craft technique make writing come alive for the reader?

One way to figure out the Why behind craft techniques is to compare each one to a more basic choice an author, whether it is a student or published writer, could have made. Thinking through other ways the text could have been written is an important aspect to seeing and understanding the craft of writing (Ray, 1999). Let's use similes as an example. It is common knowledge that similes are descriptive, and we can tell that they enhance writing somehow. To be even more specific about how they are descriptive and why we bother using them in writing, we can compare them to sentences *without* similes.

Table 3.1

WITHOUT SIMILES (THE MORE BASIC CHOICE)	WITH SIMILES
Ken's legs were skinny.	*Ken's legs were like two toothpicks.*
The cat's tongue was rough.	*The cat's tongue was as rough as sandpaper.*

Read the sentences in Table 3.1 and think about the differences between the sentences in each column. What do the sentences in the second column do for you as a reader that the sentences in the first column don't? How are the images in your mind different?

The sentences in the second column probably produced an exaggerated image in your mind. In the first example, the use of a familiar object enhances the skinniness. In the second example, the *feel* of a familiar object is what enhances the description; it makes the feel of the cat's tongue come alive.

Now consider the use of brand names, one of the craft techniques Patricia Polacco uses in *Chicken Sunday*. Years ago I could certainly identify *Band-Aid* as a proper noun in writing, but only as a brand name if I was shopping in a store. At the time, my awareness of this word related to the rules of using capital letters with proper nouns. When I first stopped and asked myself, "Well what is it about this use of a brand name that makes me like it? Why is it good?" it took some thinking to put my answer into words.

I realized that by using brand names, you can describe an object in detail with only one or two words. When reading "Band-Aid tin," in *Chicken Sunday*, I immediately could see the metal box with the hinged top, the red and blue writing with Johnson & Johnson in script against a white background, along with a picture of a Band-Aid. I even can't help but smell that unique, medicinal cotton scent of Band-Aids and recall the sound the rectangular lid makes when you close it shut. What would have taken Patricia Polacco at least four or five sentences to describe, she did in just three words! Very often effective writing has to do with packing images into sentences. Brand names can also sometimes invoke a sense of familiarity, even nostalgia. My mom used to keep a Band-Aid tin in our downstairs medicine cabinet. As far as I know, Johnson & Johnson doesn't make those tins anymore like they did when I was little. This doesn't mean that upon reading *Chicken Sunday* I paused and, looking out the window, recalled all those details and felt nostalgic about those Band-Aid tins of my past. The reading experience happens much too quickly. It is because the normal pace of reading happens so quickly that it is necessary to slow down our reaction to a sentence or phrase in order to fully understand its sometimes hidden effect.

Table 3.2 Examples of the Why of Craft

EXAMPLE PHRASE	WHY IS IT GOOD?
Band-Aid tin	Brand names give an extremely detailed image in only a few words; sometimes a brand name can also evoke familiarity or nostalgia
held our breath	Gives reader a visual of an emotion, rather than just telling the emotion
said fearfully	Gives reader a visual of how someone's face might look as they say something; can also indicate emotion
Eggs flew	Gives reader a very specific image of how something moves
glared straight at us	Produces a very specific image of how someone looks at someone else; can also convey emotion
pelted	Produces a specific image of the way the eggs hit the door
he shouted as he wagged his finger	Gives reader a visual and sound at the same time

---

Table 3.2 gives examples of how I would describe the Why with some of the craft techniques gathered from the excerpt of Patricia Polacco's writing.

Trying It Out

Keep in mind that although this chapter takes a *group* of example words and phrases through each stage together (those I chose from *Chicken Sunday*), you can also take each word or phrase you find through the three stages independently.

recognize the small part ⟶ name it ⟶ say why it is good

This process of gathering craft can be repeated with most books you typically use for writing instruction, regardless of the genre. This activity is especially good to do with colleagues during team meetings before an upcoming unit of study. For nonfiction, taking time to gather craft can help teachers move beyond teaching text features. Likewise, noticing what writers do in poems helps you make a shift from relying only on formula poems to teaching the craft of poetry.

Another benefit of gathering craft from literature is that, by taking the time to slow down your reading of text and your reaction to certain words and phrases, you get to know books very, very well. Using the same book for different lessons reinforces the concept that one piece of writing can contain many different craft techniques. You don't have to go hunting for books for all your lessons. Students also get to know the books very well, so during lessons they can focus on the craft lesson itself rather than become distracted by the story.

I also noticed that when I knew these books intimately, I could more easily refer to literature in my conferences. You might have seen videos where people confer with students and spontaneously say, "You know, you remind me of Cynthia Rylant right here in your second paragraph when you. . . ." This ability to authentically connect students' writing with that of published authors on the spot perhaps seems out of reach. But when you know books intimately—and not all the books in your classroom, just a few—these student-author connections can occur naturally.

You've probably noticed that I've repeated the concept of specificity at each step of the gathering process. This is the key to writing instruction: not the *teaching* end of instruction but the *receiving* end of instruction. It's the specificity that makes the craft so doable. One of the biggest selling points for specific craft is revealed when I have teachers try specific craft techniques themselves; it allows teachers to see how easy specific craft is to use, regardless of the subject matter.

Tables 3.3 through 3.6 provide an opportunity for you to try out a few of the specific craft techniques that I have introduced thus far. I offer my own examples with space below for readers to write their own sentences. A regu-

---

Table 3.3

EXAMPLE PHRASE	SPECIFIC CRAFT	WHY IS IT GOOD?
Band-Aid tin	brand name	Gives an extremely detailed image in only a few words; can also evoke familiarity or nostalgia

My try: *All that was in the fridge was a can of Cheese Whiz and a half-empty bottle of Heinz ketchup.*

Your try:

Table 3.4

EXAMPLE PHRASE	SPECIFIC CRAFT	WHY IS IT GOOD?
he shouted as he wagged his finger	*said* + action (using *as*)	Gives reader a visual and sound at the same time

My try: *"Let's run by the river today," Leah said as she laced up her sneakers.*

Your try:

Table 3.5

EXAMPLE PHRASE	SPECIFIC CRAFT	WHY IS IT GOOD?
said fearfully	*said* + adverb	Gives reader a visual of how someone's face might look as they say something; can also indicate emotion

My try: *"Maybe Nancy would be willing to babysit," my sister said hopefully.*

Your try:

Table 3.6

EXAMPLE PHRASE	SPECIFIC CRAFT	WHY IS IT GOOD?
glared straight at us	variation of *look*	Gives reader a visual of how someone's face might look as they say something; can also indicate emotion

My try: *Sara glanced at the clock as she walked into the lobby of the hospital.*

Your try:

lar piece of paper will work just as well. The topic itself doesn't matter. If you're stuck for an idea, you can always use the classroom or teacher's lounge as the context for a sentence. I do encourage teachers to try out at least a few in writing. Although it's possible to think through some examples, writing them out allows you to experience the instruction you will be giving.

The more time I've taken to study literature and student writing with a gathering process, the more craft techniques I learn. Noticing craft should not be an end to itself, but a way to accumulate specific craft techniques to teach in lessons or to recognize in subsequent student writing. In the following chapters, I offer different categories of craft techniques that I have developed from my own study of writing.

4

Categories of Specific Craft

When I was little, there were two things I savored. Books and chocolate. Part of my appreciation for chocolate was that I didn't have it all the time. I was one of those kids who got an apple for dessert in their lunch box and looked longingly at those who had Devil Dogs and Hostess Cup Cakes. Books, on the other hand, I could have whenever I wanted. In the summer, I loved sitting outside in a lounge chair with my pink sunglasses and my two favorite things—a book and a piece of chocolate. To this day, a few chocolate smudges still remain on pages of my most-loved chapter books.

The fact that I happened to love reading of course affected how well I did on September assessments in school. It wasn't until I got older that I realized how my natural interest in reading helped me do well, not just on reading assessments, but also on writing assignments. By doing all that reading, I had the sound of writing in my mind and more exposure to vocabulary, both in meaning and spelling.

We all know that this strong connection between reading and writing still exists. The best writers in most classrooms also tend to be avid readers. Although read-alouds are helpful in terms of exposing students to the sound of good writing, they are not nearly as powerful as when students read independently. Students will access many more words when reading by themselves, but it is the independent act of reading that is the most beneficial to writing. When students read text silently in their minds, they are the ones giving sound to the black and white print in front of them. Having a more active role in bringing printed words to life, rather than just receiving the sound of writing without seeing it, more closely mirrors the act of writing. When reading independently, we take the print and create the sound in our minds. When writing, we create the sound of words in our minds then put them into print. This relationship between reading independently and writing is the reason students, past and present, can receive little to no writing instruction and still write with lots of voice.

Students who come to our classrooms in September arrive with different levels of reading interest, reading ability, and home literacy histories. And they always will. One of the greatest assets of writing workshop is that students' reading abilities no longer predetermine what kind of experience they will have in writing. When I was in elementary school, those of us who liked to read during the summer usually got smiley faces and stars on writing assignments. This constant positive feedback affected our attitude and confidence about writing. Meanwhile, those students who needed help the most were getting the opposite—just red marks. No smiley faces. No stars. Feedback or "support" in writing was not really about instruction: it was about assigning and correcting. For the most part, this is just how writing was taught.

Writing workshop values the fact that if writing is to be an academic subject, then instruction should be part of the equation. We don't just keep assigning and correcting without offering support in how to write better, beyond spelling and punctuation. Teaching craft may be a shift for many teachers, but it is a shift reflective of a new mind-set that makes room for all students and their ability to improve.

In Chapter 3, I presented a process for noticing and collecting craft from writing. I could have jumped right into offering lots of suggestions for craft lessons, but one of the main purposes of this book is to support teachers' independence and comfort when it comes to the planning and teaching of writing. I wanted to go beyond just offering ideas for lessons and support teachers in becoming more familiar with the craft of writing itself. That being said, I also understand that seeing craft embedded in writing is a somewhat new skill for many teachers. I feel that my job, in addition to supporting teachers' autonomy in noticing and gathering craft from literature and their own student writing, should be to share the specific craft I have collected myself. Most teachers don't have the luxury of time to develop a repertoire of craft from scratch. They could, and it might take time, but I respect the fact that teachers have students they need to teach—right now.

This chapter is divided into five main topics, which are common themes when it comes to teaching the craft of writing:

The Five Senses
Show Not Tell
Dialogue
Sentence Variety
Word Choice

Within these five sections are tables describing specific craft techniques that relate to each topic. The chart below describes how these tables are set up.

SPECIFIC CRAFT	EXAMPLE SENTENCE	WHY IS IT GOOD?
A possible name for a specific craft technique	*A sentence that demonstrates this technique.*	A brief explanation of how this specific craft affects the writing or the reader

The main purpose of these tables is to support the connection between teachers' assessment of writing and their responding instruction. As I mentioned before, most people can read student writing and know when it either has or lacks things like sentence variety or visual description, and that is a fine place to start. But the key to effective writing instruction is being able to respond to students' needs with a small next step, not just presenting them with general goals. Teachers can use the charts in this chapter to plan for specific lessons in response to noticing a general need in student writing. If a third-grade teacher, for example, notices her students are telling their stories with very little showing or describing whatsoever, she could use these charts to find a specific craft technique that relates to Show Not Tell or The Five Senses. Appendix G gives an overview of all the different specific craft tables this book offers. These charts are meant to be a resource for teachers and not charts to be copied for students. Although it may be tempting to give students a piece of paper listing different craft techniques they might use, it would not support their ability to use them independently. Students need to be shown these craft techniques one at a time and see them modeled either by a teacher or in literature.

After teaching the general use of a craft skill, teachers can also use the specific craft charts to plan follow-up lessons. After teaching the concept of adding sound, for example, you could teach students several specific *ways* to use sound. It's important to point out that the specific craft presented are options to choose from, not a list of what to teach one by one. In the case of follow-up lessons, you might choose two or three, depending on the level of students in your classroom.

Some of the craft points in this chapter came from noticing what authors do in literature, and some came from gathering craft during writing conferences with students. But there are also many craft techniques here that are not necessarily from a particular source. One of the greatest benefits of creating categories was that I could think of other related craft without necessarily collecting it from anywhere. For example, when *writing with sound* became a category for me rather than just a singular craft technique on its own, I already knew of several specific craft techniques that fit within it. But I also played with different ways one could write sound, such as: *The seagulls above us were squawking as if they hadn't eaten all day*. It wasn't until I wrote it down that I could name it—describing a sound with *as if*. Upon seeing that I hadn't yet gathered this particular specific craft from published literature or student writing, I could go ahead and add it to this category in my mind. It's not that I hadn't read sentences like that at some point. I'm sure I have. But by playing with language myself, I didn't have to wait to encounter this kind of sentence during a purposeful study in order to add it to my list.

Although the tables in this chapter can be used as a resource for lesson ideas, they do not always have to be consulted to benefit the teaching of craft, particularly conferring. In fact, I would say this is probably the biggest benefit of these tables. Familiarizing yourself with different types of specific craft, whether or not you actually end up doing lessons on them, can increase the range and depth of craft you notice in student writing. The more you know, the more you will likely see.

It's also important to keep in mind that these charts are open-ended: there is always room for you to gather more craft from literature, conferences, books about writing, other teachers, and any literacy staff developers that may be in your building. I encourage teachers to do this. Gathering craft ideally becomes a personal reflection of the students you teach in addition to any resources you read and study.

The Five Senses

The five senses is a popular topic to teach when trying to help students write more descriptively. And it should be! We experience the world through each of our five senses; describing more than one sense offers a multidimensional image for the reader. The student writing in Figure 4.1 certainly allows a reader to feel and picture what it's like in the tropics.

It's probably safe to say that by third grade most students know about the five senses. They know what they are and they usually know that using the five

FIGURE 4.1

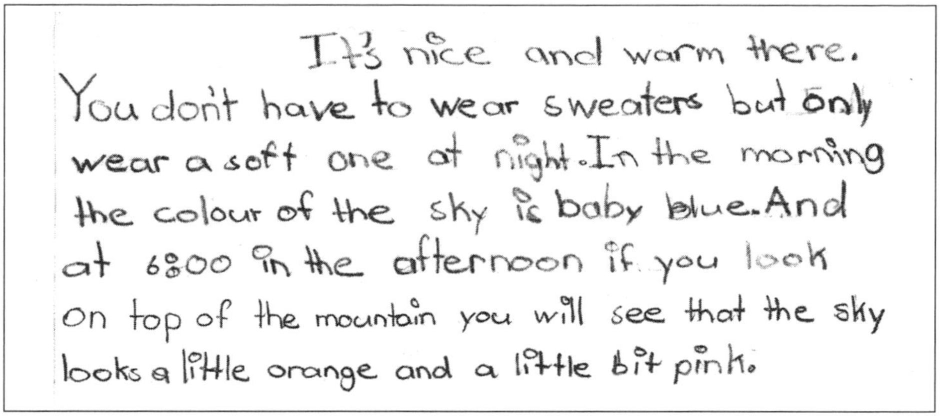

> It's nice and warm there. You don't have to wear sweaters but only wear a soft one at night. In the morning the colour of the sky is baby blue. And at 6:00 in the afternoon if you look on top of the mountain you will see that the sky looks a little orange and a little bit pink.

senses can make their writing better. But after a mini-lesson on this topic, many students revert to describing only with visual details, if any. In order for teachers to support students in using the five senses when writing independently, without teacher prompting, I have found it best to focus on one sense at a time.

The Sense of Sound

I was recently conferring with John, a third grader who was in the middle of writing about a Celtics basketball game he had recently attended with his dad. He was writing mostly about the halftime show, which was his favorite part. In his notebook entry, he included a few good visual details—how the mascot, Lucky, flipped ten times and how he later stood on stilts. I noticed John wasn't using sound in this entry or any other recent entry. I saw this as a good opportunity to show him how he could bring sound into his writing. Now, I have been to basketball games, so I know in general what they sound like. When I first read his entry, my mind was mostly filling up with whatever visual images he gave me. Readers are supposed to fill in *some* information with their own visualizing; we wouldn't want every single thing described for us. But I find that most students are still working on offering the reader enough details to create a healthy balance. When reading John's entry, I might have had a few basketball sounds in the back of my mind, but in a very hazy way.

After talking with John about this memory and talking with him about how sounds make a story come alive for the reader, I asked him to think back and remember some sounds that he could include in this entry. He added: "the bozzer went of dinggg." A few sentences later he wrote, "Then the music turned on." Every time I teach the concept of including sounds in writing, I am reminded just how much magnifying particular sounds helps a memory (or story) come alive for the reader. As soon as John added that first sentence, I suddenly and very clearly heard that loud, monotone buzzer that occurs only at basketball games.

Table 4.1 Sense of Sound

BASIC CRAFT SKILL	EXAMPLE SENTENCE	WHY IS IT GOOD?
Including sound in writing	*I heard seagulls.*	Basic sound: makes the story come alive for the reader

SPECIFIC CRAFT	EXAMPLE SENTENCE	WHY IS IT GOOD?
Writing *I could hear* (instead of *I heard*)	*I could hear seagulls.*	Sentence variety: avoids repetition of *I heard*
ing verb after the sound	*I heard seagulls squawking.*	Specifies the sound
Sound without writing *I heard*	*In the air, seagulls were squawking.*	Gives reader the sound without taking up the whole sentence to say so—more room for other information
Writing a sound (even if it's not a real word)	*"Kaaa kaaa," the seagulls cried as they circled in the air above us.*	Brings the sound to life
Describing a sound using a simile	*The seagulls above us were squawking like an unrehearsed chorus.*	Gives a precise and somewhat exaggerated sound
Describing sounds with *as if*	*The seagulls above us were squawking as if they hadn't eaten all day.*	Gives an emotion or motive to sound (even if hypothetical); can indicate a more precise sound
Sound and visual using *as*	*Seagulls squawked above us as we walked onto the beach.*	Gives reader a sound and a visual at the same time

Very often, if I am introducing the concept of adding sound, either in a conference or a mini-lesson, I begin with just the basic idea that adding sound can help make a memory or story come alive for the reader. It's only after this foundation is created that I introduce some of the smaller, more specific craft skills that relate to sound. Although the differences among the ways to write sound listed in Table 4.1 may seem subtle at times, legitimizing them as separate craft techniques means you have more specific instruction at your disposal. Specific craft is based on the fact that the subtle difference between craft skills matters. When students (and adults) understand that there are different ways to write a sound, they can make choices as writers, thereby creating variety in writing.

As with most charts in this chapter, Table 4.1 first introduces the use of a basic craft skill. The rest of the chart illustrates the related specific craft. The "Why Is It Good?" column highlights how subtle differences in craft create subtle differences in what each one does for the reader. Putting the Why in words will also be important when we come back to the actual instruction of craft, both in whole-class lessons and conferences.

Very often these charts move from basic specific craft toward more advanced craft techniques. One benefit of this range is that it legitimizes even the simplest use of craft that can be found in student writing. Another benefit of this developmental range is that it identifies slightly more complex craft techniques for students who are already including sound in their writing. Ideally, craft instruction in lessons and conferences does not just help students use craft that seems to be missing, but also shows students ways to *enhance* craft they are already using. These more advanced craft techniques are particularly useful when conferring with students who write very well and often leave teachers wondering what to teach.

I do find that if students are writing with only visual details, sound is often the first sense I teach. There seem to be more opportunities for students to use sound than other senses in their writing because sound is something that is almost constantly a part of our everyday experience. Very rarely is life absolutely silent. In quiet places there are still sounds—they are just smaller. In a library, for example, even when there is no one talking or whispering, there is still the sound of moving chairs, cars outside, the wheel of a book cart, or the ticking of a clock. These small sounds, ironically, can emphasize just how quiet a place is.

The Senses of Smell, Taste, and Touch

The senses of smell, taste, and touch, on the other hand, are not as much of a constant part of life. Even as I sit in my office, I hear and see plenty, but it would be hard to describe any particular smell or taste. Even though I am sitting in a chair and typing on a keyboard, there is nothing at the moment worth describing in terms of feel or touch either. There are certain experiences we all have when one or a few of these three senses are highly active. Describing a snowstorm or rainstorm, for example, invites the sense of touch. Any meal or food experience is a great opportunity to describe both taste and smell. One reason I sometimes like writing about the beach in lessons is that writing about this place invites so many different kinds of details from all the senses. The same is true when I write about going to the dentist: my experience of this place involves so many of my senses—the feel of the cool plastic chairs, the taste of the fluoride goop and of the bubble gum toothpaste on the high-speed toothbrush. I can write about all the senses because they are all so heightened when I'm sitting in the dentist's chair. We can't force students to mention senses that were not strong parts of a memory, but we can certainly help them understand that when the opportunity presents itself, these other senses—smell, taste, and touch—are wonderful details that can enliven a memory or story. Tables 4.2, 4.3, and 4.4 offer craft lessons for each of these senses.

Table 4.2 Sense of Smell

BASIC CRAFT SKILL	EXAMPLE SENTENCE	WHY IS IT GOOD?
Including smells in writing	*I smelled coffee.*	Basic smell: helps the story come alive for the reader

SPECIFIC CRAFT	EXAMPLE SENTENCE	WHY IS IT GOOD?
Writing *I could smell* (instead of *I smelled*)	*I could smell the coffee.*	Sentence variety: avoids repetition of *I smelled*
Including an adjective with the smell	*I smelled the freshly brewed coffee.*	Describes a more specific smell
Describing the air or place	*The smell of freshly brewed coffee filled the kitchen.*	Makes the smell the focus of the sentence; sentence variety: a different way to describe a smell
Describing a reaction to the smell	*As soon as I smelled the coffee, I felt so much more awake.*	Combination: gives a smell and an emotion at the same time
Using the smell as an adjective	*The freshly brewed coffee smell drifted into everyone's bedroom.*	Gives the reader a smell without taking up the whole sentence to do so—more room for other information

Table 4.3 Sense of Taste

BASIC CRAFT SKILL	EXAMPLE SENTENCE	WHY IS IT GOOD?
Naming something you tasted	*Then we ate some pizza.*	Basic taste: helps bring story alive for the reader

SPECIFIC CRAFT	EXAMPLE SENTENCE	WHY IS IT GOOD?
Describing the taste	*Then we ate some pizza. It was so cheesy and delicious.*	Reader can better experience the taste
Giving visual details of the food	*Then we ate some pizza. It had cheese all over and was sprinkled with peppers and mushrooms.*	Gives visual and taste
Describe the ingredients	*Then we ate some pizza. My uncle puts oregano in the tomato sauce and uses two types of cheese—mozzarella and a little bit of cheddar.*	Gives a visual and more specific taste
Showing reaction to the taste	*Then we ate some pizza. I couldn't believe how cheesy it was. I already wanted another slice.*	Shares a feeling along with the taste

Table 4.4 Sense of Touch		
BASIC CRAFT SKILL	**EXAMPLE SENTENCE**	**WHY IS IT GOOD?**
Including the sense of touch in writing	*I felt the warm sand on my feet.*	Basic description of how something feels: helps the story come alive for the reader
SPECIFIC CRAFT	**EXAMPLE SENTENCE**	**WHY IS IT GOOD?**
Writing *I could feel*	*I could feel the warm sand on my feet.*	Sentence variety: avoids repetition of *I felt*
Starting with the object	*The sand felt warm on my feet.*	Shifts the emphasis from the person to the object
Adding a visual adjective	*The white sand felt warm on my feet.*	Provides a more specific visual in combination with the sense of touch
Describing the "touch" without using the words *feel* or *felt*	*The white sand warmed the bottoms of my feet.*	Avoids repetition of *I could feel*; less informational
Describing two different ways something feels	*The sand warmed the bottoms of my feet and stuck in between my toes.*	Describes two different senses for the reader
Using a simile to describe how something feels	*The sand was as soft as flour.*	Gives a precise and somewhat exaggerated feel by comparing to a familiar object.
Sense of touch and visual using *as*	*The white sand warmed the bottoms of my feet as we walked onto the beach.*	Gives the reader two senses in one sentence.

Sense of Sight: Visual Description

There may not be a particular order to the five senses, but I saved the sense of sight for last on purpose. Because most of us take in so much information through our sight, this sense needs more than one chart to cover related specific craft. There are so many things to consider when recreating visual images for a reader. The other four senses, although powerful, are more limited in choice. If I were writing about going into a doughnut shop, for example, I might mention the smell of the doughnuts themselves and maybe the scent of brewing coffee. After that, my choices as a writer are really about *how* to write about those smells. I might spend several sentences describing the smells or sneak in the sense of smell here and there with a few words, but the number of smells I can write about at one time is usually not that extensive.

If I were to think about what to describe visually in the doughnut shop, however, the list would feel endless. I could describe everything from the '70s beige cash register to the display of doughnuts sitting in metal racks to the three regulars sitting in the corner reading the *Boston Globe*. Whichever one I decide to write about, there are then smaller visuals to consider: the tip jar made from a plastic cup sitting on the cash register; cinnamon dust on the wax paper left from doughnuts already bought; the POW buttons on one customer's jacket.

During writing lessons, teachers commonly give the directive to create a mental picture or make a mind movie for the reader. Although these are accurate ways to describe what good writers often do with visual details, it's more complicated than simply writing what you see in your mind. Good writing doesn't entail describing every single thing all the time. Talking about creating a mind movie can help, but this doesn't necessarily translate into skillful use of visual description. By using specific craft, you can show students tangible ways of going in and out of detailed description. Some categories of craft that create different but specific types of visual description in writing follow.

Colors

Using color to paint a visual image for a reader is one of the more basic ways of describing. Even in first grade some students are describing objects by mentioning their colors. As students' writing develops throughout the grades,

Table 4.5 Colors

BASIC CRAFT SKILL	EXAMPLE SENTENCE	WHY IS IT GOOD?
Including colors in writing	*The water was blue.*	Basic colors: helps reader create a better visual image

SPECIFIC CRAFT	EXAMPLE SENTENCE	WHY IS IT GOOD?
Using color as an adjective	*I wanted to dive into the blue water.*	The color is not the purpose of the sentence: leaves room for other information
Mentioning a particular shade of a color	*I wanted to dive into the aqua blue water.*	Gives a more precise color
Using a simile to describe a color	*The water was as blue as the night sky.*	Conveys a shade of a color without saying it
Using a familiar object to describe the exact color.	*The water was the color of Windex.*	Conveys an exact shade of a color without saying it
Using a familiar object as an adjective	*I couldn't wait to dive into the Windex blue water.*	Conveys an exact shade in the sentence while leaving room for other information

Table 4.6 Comparing		
BASIC CRAFT SKILL A simile	**EXAMPLE SENTENCE** *Olivia's hands were as sticky as cotton candy.*	**WHY IS IT GOOD?** Basic simile: compares to a familiar object so you can feel (in this case) the stickiness
SPECIFIC CRAFT "One upping" a simile	**EXAMPLE SENTENCE** *Olivia's hands were stickier than cotton candy.*	**WHY IS IT GOOD?** Heightens the stickiness
Using *as if* to give a description	*Olivia's hands were sticky, as if she had just washed them in honey.*	A made-up action creates a visual image to enliven the description
Using *so . . . that* to give a description	*Olivia's hands were so sticky that her hand almost stuck to the doorknob.*	Using an action gives a visual and enlivens description

there are several different ways they can enhance the way they describe colors, as shown in Table 4.5.

Comparing

Comparing, which is presented in Table 4.6, is another category that falls under visual description. This particular category was also used in Chapter 2 to demonstrate the nature of specific craft.

Specific Versus General

In Chapter 3, I described how brand names offer a packed visual image for the reader in just a few words. The image is detailed because the product itself is so specific. When a writer chooses to use a brand name, very often a general word could have been used instead. If I were writing about going to the movies, for example, I could mention that I bought some candy and popcorn. There is nothing really wrong with that detail. But as soon as I use a brand name, such as Snickers or Junior Mints, instead of candy, the specificity of the product automatically provides much more description.

Brand names are not the only way a writer can choose a specific name over a more general word to give a more detailed image. The list in Table 4.7 illustrates some of the different topics that present opportunities for using specific names. Some of these examples also show how specificity can enhance descriptions with senses other than sight. This is one of several tables that does not include a basic craft technique. As demonstrated in the example sentences, each specific craft technique in this category relates to its own more basic choice.

Table 4.7 Specific Versus General

SPECIFIC CRAFT	EXAMPLE SENTENCE	WHY IS IT GOOD?
Names of people	*Leah and Jessica came over for dinner to meet my cousin Quincy.* (vs. *My friends came over for dinner to meet my cousin.*)	Gives a more specific image to the reader
Name of a restaurant	*Before I got my braces, my mom took me to Friendly's for lunch.* (vs. *Before I got my braces, my mom took me out for lunch.*)	Gives a more specific image to the reader
Name of a store	*Yesterday my mom and I went to Marshalls and then DSW to look for shoes.* (vs. *Yesterday my mom and I went to some stores to look for shoes.*)	Gives a more specific image to the reader
Brand names for any type of food	*Joseph threw a handful of Kraft Macaroni & Cheese on the floor from his high chair.* (vs. *Joseph threw food on the floor from his high chair.*)	Gives a more specific image and taste to the reader
Specific type of food (not brand name)	*We had turkey and Swiss sandwiches for lunch.* (vs. *We had sandwiches for lunch.*)	Gives a more specific image and taste to the reader
Specific type of candy	*After we ordered popcorn, Sondra decided to get some Skittles and Junior Mints.* (vs. *After we ordered popcorn, Sondra decided to get some candy.*)	Gives a more specific image and taste to the reader
Brand names for clothes	*After seeing how fast the snow was coming down outside, Mike put on his Timberland boots.* (vs. *After seeing how fast the snow was coming down outside, Mike put on his boots.*)	Gives a more specific image to the reader
Brand names for drinks	*Nikki grabbed a Sprite and two Cokes and stuffed them into her beach bag.* (vs. *Nikki grabbed some sodas and stuffed them into her beach bag.*)	Gives a more specific image and taste to the reader
Type of animal	*Sitting in front of the supermarket were two poodles and a German shepherd.* (vs. *Sitting in front of the supermarket, were three dogs.*)	Gives a more specific image to the reader
Title of a song (or name of an artist)	*I started to do my taxes as I listened to Pavarotti.* (vs. *I started to do my taxes as I listened to music.*)	Gives a more specific sound to the reader

Table 4.8 Describing the Background

SPECIFIC CRAFT	EXAMPLE SENTENCE	WHY IS IT GOOD?
Telling the season	*It was a spring day.*	Provides reader with a general picture of the time of year.
Showing the season	*Tree branches were just starting to show little green buds.*	Gives a specific visual image and indicates time of year
Telling the weather	*It was a sunny but cool day.*	Relates to sense of touch
Showing the weather	*The sun felt warm on my face but I was glad I had put on an extra sweater.*	Recreates specific feeling of weather (sense of touch) without being told information
Describing nature in the background	*Trees lined the sidewalks and every now and then little purple crocuses stuck out from the ground.*	Gives reader a fuller image
Describing small objects in a room	*Black and white photographs of relatives lined the mantel above the large fireplace.*	Offers detailed images that also tend to reflect personality of the owner or owners

Describing the Background

When it comes to visual description, many students at first tend to write details based only on the action of the story. This is a good start, but we want students to understand that describing the scenery, or background of the story, makes for a fuller, more descriptive image. Craft skills for describing the background are listed in Table 4.8. This is another table that does not include a basic craft example. As with other categories discussed later in this chapter, the alternative to using this kind of craft technique is to not use any at all—in this case, the writing would not mention the background in any way.

Show Not Tell

"Show not tell" is one of the most well-known writer sayings. There is a good reason we hear these three words from elementary school all the way up to the college level. When we pick up a piece of writing, we don't just want to be told a story, we want to see it in our minds and experience it. I don't read novels at the beach, for example, just so I can know the plot. I read them for entertainment, as much as I see a movie for entertainment. Writers need to use words that create images and emotions for other people in addition to telling a story. Figure 4.2 is a good example of student writing that conveys feelings—both emotional and physical—with show not tell.

FIGURE 4.2

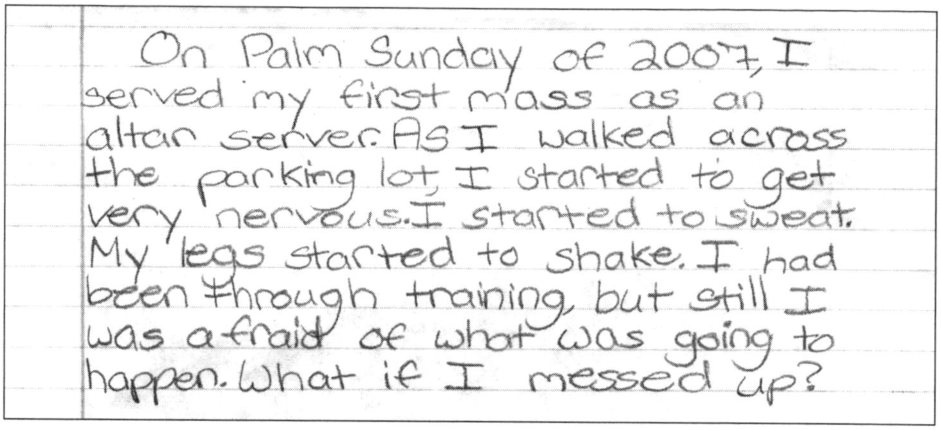

> On Palm Sunday of 2007, I served my first mass as an altar server. As I walked across the parking lot, I started to get very nervous. I started to sweat. My legs started to shake. I had been through training, but still I was afraid of what was going to happen. What if I messed up?

It makes sense that elementary teachers find themselves teaching many lessons about show not tell. Developmentally, it's where students of this age should be: they are supposed to be in the midst of shifting from telling to showing in their writing. Think of where they are coming from in terms of expectations. In the primary grades, one aspect of doing a "good job" in writing means a student can tell a story in order. The younger grades also have a lot more emphasis on the more foundational skills of writing. Students can start adding basic craft such as using colors, adding dialogue, and sharing basic feelings such as *I was so sad*. By the end of second grade and at the beginning of third grade, students are typically ready to move on to what it means to show not tell. But I wouldn't expect my students to go from writing sentences such as *I was so sad* to *Tears were streaming down my face*. That's quite a leap, both in vocabulary and in concept. This is not to say we should not have expectations that students in the elementary grades are capable of writing that way. What I am saying is that if this type of show not tell is not happening naturally in their writing, then we can show students specific next steps that will help them move beyond *I was so sad*. The eventual goal would still be for students to consistently and skillfully "show not tell" on their own, but what I think needs more validation are the smaller steps in between basic skills and the desired goal. Specific craft can help students *develop*, not just automatically obtain, the ability to show not tell.

Feelings

Students in the elementary grades are often overly aware of telling a story in terms of what happened. Adding sentences about how someone was feeling or what they were thinking, what I commonly refer to as *inside sentences*, are particularly useful in helping students move away from just telling a story and explaining what happened. Feelings help the reader connect with the experience being told on an emotional level. Tables 4.9, 4.10, and 4.11 give some craft techniques for writing inside sentences.

Table 4.9 Feelings

BASIC CRAFT SKILL	EXAMPLE SENTENCE	WHY IS IT GOOD?
Including feelings in writing	*I was sad.*	Basic inside sentence: helps reader experience a story on an emotional level

SPECIFIC CRAFT	EXAMPLE SENTENCE	WHY IS IT GOOD?
Telling a feeling, then giving a reason (using the word *because*)	*I was so sad because I couldn't find my dog.*	Connects the feeling to a reason: gives reader something to relate to
Using *so . . . that* to describe a feeling	*I was so sad that I wanted to cry forever.*	Gives the emotion a specific level of intensity
Telling a feeling, then showing it	*I was so sad. Tears came streaming down my face.*	Includes a visual image for the reader
Showing a feeling instead of telling it	*My heart sank and tears ran down my cheek.*	Describing only the visual image creates a direct feeling, not so informational

Only in the last example does my sentence show an emotion without any telling whatsoever. The appeal here is that rather than receiving information about how someone feels, the reader just experiences the emotion. By offering visual images of an emotion, the reader can infer the feeling and doesn't need to be told.

Thoughts and Feelings

Although feelings and thoughts are separate concepts, they are often closely connected. Whenever we feel something emotionally, there is an affiliated thought, whether on a conscious or subconscious level. We don't feel things in a vacuum. The craft techniques in Table 4.10 reflect this close connection.

Table 4.10 Thoughts and Feelings

SPECIFIC CRAFT	EXAMPLE SENTENCE	WHY IS IT GOOD?
Telling a feeling then a related thought	*I was so sad. I thought I would never see my dog again.*	A double "inside story": reader understands what another person is feeling and thinking
Showing a feeling and then a related thought	*My heart sank and tears ran down my cheek. I thought I would never see my dog again.*	A double "inside story": gives reader a visual rather than information about a feeling
Showing a feeling, then showing a thought through a question	*My heart sank and tears ran down my cheek. How would I ever go on?*	A double "inside story": experience of the thought is more natural rather than informational

	Table 4.11 Thoughts	
BASIC CRAFT SKILL	**EXAMPLE SENTENCE**	**WHY IS IT GOOD?**
Including thoughts in writing	*I thought the spinach lasagna my aunt made was terrible.*	Basic inside sentence: creates a closer connection to the reader
SPECIFIC CRAFT	**EXAMPLE SENTENCE**	**WHY IS IT GOOD?**
Writing a thought with *I wondered . . .*	*I wondered how Marlene could have made such a terrible lasagna.*	Sentence variety: avoids repetition of *I thought*
Writing a thought without the words *I thought*	*The spinach lasagna tasted terrible!*	Experience of the thought is more natural rather than informational
Using inside/outside sentences (first share the thought, then show how you appeared)	*I thought the spinach lasagna was terrible. When Marlene looked at me, I forced a big smile as I managed to swallow another bite.*	Creates a visual but also a close connection: the reader is "in" on what is real and what is apparent
Talking to yourself	*"What on earth did she put in this?" I thought to myself.*	Makes inner dialogue more animated
Using a question to convey a thought	*How did she make such a terrible lasagna?*	Shares a thought rather than telling it; less informational; illustrates inner dialogue
Offering a possible answer after asking a question	*How did she make such a terrible lasagna? She probably experimented with tofu again.*	Shares a thought but also offers additional information

Thoughts

Some thoughts we have, on the other hand, are on a purely practical, intellectual level and don't emit strong emotions. While the previous category reflects the overlapping of thoughts and feelings that occur in life, the craft in Table 4.11 reflects more pragmatic thoughts that can be included in writing.

Words That "Tell"

A common reason teachers plan lessons that fall under the category of show not tell is because they see students write a lot of sentences like these:

> *The ride was fun.*
> *The dinner was good.*
> *Her dress was pretty.*

These are great opportunities for students to offer description, for them to show rather than tell. But often students just move on to the next thing that happened. When teachers read these types of sentences, they often picture the missed opportunities. This is especially true if you talk with students in conferences and get them to mention details they could have written. If a student wrote "The dress was pretty," for example, it might not be until you talk with her that she mentions all the wonderful details: the light green color of the dress, the shiny material, and the ribbons on the back.

Chances are that this student *was* picturing that dress with all the ribbons and shiny material when she described it as "pretty." Many elementary students are in the midst of learning that their new job as writers is to create images for a reader and learning how to do that job well. This shift requires them to move outside their own experiences, which is not an overnight process.

When it comes to students using vague descriptors such as *good, fun,* and *pretty,* I have found it helpful, especially in a conference, to teach students to add one more sentence as a next step. This strategy is similar to some of the specific craft techniques that involve thoughts and feelings. In one example, the telling of a feeling is followed by a second sentence that describes the feeling; it doesn't yet ask the student to let go of the telling. Keeping a foot in both telling and showing provides a comfortable transition. It is also a very doable, tangible next step. From these "dual" sentences, it is not such a leap for a student to soon move on to just showing feelings without telling the reader at all.

This same concept of adding one more sentence to a "telling" sentence can be used with vague descriptors such as *fun, good,* and *pretty,* as shown in Table 4.12.

I made a point not to write absolutely fabulous second sentences. If students are at the point of writing "It was fun" or "The dinner was good," then typically these second sentences aren't always unbelievably descriptive, which is developmentally appropriate. But in writing a second sentence, no matter

Table 4.12 Showing After Telling

BASIC CRAFT SKILL	EXAMPLE SENTENCE	WHY IS IT GOOD?
Telling a feeling, then showing it	*I was so sad. Tears came down my face.*	Includes a visual image for the reader

SPECIFIC CRAFT	EXAMPLE SENTENCE	WHY IS IT GOOD?
After saying it's *fun,* writing one sentence to show it's fun	*The ride was fun. It went up and down really fast.*	Includes a visual image for the reader: the reader understands why it's fun
After saying it's *good,* writing one sentence to show it's good.	*The dinner was good. We had homemade gravy.*	Includes a visual image for the reader: the reader understands why it's good
After saying it's *pretty,* writing one sentence to show it's pretty	*Her dress was pretty. It was green and long.*	Includes a visual image for the reader: the reader understands why it's pretty

how simple, students take an important next step—they are taking a moment to give the reader a description before moving onto the next topic.

Students can easily take ownership of this next step of adding a second sentence and use it regardless of what they write about. For example, if I were conferring with the student who wrote "The dress was pretty," I could spend several minutes fishing for details about her dress. If all she does is write down the details that come out in our conference, I have not really taught her anything she can own. Although that kind of conference might help in demonstrating the thinking process behind adding details and might make her feel good that she made her writing better, this kind of support leans more toward the writing rather than the writer.

If, however, after fishing for details, I move on to a teaching point about adding one or two more sentences after writing the word *pretty* so the reader can understand why something is pretty, I have helped her beyond this particular piece of writing. Imagine that a few days later this same student is working on another notebook entry and writes, "The flowers were pretty." Because the word *pretty* had been the focus of my instruction, it has a chance of acting as a trigger for this craft technique. This student will more likely remember she can follow her sentence about the flowers with a second sentence that describes why and in what way the flowers were pretty.

Another way to help students move beyond general descriptors is to focus on what they are saying is fun or pretty, rather than the actual words. In the *pretty dress* example, I could follow fishing for details with a teaching point that focuses on the topic of clothes. I would want the student to understand that whenever she writes about clothes, she can write a few sentences about what they look like so the reader can see them too. Then the topic of clothes, rather than the word *pretty*, can act as the trigger. The next time this student is writing about clothes, there is a greater chance she will remember she could add a few sentences that show what the clothes look like. Teaching specific craft of course does not guarantee students will always remember and use what was taught in a conference or mini-lesson on craft. But because specific craft techniques are so tangible, they are easier for students to remember as they write.

After students start becoming more aware of how important it is to provide the reader with visual images, even by adding only one sentence, they can then move on to strengthening the quality and length of their descriptions. Next steps at this point could focus on specific types of visual descriptions and other craft skills such as describing feelings and sounds. The more options students have for bringing description into their writing, the more they will be showing the reader, and the less they will need to hang on to telling the reader.

Revision Strategies for Show Not Tell

Revision strategies, in addition to specific craft techniques, can help students move beyond just telling the story. It's important to note that I mean a specific

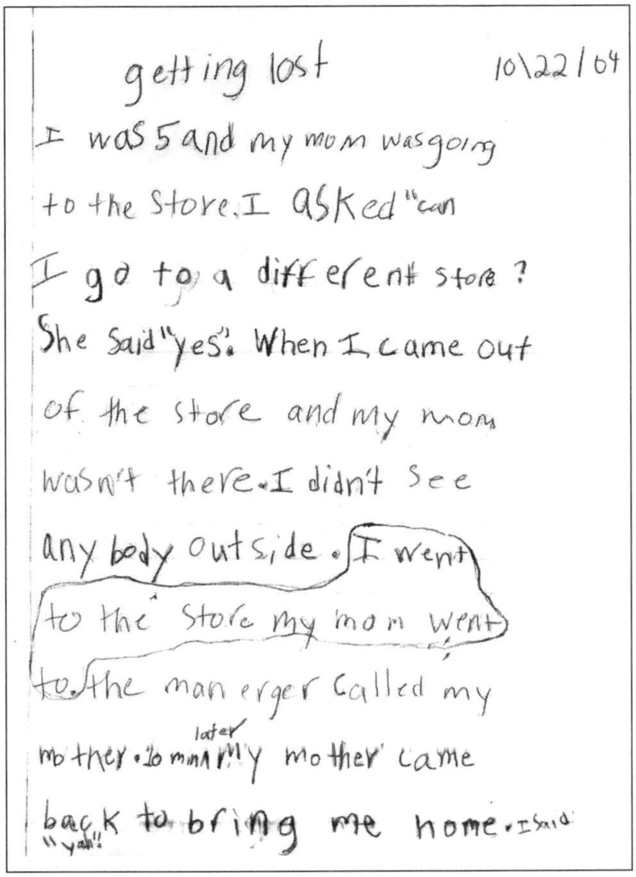

getting lost 10\22\04

I was 5 and my mom was going to the store. I asked "can I go to a different store? She said "yes". When I came out of the store and my mom wasn't there. I didn't see anybody outside. I went to the store my mom went to the man erger called my mother. 10 mins later My mother came back to bring me home. I said "yay!"

FIGURE 4.3 Original Entry

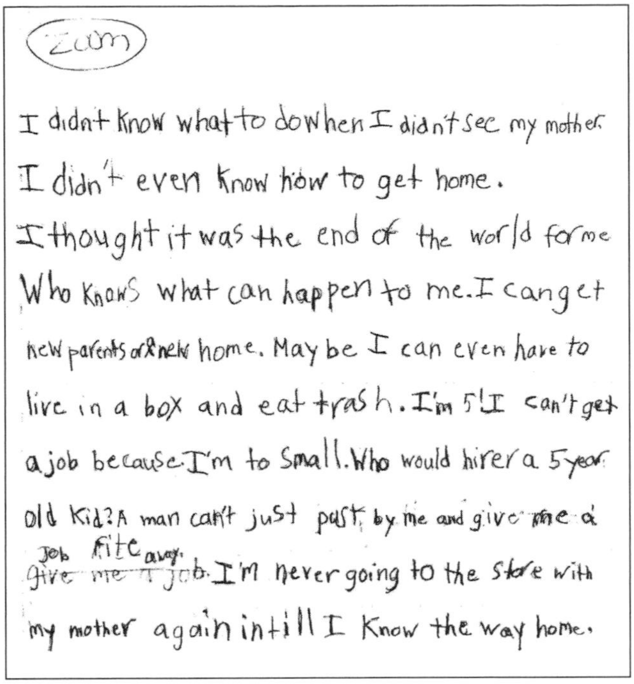

Zoom

I didn't know what to do when I didn't see my mother I didn't even know how to get home. I thought it was the end of the world for me Who knows what can happen to me. I can get new parents or new home. Maybe I can even have to live in a box and eat trash. I'm 5! I can't get a job because I'm to small. Who would hire a 5 year old kid? A man can't just past by me and give me a job right away. give me a job. I'm never going to the store with my mother again intill I know the way home.

FIGURE 4.4 Zooming In

FIGURE 4.5 Letter

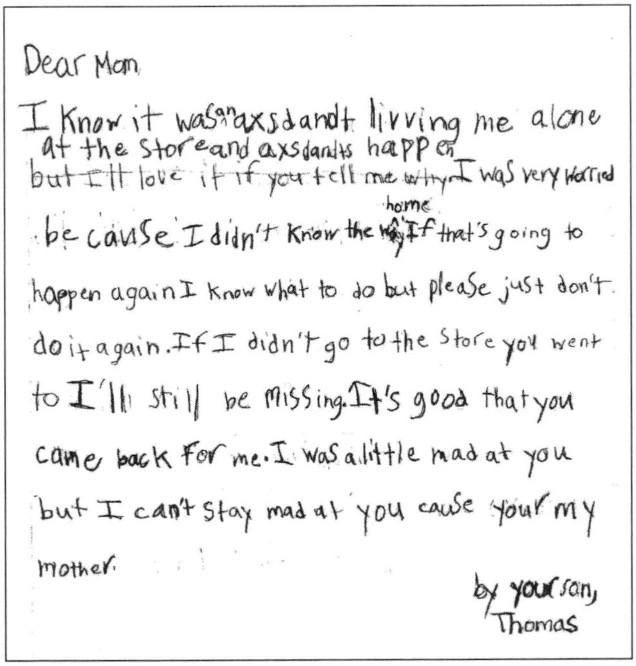

Dear Mom

I know it was an axsdandt livving me alone at the store and axsdandts happen but I'll love if if you tell me why I was very worried be cause I didn't know the way home If that's going to happen again I know what to do but please just don't do it again. If I didn't go to the store you went to I'll still be missing. It's good that you came back for me. I was a little mad at you but I can't stay mad at you cause your my mother.

by your son,
Thomas

kind of revision, revision being a very elastic term when it comes to the writing process. To many teachers and writing programs, revision means fixing a piece of writing by squeezing in sentences and words here and there. The revision strategies I learned from Lucy Calkins, however, are ones that free students from their original writing notebook entry. For example, one strategy has students zoom in on certain parts of an entry by taking that part and expanding it on another piece of paper or in another part of their notebook.

Another revision strategy I often teach students is to write a letter to someone who was mentioned in their original notebook entry. Each person they write to brings into focus a different relationship as well as a different perspective of any memory. The form of a letter naturally gets students to write in the second person, which in turn brings emotions and feelings to the surface.

Figures 4.4 and 4.5 are examples of how both zooming in and writing a letter helped a student bring out details and inside feelings and thoughts that were not in his original entry, shown in Figure 4.3, where he was just telling the story.

Teaching students to write with more detail ideally includes both larger writing strategies as well as specific craft techniques.

Dialogue

Dialogue, like many other craft techniques, helps to make a memory or story come alive for the reader. In Figure 4.6, it's the dialogue that makes the mother's reaction lifelike for us. The words inside the quotation marks are, of course, the words that were actually spoken (or in the case of fiction, words the writer wants us to imagine as being spoken). Although some lessons can certainly focus on writing authentic dialogue, it is the words outside the quotation marks that give life to the dialogue. Writers can use different types of words and phrases, as demonstrated in Table 4.13, to convey different images for the reader.

One of my favorite craft techniques to teach is the use of *as* with dialogue. It's very attainable for children and it immediately lifts up the complexity of

Table 4.13 Words Next to Dialogue

BASIC CRAFT SKILL	EXAMPLE SENTENCE	WHY IS IT GOOD?
Including dialogue in writing	*"Let's have pizza for dinner," Joseph said.*	Basic dialogue: helps bring the memory or story alive for the reader

SPECIFIC CRAFT	EXAMPLE SENTENCE	WHY IS IT GOOD?
Said before the name	*"Let's have pizza for dinner," said Joseph.*	Sentence variety: offers a different rhythm than *Joseph said*
Variations of *said* that show volume	*"Let's have pizza for dinner," shouted Joseph.*	Specifies how loudly or quietly something is said
Said with an adverb to show volume	*"Let's have pizza for dinner," Joseph said loudly.*	Specifies how loudly or quietly something is said
Said with adverbs that show pace	*"Let's have pizza for dinner," Joseph said quickly.*	Specifies how slowly or quickly something is said
Said with an adverb to show emotion	*"Let's have pizza for dinner," Joseph said excitedly.*	Conveys emotion along with what is said
Using *as* to add an action	*"Let's have pizza for dinner," Joseph said as he jumped up and down.*	Gives reader a sound (dialogue) and visual (action) at the same time
Using *while* to add an action	*"Let's have pizza for dinner," Joseph said while his mom wrote a grocery list.*	Gives reader a sound (dialogue) and visual (action) at the same time

FIGURE 4.6

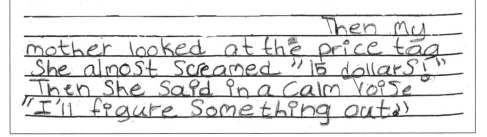

their writing. This technique lets students create those packed images I have mentioned previously. Whenever we say something, we are almost always *doing* something, whether it's holding an object, moving a certain way, making gestures with our arms or hands, or making more subtle gestures with our facial expressions. In teaching students about using the word *as*, I am encouraging them to slow down their thinking and take advantage of all the images that are available in their own minds.

Using *Said* in Dialogue

I want to take a moment to speak in defense of the word *said*. This word is sometimes given a bad reputation when it comes to dialogue and is often accused of creating mediocre writing. I've even been in several classrooms that have a poster with *said* sitting inside a big, red circle with a red slash in front of it. All around *said* on the poster are more "exciting" words to replace *said*. The more I've accumulated specific craft by noticing what good writers do, the more I've realized just how much this word does not belong behind red bars. Of course we don't want students to use *said* over and over, and it is true that one way students can make dialogue more lively is to use other words besides *said*, such as *shouted* and *whispered*. But *said* can also be enhanced. Adding to the word *said*, instead of always replacing it, will lead to greater variety in writing. In fact, it's *said*'s bland complexion that allows a writer to add description to dialogue without overdoing it. Understanding how to enhance *said*, in addition to replacing it with other words, means students have more choices at their disposal as they write dialogue.

Dialogue Structures

Most of the dialogue craft techniques we've looked at so far would appear after dialogue in student writing, which tends to be the most common way of structuring dialogue. Table 4.14 shows other ways of structuring dialogue, each one creating a different rhythm. The Why column is not included in this table because the Why relates not to the singular use of any one structure, but to the skill of alternating among different dialogue structures throughout a piece of writing.

Table 4.14 Dialogue Structures	
SPECIFIC CRAFT	**EXAMPLE SENTENCE**
Dialogue first	*"You know, we could just store some of the tomato sauce in the freezer," Tony suggested.*
Sandwich dialogue	*"You know," Tony suggested, "We could just store some of the tomato sauce in the freezer."*
Dialogue last	*Then Tony said, "You know, we could just store some of the tomato sauce in the freezer."*

Sentence Variety

Sentence variety is an aspect of craft that has to do with the sound and rhythm of writing. When we read the writing in Figure 4.7, the words sound lively—there's the thoughtful intonation of a question, the repeated staccato of a short sentence and an intentional sentence fragment, and a straightforward declarative sentence. One of the best ways to help students get a sense of what good writing sounds like is for them to hear lots and lots of writing. Teachers help support this exposure by choosing read-alouds and modeling the lyrical variety writing can offer, whether in picture books or chapter books. The end goal of all this modeling is not simply listening to read-alouds but growth in students' ability to hear sounds and rhythms of words in their own minds when they read by themselves.

One skill that provides an important foundation for writing with sentence variety is the ability to write complete sentences. In my experience, run-on sentences, especially those with lots of *and then*'s are one of the biggest frustrations for teachers at the elementary level. This habit is indicative of students who are still primarily focused on telling their stories. Many children tend to think of one thing at a time as they write whether that thing is an action, a sound, or a feeling. The phrase *and then* allows students to mention one thing *and then* move onto the next thing, regardless of how short or long the actual sentence is. Writing sentences this way, however, does not allow much room for either sentence variety or description. The next chapter, which focuses on craft that involves punctuation, looks more closely at the skill of writing complete sentences with periods and other end punctuation.

FIGURE 4.7

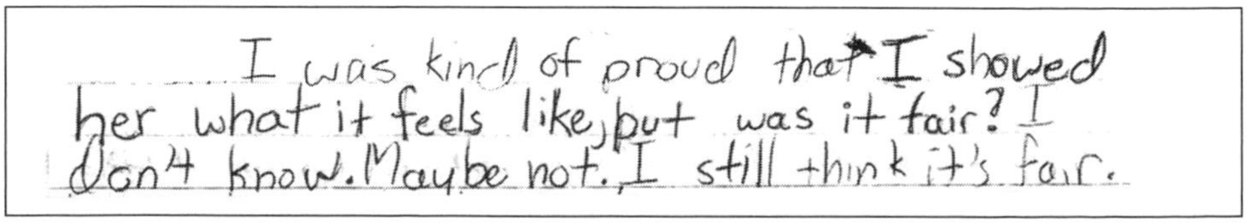

I was kind of proud that I showed her what it feels like, but was it fair? I don't know. Maybe not. I still think it's fair.

Although the following categories may at times relate to other types of craft, they are particularly effective when it comes to looking at writing through the lens of sentence variety.

Sentence Length and Sentence Beginnings

When every sentence in a piece of writing is the same length or starts with a similar kind of word, monotony puts a ceiling on the voice of the writing, regardless of how craftlike the words are. Table 4.15 gives a few types of sentences that writers can use to bring variety to their writing. Although I could have given only isolated examples for each craft technique, I wrote a paragraph that includes the different types of sentences mentioned in the table. The whole purpose of sentence variety is that it provides variety within a paragraph or whole piece of writing. It is easier to understand the effects of different types of sentences in relation to each other rather than in isolation. Keep in mind that, for now, we're only looking at sentences that do not have commas in them. The more multi-layered sentences that require punctuation will be discussed in the next chapter.

Josh hoped it would not start raining while he was swimming. He looked up at the sky. The clouds were getting darker and darker over the ocean. Still, he really wanted to get in just a quick swim before the long drive and the long weekend that would be filled with relatives and talking and eating. Waves crashed against his legs as he waded in up to his hips. Then, after putting on

Table 4.15 Sentence Length and Sentence Beginnings

SPECIFIC CRAFT	EXAMPLE SENTENCE	WHY IS IT GOOD?
Two- or three-word sentence	*Josh smiled.*	Puts more emphasis on a small action or thought
A long sentence followed by a short one	*He swam for a few moments and then paused as the waves bobbed him up and down under the dawn-filled sky. Josh smiled.*	Offers a contrasting length and rhythm
Different-sized sentences	See paragraph above: short, medium, and longer sentences.	Keeps writing from having the same sound
Starting sentences with different words	See paragraph above.	Avoids repetition
Starting a sentence with an object	*The clouds were getting darker and darker over the ocean.* *Waves crashed against his legs as he waded in up to his hips.*	Emphasis on object instead of person creates variety in focus and often in rhythm

and adjusting his goggles, he took a deep breath and dove in. He swam for a few moments and then paused as the waves bobbed him up and down under the dawn-filled sky. Josh smiled. Ocean swims always made him feel better.

The craft technique of starting sentences with different words is particularly effective in strengthening sentence variety, both for narrative and expository writing. Sometimes it may be tempting to give students suggestions for different words they could use to begin sentences, such as *After that* or *Also*. But then students tend to cling to whatever you give them. When students are given just the expectation to not start sentences with the same word, then what they come up with is always better: they tend to use many different words to begin sentences, and in order to do that, they learn to play with language in their mind before they write, both in terms of word choice and word order. An example of how this technique might be taught in a lesson can be found in Chapter 7. When it comes to nonfiction and other expository text— persuasive essays, for example—it's certainly beneficial to teach beginning phrases such as *Also . . .* and *For example . . .* that go along with facts. It's not that certain sentence starters shouldn't be taught; I would just recommend first teaching a lesson that supports students playing with word order themselves to create variety, before introducing genre-specific phrases.

Combinations

Along with setting an expectation that writing should contain different-sized sentences, it's important to teach students specific ways to write longer sentences in particular. There is a limit to the ways one can write a short sentence. When it comes to writing long sentences, however, not only are there many more possibilities, but students also need support in not letting length lead to lack of control with sentences. The concept of including some longer sentences but not writing run-ons can appear contradictory to some students. If you look carefully at some of the longer sentences in literature, you'll see that although they may not be full of *and then*'s, they do sometimes "run on" a bit. The difference of course is that the author has a command of language: he or she not only writes longer sentences intentionally, but the length is used to deepen description or reflect pacing, rather than to hop from one event to the next.

Combination sentences, which were introduced in Chapter 3, are one of my favorite craft techniques to teach to students who are ready to move beyond simple sentences and write more complex, descriptive sentences. A few combination sentences also appeared in some of the preceding tables in this chapter. As with other specific craft, I have found students are more apt to understand and use combinations when they are presented with a particular word or phrase as an anchor. As Jeff Anderson points out in his book *Mechanically Inclined* (2005), certain key words indicate a relationship of time

Table 4.16 Combinations with *As*

SPECIFIC CRAFT	EXAMPLE SENTENCE	WHY IS IT GOOD?
Two actions with *as*	*Genevieve washed the dishes as Juliette arranged the cheese and crackers on a plate.*	Gives reader two visuals at the same time
Sound+ *as* + action	*My dog started barking as our friends pulled into the driveway.*	Gives reader a sound and visual at the same time
Feeling + *as* + action	*A wave of nostalgia came over me as I saw my old roommate from college getting out of the car.*	Gives reader an emotion and visual at the same time
Smell + *as* + action	*I could smell the fireplaces of nearby houses as I walked onto the porch.*	Gives reader sense of smell and a visual at the same time
Thought + *as* + action	*Eva wondered if she should have gotten more bread as she put the two loaves in the oven to warm.*	Gives reader inside thought and visual at the same time
Dialogue + *as* + action	*"Jake, can you put some music on?" Peter asked as he started setting the table.*	Gives reader sound and visual at the same time

between two events or concepts. These words include *while, as, during, before,* and *after.* Words such as these create more complex, multi-layered sentences that sometimes require the use of the comma, which will be explored in the next chapter. The more simple combinations, those that do not need a comma, are presented in Tables 4.16, 4.17, and 4.18. Because each specific craft technique in these tables has the same structure, the Why in each category is very similar: their effectiveness has to do with giving the reader two experiences at once.

Combinations with As

Although there may be other combinations with the word *as,* actions tend to be the most natural to use with combinations because they provide a visual. The two concepts you decide to link can be led by what other craft you are teaching at that time and what craft students are using already.

Combinations with While

The words *while* and *as* are similar in that they both imply that two things are happening simultaneously. Because variety is important, it's beneficial to use both words as you write. Although there is very little difference between the two, I do find that these two words are not completely interchangeable. For example, I could see myself writing, "'Where have you been?' her mother

Table 4.17 Combinations with *While*

SPECIFIC CRAFT	EXAMPLE SENTENCE	WHY IS IT GOOD?
Two actions with *while*	*My sister set the table while I arranged the cheese and crackers on a plate.*	Gives reader two actions at the same time
Sound+ *while* + action	*I listened to my new CD while washing the dishes.*	Gives reader a sound and visual at the same time
Smell + *while* + action	*The smell of bread slowly filled the room while Andrew and I were playing Scrabble.*	Gives reader a smell and action at the same time
Dialogue + *while* + action	*"Who would like coffee?" I asked while my sister started clearing dishes.*	Gives reader sound and action at the same time

asked as she put her hands on her hips." That small action with the hands not only gives a visual but also hints at the not-so-happy tone of the mother's voice. Writing "'Where have you been?' her mother asked while she put her hands on her hips," on the other hand, doesn't seem to fit quite right. Without trying to overanalyze the difference between these two words, *while* seems to fit better when the two concepts in question are somewhat ongoing. Clearly, this difference between *as* and *while* is not essential in order to use them properly, or at least use them in ways that don't sound awkward. Word usage is developed naturally through oral speech starting in childhood. But in keeping with the concept of considering how different words affect writing, I wanted to at least note the difference.

Combinations with Until

Using the word *until* in a combination implies a continuing action that gets stopped by something else. To reflect this ongoing motion, *ing* words are typically found in the first part of the combination.

Table 4.18 Combinations with *Until*

SPECIFIC CRAFT	EXAMPLE SENTENCE	WHY IS IT GOOD?
Two actions linked with *until*	*We had the music blaring until a neighbor came by and asked us to turn it down.*	Gives a continuing action and an abrupt one
Feeling + *until*	*I was feeling so happy about how the dinner party was going until I dropped the entire cake on the floor.*	Gives a continuing action and an abrupt one

Word Choice

As elementary students develop as writers, they become more aware of the choices they can make as they write their sentences. Word choice, of course, relates to the variety and complexity of the words children choose. As discussed in Chapter 3, looking at the variations of words that exist within a particular context can help students take more ownership in reaching for "more exciting" words. Variations are doubly effective in that they not only avoid repetition of words, but they help writers pinpoint an exact image.

Variations of words reflect variations in life. Ideally, teaching variations helps students recall more precise images as they write and then use the vocabulary they have to name that image to the best of their ability.

Teaching variations should not be confused with giving students a list of options for more common words or with having students look up words in a thesaurus. It is essential that the words students choose are already a part of their own oral vocabulary. I was once in a classroom where a teacher had given students a student-friendly thesaurus. In the left-hand column was a list of basic words that students frequently use, such as *pretty, good*, and *said*. In the right-hand column were about eight different "exciting" words students might choose instead of each basic word. While there was no question the teacher had anything but good intentions in supporting her students' writing vocabulary, it helped only in a surface way. For example, as one third grader was reading his writing to me, he came to the word *glorious*, which he had gotten from his student-friendly thesaurus. His original sentence, "The dinner was really good," now read "The dinner was really glorious." He stumbled several times over the word *glorious* until I finally pronounced it for him just so he could continue. As he read on I thought to myself, "What good is this 'exciting' word if this student can't even pronounce it, let alone bring it into his writing in a natural, independent manner?" The message behind giving students this tool was that any substitution of a "boring" word would be an improvement. But this is not always the case. The word *glorious* here not only sounded contrived in this student's writing but just plain awkward. Even when a substitution from a list like this makes sense, it still does not really encourage students to stretch their minds to think of their own words.

Teaching variations stresses the same idea of elevating word choice but supports students in using their own vocabulary to do so. When writing independently, students can only choose from vocabulary that they know at that time. This includes both words easily within their reach and more advanced words in the back of their minds that they actually need to reach for and may not even be able to spell very well but still understand. The images students see in their minds, in combination with making an effort to think of more precise words to reflect that image, should be the driving force of their word choice. For adults, this retrieval of words happens so fast when we write that we're not always aware of it. I remember one time in particular when I was aware of this thought process. I was writing an article about my experiences teaching writing workshop and was describing the way my students came up to the microphone during our first official writing celebration. First I described Tové, who had been nervous all day about reading in front of people. I wrote: "Tové, on the other hand, is visibly shaking when she comes up. Her eyes are wet with fear, and she slowly shakes her head at me." The way she walked up to the microphone was not average, so it was easy for my description not to be average. Then I described how Kevin walked to the microphone. I actually remember looking up from my keyboard and replaying that image in my mind with a more focused lens, looking for a better word than *walked*. How exactly did he walk onto the stage? I saw the overly confident smile and the slight bounce in his step. He wasn't just walking; he was . . . strutting. My sentence about him became: "Some students, like Kevin, strut up to the microphone, savoring the spotlight."

Word choice is often more powerful when it reflects subtleties, which students are initially less likely to notice when they replay images in their mind. For example, if a student is writing a memory about someone running or jumping or crawling, he or she would more likely use these words rather than just *walking* because those actions are so different than walking. However, when recalling an action similar to walking, it takes a little more effort and thinking to reach for a more specific word than *walking*, such as *marching, strutting,* or *gliding*. It's only when they begin to grow into their new job as writers, when they are thinking from the reader's point of view about how word choice can create different and more precise images for someone else, that students begin to take time to look carefully at the picture in their own mind and search for a more precise word. Students can only use what words they know, whether those words are at the forefront of their minds or at the periphery. So, teaching variations is not so much about supplying vocabulary, but teaching students a strategy so they can better draw on their own range of vocabulary when they write.

Variations of Common Verbs: *Walk, Look, Said*

Because there are many more variations than I could possibly include in this chapter, I've chosen a few that I most typically teach in lessons or conferences. This concept of teaching a variation can of course be used with any basic or nondescript word students seem to be repeating.

Variations for *Walks* (or *Goes*)

| tiptoes | strolls | sneaks | scampers | jogs | **walks** | struts | marches | runs | darts | dashes | races |

In a whole-class lesson, after I introduce the concept that there is a range of ways we walk and perhaps offer a few examples, I ask for some ideas from the class and we list them on chart paper, the board, or an overhead. Sometimes I draw a diagonal line and write the word variations next to the diagonal line instead of writing a simple list. A diagonal line can help to visually depict the fact that the words are a range of related words. Unlike most of my mini-lessons, which do not involve a lot of upfront dialogue with students, the involvement of students in this particular lesson is important. I want most of the words on any kind of visual to come from my students' vocabulary. I may or may not keep a public display of the words they suggest after the lesson is over. I do want students to benefit from being exposed to their peers' vocabulary, and providing a poster or chart paper with a record of these lessons may provide some scaffolding. But when teaching variations, my main goal is for students to go through that thinking process of reaching for words from within their own vocabulary when they are writing later that day or another day.

The "Variations of *Look*" list reflects the different intensities with which we look at something or someone. Very often, but not always, the level of intensity can depict emotion. A person glaring at you tells you something about the way that person is feeling, as does a person gazing at you. Depending on the context, it can even tell you what they might be thinking. Some variations of *look* are less about emotion and more about how long or how briefly someone looks. Peeking at the clock to see the time is much more subtle than staring at the clock. Even though some words relate to emotion and some to time, all words reflect a precise way we look at something.

Variations of *Looks*

peeks	*glimpses*	*glances*	**looks**	*gazes*	*peers*	*stares*	*glares*

The variations of *said* listed here were discussed in Chapter 3.

Variations of *Said*

whispered	*murmured*	*mentioned*	*commented*	**said**	*declared*	*barked*	*exclaimed*	*shouted*	*screeched*	*hollered*	*screamed*

Moods and Feelings

When beginning writers talk about feelings, either those that pertain to themselves, to a friend, or to a character in a story, there tends to be three popular choices: *sad, mad,* and *glad* (or *happy*). In response, teachers sometimes give great lessons on words that represent different moods and feelings. Giving students the tools to pinpoint how they are feeling can help them better communicate with their peers, because they can describe an exact feeling. Sometimes students can still cling to *happy* and *sad* in their writing when it comes to representing various levels of happiness and sadness. Teaching variations is a great way to avoid the repetition of these words. As with other variations, the actual vocabulary offered in lessons ideally is chosen by the students. For the sake of creating a visual, I used my own vocabulary in these examples.

Variations of *Happy*

content	glad	pleased	**happy**	delighted	thrilled	overjoyed	ecstatic

Variations of *Sad*

down	blue	melancholy	**sad**	unhappy	gloomy	miserable	devastated

Although the variations of *happy* and *sad* here contain many different words, they reflect only two emotions—happy and sad. The range of words reflects the different levels of *intensity* for each emotion. We have the potential to feel so many different emotions that it can be beneficial to list just a few of the vocabulary words that reflect the different types of emotions people can feel:

hopeful   anxious   embarrassed   confused   frustrated   disappointed

I love the posters that are titled "How Do you Feel?" and have little round faces expressing all the different emotions listed. In addition to being entertaining and providing a tool for students to express themselves when they are upset, the use of visuals reinforces the connection between word choice in writing and variations in life.

This emphasis on teaching students to rely on their own vocabulary during independent writing in no way precludes the need for direct vocabulary instruction in schools. Even when it comes to teaching vocabulary, though, merely presenting new words to students does not support students' ownership and authentic use of the new words. In their book, *Bringing Words to Life* (2002), Isabel Beck, Margaret McKeown, and Linda Kucan describe different ways to bring authentic vocabulary instruction into the classroom. The strategies they present, which value usage over memorization, help students make connections between newly introduced words and concepts they already know. For example, the authors point out that the word *required* might be a good word to teach, because students already use the phrase *have to* quite often. Students have a reason to use this new word, both in speech and in writing. One of the best effects of this kind of vocabulary instruction, from my own personal experience as a teacher and staff developer, is that it can cause students to become truly interested in the relationships between words and word meaning.

The emphasis on authentic and meaningful acquisition of vocabulary also greatly supports the link between vocabulary and a writer's ability to create images for a reader. Learning more advanced words "allows students to describe with greater specificity people and situations with which they already have some familiarity" (Beck, McKeown, and Kucan 2002, 17).

Using Specific Craft in Writing

The concept of variety in writing, both at the word and sentence level, can also relate to just about all craft presented in this chapter. The more choices students have at their disposal, the more students will naturally write with variety. For example, instead of writing *whispered* every time someone talks softly, I would rather my students mix it up, sometimes writing *whispered* (a variation of talking) and sometimes writing *said softly* or *said quietly* (*said* + adverb). I would also want them to eventually develop an awareness that they could end the sentence there or choose to add a visual detail using the word *as*.

This chapter looked at craft in separate categories to support the teaching of writing even though the use of craft in writing is a much more fluid process. This difference between instruction and actual use also exists in the visual arts. An art professor may give lessons that fall into categories such as color scheme, shading, and contrast. But once the students begin the act of painting, they are all using different skills they have learned in different ways. Artists aren't always making conscious decisions to paint using skills from particular categories.

The act of painting is an art, but instruction has to be somewhat concrete in order to isolate and strengthen skills that help students improve. An art professor would not get very far just showing his or her students wonderful examples of paintings and asking students to be more "expressive" or to paint with more "exciting brush strokes." The same is true with descriptive writing. Even though it is an art form, instruction is more beneficial when it isolates specific skills that relate to different aspects of writing.

The next chapter looks at the mechanics of writing as well as additional specific craft that use both punctuation and words to create descriptions.

5

Crafting with Punctuation

Several years ago Jose, a first grader at one of my schools, came up to me holding a small square of manila-colored paper. He was clearly eager to show me something. Even though I was talking with another student, he reached up and starting tapping my elbow. At first I ignored him, knowing he would understand I couldn't talk to him at the moment. But then he upped the ante by adding verbal taps: "Ms. Hale . . . Ms. Hale . . . Ms. Hale . . ."—about one "Ms. Hale" for every five taps. I closed my eyes and quietly laughed to myself. I finished up with the student I was talking with and turned to Jose.

"Jose, what's going on?" I said smiling.

"I made this for you," he replied as he held out his little piece of paper. On it was the drawing in Figure 5.1.

Figure 5.1

Figure 5.2

"Jose that's so great! Is that me?" I asked. Jose smiled proudly and nodded his head.

"Well, you need to sign it," I said. "Then I can remember it's from you!" His eyes lit up at this suggestion, and he ran back to his desk. In about two minutes he was back with his new and improved picture (see Figure 5.2).

I still have this portrait of me for sentimental reasons, but I've also started using it in my undergraduate literacy course. In one of my first lectures, I put this drawing on the overhead and ask my students what they notice about what Jose can do in writing. It's a fun way to introduce the developmental stages of writing—scribbling to letters to inventive spelling. I also do this to get my undergraduate students used to noticing small strengths in student writing, regardless of where the student is developmentally.

My students comment on the letters, spacing, and inventive spelling of *from*, but of course what they notice most is the abundance of punctuation. Perhaps because Jose had seen his teacher's name spelled everywhere, from the classroom door to worksheets, he knew to put a period after the word *Ms.* The other punctuation marks are formed correctly but are clearly not in the right place. This kind of experimentation with punctuation is to be expected in the primary grades, especially after it's first taught. Jose is still making sense of which punctuation marks go where. After all, this is what happens with inventive spelling. When Jose spells *from* as *fum* he is using what he knows so far about letter-sound correlations to create a word. If you look at Jose's drawing, you'll see he is doing the same thing with punctuation. *From Jose* does have a natural pause in the middle. At the end of a formal letter there would be a comma after *From*, and on a preprinted birthday present tag there might be a colon. In terms of how to represent this pause in writing, Jose can only use punctuation he knows. As for the question mark, I can't really say why he put that in there, except to exercise his recently acquired question mark-making skills.

When it comes to the rules of writing, it does not take very long for students to understand the definition and purpose of basic punctuation. Most students in the primary grades know that a period means a sentence stops and a comma means a pause. Understanding punctuation through the lens of reading is an important foundation, and writing and reading are, in a sense, mirror processes, but writing is a different activity. Instruction around punctuation will be stronger if it is taught through the lens of a writer rather than a reader.

One of the best ways to support students with the rules of punctuation, ironically, is to not focus on the rules. It's not that the rules of mechanics, both in terms of grammar and punctuation, are not important to know. But in writing, our goal is to help students use punctuation to shape sentences *as* they write. There is a difference between knowing a rule and following that rule as you write. There is also a difference between adding punctuation to preexisting sentences and using punctuation when writing independently. Although it may not be teachers' intentions, this kind of activity leaves it up to students to transfer one kind of skill (rules and fixing preexisting sentences) to another type of skill (writing with punctuation).

When lessons on teaching punctuation focus on the thought process that occurs *as* students are writing, there is less of a gap for students to cross by themselves. Although it may seem obvious, the act of writing involves filling up white space, one sentence at a time. We think about what words we want to write, and then with a pen, pencil, or keyboard, we fill in the white space with a mixture of words and punctuation. Thinking about the act of writing in terms of "filling up the white space" is important, because then instruction can more closely align with the internal moments when words and punctuation are first written.

Periods

Just about every student knows that a period goes at the end of a sentence. Several times I've been in a first-grade classroom when the teacher is doing shared writing. As she comes to the end of a sentence, she asks the students, who are clustered on the rug in front of her, "And what do you put at the end of a sentence?" All twenty-five of them, some with eyes shut for maximum volume, shout in unison, "A period!"

By the upper elementary grades, teachers' tolerance for run-on sentences goes down. And understandably so. Students have had instruction and expectations around ending sentences with periods for several years by the time they get to third and fourth grade. I remember one time when I was standing next to Ms. Connolly, a fifth-grade teacher, who was handing a draft back to a student and said, "Toni, you're missing so many periods."

Toni took back the paper, scanned her writing, and nonchalantly replied, "Oh yeah," Then, *right then and there*, she fixed her draft. Very often, it's not that students don't understand the concept of adding periods, it's just that they've developed a habit of not including them as they write. This is especially true when students are writing in notebooks, where their writing is (fortunately) not corrected every time they write a page. While it is important to validate that students will need to use trial and error as they learn more complex ways of writing, the lack of periods I see in the elementary grades is, more often than not, a reflection of a habit rather than a result of a student still getting used to writing more advanced sentences.

I mentioned in Chapter 4 that ending sentences with periods is a prerequisite for more advanced description and voice. There is an automatic ceiling to how much students can "craft" their writing when sentences don't really end. As I say to my students, "There's a lot of cool craft you can't do when you write with lots of run-ons!" I do validate and make public that it might be tempting to write with a lot of *and then*'s because sometimes that's how we talk, especially when we are retelling an event. But I also firmly emphasize that talking and writing are different things.

I believe that one reason complete sentences, or lack thereof, frustrate teachers so much is that they spend a good deal of instruction time responding to this need. Most instruction that I see that relates to periods and complete sentences, however, is not directed to the root of the problem, or rather, the root of the desired skill. A common activity done in response to run-on sentences involves students reading a paragraph and inserting the missing periods. Although there is some value to this activity, it strengthens editing skills more than it strengthens writing skills. Writing entails placing words down with nothing but blank space ahead. So the actual skill behind ending sentences with periods involves writing a series of words, being aware of the sound of the sentence as you write, and then lifting your hand a little bit before making a dot. If students only practice filling in missing periods, then they are getting better at filling in missing periods, not using them *as* they write.

Similar to the preparation of craft instruction, it's important to consider the Why—why do writers use periods? What I most often hear teachers and students say is, "You have to put periods in so the reader knows when to stop. The reader has to take a breath." But this is looking at periods from the point of view of a reader, not a writer. It took some reflection to come to my own conclusion of how writing with periods benefits the writing process. After all, it had just been a rule for me as long as I can remember. It is true that a writer

Table 5.1 Periods		
SPECIFIC CRAFT	**EXAMPLE SENTENCE**	**WHY IS IT GOOD?**
Period (.) at the end of a thought/sentence	*We decided to build a sand castle.*	Lets the writer pause and think about what details could be added before continuing

does want to let a reader know where one sentence starts and the next begins. But I also realized that when you stop a thought with a period, it gives you a brief but very important pause to consider what else you might want to write. This pause gives the *writer* time to think about the much-coveted practice of *adding details*. Table 5.1 presents this idea as specific craft.

Looking at the Why from the point of view of a writer has helped me more effectively model in lessons the thinking I want my students to do when they write. I focus on the sound of a complete thought, make a period, and then think aloud in order to demonstrate how this pause gives me time to think about what else I want to write. Students are more apt to comply with the rule of using end punctuation when they are given a deeper reason than *because you have to*. This lesson on ending sentences with periods is explained in more detail in Chapter 7.

Other End Punctuation

A period, of course, is not the only way to end a sentence. There are also question marks and exclamation points. Which mark a writer decides to use depends on the meaning of each sentence. Exclamation points all look the same, as do question marks, but there are a few subtle differences in how they are used in writing. Their effects, both on meaning and sound, are slightly different in narrative as opposed to when they are used in dialogue. Tables 5.2 and 5.3 offer some examples of these differences.

Table 5.2 Exclamation Points		
SPECIFIC CRAFT	**EXAMPLE SENTENCE**	**WHY IS IT GOOD?**
Exclamation point (!) in narrative	*After the storm the waves were gigantic!*	Emphasizes the strength of a thought or reaction
Exclamation point (!) in dialogue	*"Owen, watch out for the wave!" I shouted.*	Raises the volume of the dialogue

Table 5.3 Question Marks

SPECIFIC CRAFT	EXAMPLE SENTENCE	WHY IS IT GOOD?
Question mark (?) in narrative	*Where were all the seagulls?*	Shows internal question; reader can connect with the "inside story"
Question mark (?) in dialogue	*"Owen, do you and Olivia want your sandwiches now?" I asked.*	Tells reader that what was spoken was a question and not a statement

Questions and exclamations have different intonations in oral speech that are far more varied than the typical statement sentence that needs a period. Using all three ways to end sentences throughout a piece of writing contributes to sentence variety. Of course, if you've ever read the writing of a second grader who has just discovered exclamation points, you know that using too many exclamation points takes away from the quality of a piece of writing. An exclamation point is meant to be reserved to make a strong point—use it too much and its emphasis gets diluted. Although it is important to validate that children will need to play and experiment with punctuation marks when they first learn them, we do want students eventually to understand that, like any craft technique, even exciting punctuation like exclamation points should not be overused.

Quotation Marks

Quotation marks are very familiar to most elementary students. With all the dialogue that exists in books, most children are exposed to quotation marks long before they start attempting to bring them into their own writing. Dialogue can begin simply with words like *she said*, at which point teachers might start giving lessons on how quotation marks go around the words that were actually said, as shown in Table 5.4.

Writing dialogue is unique in that it requires several little rules, not just one. The main purpose of quotation marks is to show which words are part of the dialogue and which words are part of the narrative. There is also the rule about

Table 5.4 Quotation Marks Around Dialogue

SPECIFIC CRAFT	EXAMPLE SENTENCE	WHY IS IT GOOD?
Quotation marks around dialogue	*"I think I'm going to go swimming first," I told my sister.*	Keeps the reader from being confused; shows which words were actually spoken

Table 5.5 Quotation Marks Around Personal Names or Phrases		
SPECIFIC CRAFT	**EXAMPLE SENTENCE**	**WHY IS IT GOOD?**
Quotation marks around a personal name or phrase	*I dug through my "memory box" to see if I could find the letter from my grandmother.*	Tells the reader that a name is personal

starting dialogue with a capital letter and the rule about where the commas go. Later still, usually not until middle school or high school, students learn the rule about starting a new paragraph when a new person is speaking. As with many aspects of writing, it's important to validate the steps of development when it comes to writing dialogue. If students can first focus on getting the quotation marks around what is actually said, then they are creating a solid foundation for learning the smaller, more advanced rules of dialogue.

Although quotation marks are most well known for dialogue, they are also used for other purposes. This is a good time to bring back a phrase that uses quotation marks in the *Chicken Sunday* excerpt we looked at in Chapter 3.

Stewart reached into the hole in the trunk of our "wish tree" in the backyard.

When I was gathering craft from *Chicken Sunday*, it took me a minute to think about why quotation marks were used here. Similar to times when I compare the use of a craft technique to a more basic choice, I imagined what this sentence would be like without these quotation marks. And again, I had to slow down my reaction and notice the almost subliminal effect the absence of those quotation marks would have if I were reading that sentence at a normal pace. I realized that, without quotation marks, I might think, "Wait . . . what's a wish tree? Is there something I'm missing?" I realized that by adding quotation marks, Patricia Polacco lets me know that *wish tree* is a special name or phrase that I'm not necessarily supposed to know. Once again, punctuation is used to avoid confusion. See Table 5.5 for another example.

A few months after gathering craft from *Chicken Sunday*, I was reading a nonfiction entry about babysitting, written by a third-grade English language learner (ELL). She did the same thing I noticed Patricia Polacco doing with "wish tree," except this time it was about a name her family had for a pacifier (see Figure 5.3). I am guessing that no one taught her a lesson on using quotation

FIGURE 5.3

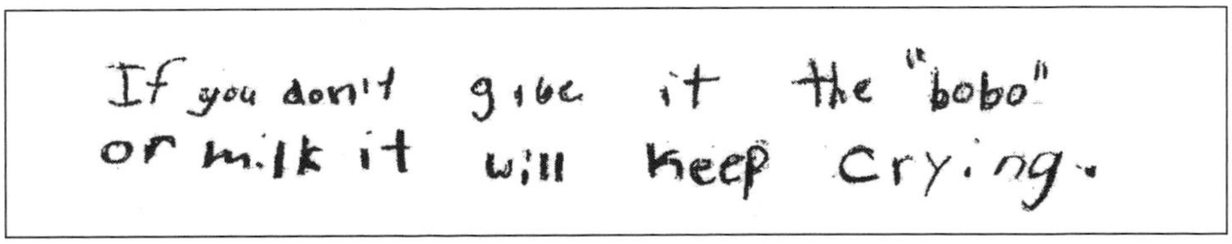

If you don't gibe it the "bobo" or milk it will keep crying.

Table 5.6 Quotation Marks to Show a Term Is Used Loosely		
SPECIFIC CRAFT	**EXAMPLE SENTENCE**	**WHY IS IT GOOD?**
Quotation marks around a statement you mean loosely	*Renaldo sat down for his "dinner" of crackers and peanut butter.*	Tells reader not to take a word or phrase completely literally

marks this way. Perhaps she just picked it up through reading or maybe she just intuitively knew she had to make those words different, because not everybody calls a pacifier a "bobo." Of course, not everything our students do in their writing will be a result of direct teaching. But the fact that I had already thought about this particular use of quotation marks meant that I could help her become more aware of what she was doing as a writer when we met for a conference.

Quotation marks are also used in a slightly similar way to imply that a word or phrase should not be taken literally, as in the sentence in Table 5.6.

Using quotation marks with phrases like "wish tree" is an intentional way to avoid confusion. It's the writer saying, "You're not really supposed to know what this means" or "Just so you know, this is a personal or specialized term." However, using quotation marks as in Table 5.6 is more like the writer saying, "I'm using that word loosely." Another example is when I was talking about reading like a writer in Chapter 3 and wrote: *"hang on" to what you see.* I didn't think too much about it when I wrote those quotation marks. I just intuitively knew I wanted to convey that *hang on* was not meant literally, but as a metaphor to describe the process of studying text. It wouldn't take long for the reader to understand what I meant without the quotation marks. But because the reading process happens so quickly, punctuation avoids even the briefest pause in comprehension.

Commas

Although the punctuation marks discussed thus far can help craft a piece of writing, the comma is the one punctuation mark I have come to favor teaching lately. This small mark has amazing potential to lift up the writing skills of students, particularly those who are ready to move beyond basic sentences.

Most students know that a comma indicates a pause when reading. The purpose of using commas as a writer is to communicate which words belong together. Using commas to keep writing clear is evident in one of the more common teaching points about punctuation: using commas in a series or list (see Table 5.7).

Without the commas, the reader would be expecting the sentence in Table 5.7 to just continue naturally after the word *sunglasses.* Looking at this sentence

Table 5.7 Commas in a Series		
SPECIFIC CRAFT Using commas in a series	**EXAMPLE SENTENCE** *In my oversized beach bag I put my sunglasses, a towel, two books, a chocolate bar, and my cell phone.*	**WHY IS IT GOOD?** Reader understands that words are separate items in a list

through a craft lens, the use of commas here is desirable because it provides a detailed picture for the reader. A more basic choice of writing this sentence would be, "In my oversized beach bag, I put all my things for the beach." Using the word *stuff* instead of *things* would provide an equally general and nondescript image.

Listing objects in a series is not the only way commas can help writers write more descriptively. Phrases that act as dependent clauses in sentences, which require commas, clearly add a richness to text, both in terms of sentence variety and description. These qualities of writing, in turn, affect the voice of writing: when students know more ways to vary sentence structure, there is more of an opportunity for them to create rhythms that are already a natural part of their speech.

Commas can allow a writer to pack more ideas into one sentence, whether they are thoughts or descriptions. Although a basic sentence can be descriptive, there is only so much information a writer can give to a reader in one sentence before commas will be needed to avoid confusion. There are also ways to be descriptive without a lot of words and without using commas. Brand names offer packed images in just a few words. Variations such as *glanced* are descriptive in that they give the reader a very precise image. And not every sentence needs to be, or should be, very descriptive. Too much description is like putting too much maple syrup on your pancakes. Maple syrup is wonderful and pancakes would be bland without it (in my opinion), but at some point there's too much of the good stuff and the ratio is off balance. Once in a while, I read student writing that is so overloaded with adjectives and similes it is overly descriptive, especially because there is not much variety in the *way* they are being descriptive. But I would say the majority of teachers are still working on getting their students to be *more* descriptive, not less.

Many students, especially those in the upper elementary grades, are ready to write more complex sentences. But unless there is explicit instruction on ways to write dependent clauses, many of them tend not to venture past single-idea sentences. They can get stuck on the one-thought-per-sentence writing. This is yet another area in which students who are avid readers will more likely be ahead of their peers because they have been more frequently exposed to the sound and structure of more complex sentences. Although we want to encourage students' authentic interest in reading as much as possible, we don't have to wait for this to happen completely in order to help students move past the basic sentence barrier.

One way to support instruction around comma usage is to focus on the relationship between commas and the words around them. We don't use commas for the sake of it; we use them because what we are writing requires us to do so. The more complex the sentence, the more likely it is that commas will be needed to keep the meaning clear. Teaching commas *with* craft takes advantage of this relationship. There are certain words that seem to just bring a comma along with them naturally, because they allow a writer to connect two different ideas. There are also phrases that can be inserted to add another layer to a sentence and require a comma. The following sections describe some specific craft techniques that use both words and commas to add description to sentences.

Reverse Combinations

Chapter 4 presented combination sentences that use *as* or *while* to connect two different events or descriptions. These small connecting words imply a sense of time in that the two events or descriptions are happening simultaneously. These are the simplest combinations. A comma is not needed, because the connecting word is in the middle and there is an easy and clear symmetry. Here is one example from Chapter 4.

I could smell the fireplaces of nearby houses as I walked onto the porch.

If I were to write the same sentences in reverse and still not use a comma, it would look like this:

As I walked onto the porch I could smell the fireplaces of nearby houses.

This sentence certainly does not cause total confusion. It wouldn't take very long to make sense of it. But clarity is as important as description. As you read along, *As I walked onto the porch I* suddenly does not make sense as a single sentence. You have to slightly adjust the way your mind takes in the words. When a comma is missing, it's like we are self-correcting the error in the text. This process of making sense of text happens so quickly that we may not even be aware of this brief self-correcting. But any extra effort a reader has to use to clarify the meaning of what is written, even if it is on a practically subconscious level, takes away from the reading experience. Commas in the right place keep this sometimes minuscule self-correcting from being necessary.

As I walked onto the porch, I could smell the fireplaces of nearby houses.

So, what's the difference between writing a combination sentence and writing one that is in reverse order? Reread each of the first two versions above and, as you read, notice how each one affects what you picture.

You might notice that whatever image is mentioned first is the one you first picture. In the first sentence, which begins with *I could*, the smell of fireplaces takes center stage. In the second sentence, the action of walking onto the porch is most prominent. Sometimes, decisions about which order to write these combination sentences in is based on which of the two concepts you want to stand out—in this case, the walking onto the porch or the smell of fireplaces. Although these two versions are very similar, discriminating between the two means I can eventually teach my students several different ways to get the same idea across to the reader, which in turn increases the number of choices my students can make as writers. See Table 5.8 for examples of reverse combinations.

One of the most exciting transitions in elementary writing is when students move beyond deciding the content of the sentence and begin to play with the order of words in a sentence in their mind before writing it. This is not to say that children, and even adults for that matter, are supposed to stop and analyze their decisions every time they write a sentence. That would be quite tiring. Sometimes we are more aware of our decision-making in the way we are adding descriptions and playing with word order, and sometimes writing feels more like intuition than decision-making. Even when it doesn't feel like it, decisions are always being made at some level much in the way artists make decisions with different levels of awareness when they paint a picture. Helping students understand how different choices affect writing supports decision-making at all levels.

Although all the words and phrases that begin each sentence in Table 5.8 are similar in that they indicate time, there are subtle differences. Once again, the different words reflect the slight variations that occur in life. Things don't always happen at the same exact time:

As and *While* imply that two things are happening at the same time.
When implies a cause and effect relationship.
Just as implies the slightest overlapping of two things.
As soon as implies that one thing happens right after the other.
Once and *After* imply a sequence of events.

Notice these craft techniques intentionally focus on particular words rather than a part of speech. These example sentences could certainly fit within a lesson called "using a comma when you start a sentence with a conjunction." That description may be accurate. And it is true that students should know the names and purposes of different parts of speech. As mentioned previously, however, knowing the parts of speech of words is not really

Table 5.8 Commas with Reverse Combinations

SPECIFIC CRAFT	EXAMPLE SENTENCE	WHY IS IT GOOD?
Starting a sentence with *As*	*As Keon handed out his birthday cupcakes, his teacher got cups ready for the juice.*	Gives reader two actions in one sentence
Starting a sentence with *While*	*While Keon handed out his birthday cupcakes, his teacher got cups ready for the juice.*	Gives reader two actions in one sentence
Starting a sentence with *When*	*When Keon realized there was one person who didn't get a cupcake, he offered to give up his.*	Gives reader two actions in one sentence
Starting a sentence with *Just as*	*Just as Keon was about to give Ameina her cupcake, he tripped and it went flying in the air.*	Gives reader two actions in one sentence
Starting a sentence with *As soon as*	*As soon as he finished passing out all the cupcakes, his class sang "Happy Birthday" to him.*	Gives reader two actions in one sentence
Starting a sentence with *Once*	*Once everyone finished their juice, they could ask for seconds.*	Gives reader two actions in one sentence
Starting a sentence with *After*	*After everyone finished their juice, the teacher went around with the garbage can.*	Gives reader two actions in one sentence

the skill students use *when they write*. This is true for adults as well: we are more in touch with the words we write than what parts of speech we write.

Ing Phrases

Starting a sentence with a participial adjective—an *ing* word used as an adjective—is another craft technique that usually brings along a comma. Sometimes the part before the comma is one word and sometimes it is a phrase.

Grinning, Rich walked up the stairs to accept his diploma.
Grinning from ear to ear, Rich walked up the stairs to accept his diploma.

In his book *Mechanically Inclined* (2005), Jeff Anderson calls these introductory phrases "openers." They set the stage for the main part of the sentence by offering an extra description. This is yet another way to offer a more three-dimensional image to a reader in one sentence. One could create just about the same image using a combination sentence:

Table 5.9 Commas with *Ing* Phrases

SPECIFIC CRAFT	EXAMPLE SENTENCE	WHY IS IT GOOD?
Ing phrase describing a big action	*Running as fast as her legs could carry her, Jessica flagged down the number 2 bus.*	Gives reader two descriptions about the same person
Ing phrase describing a smaller action	*Holding her new dress in front of her, Cheryl looked in the full-length mirror.*	Gives reader two descriptions about the same person
Ing phrase describing a sound	*Humming his favorite song to keep him calm, Larry ventured into the dark woods.*	Gives reader two descriptions about the same person
Ing phrase describing a facial expression/emotion	*Tearing up, Shantel reached for another Kleenex.*	Gives reader two descriptions about the same person
Ing phrase describing a thought	*Wondering if everybody would laugh at her costume, Shannon walked slowly out on stage.*	Gives reader two descriptions about the same person
Ing phrase with dialogue	*Looking through a menu, Joseph said, "Let's have pizza for dinner."*	Gives reader two descriptions about the same person

Rich grinned from ear to ear as he walked up the stairs to accept his diploma.

Starting the sentence with the verb *grinning,* however, is probably a lot less likely to occur in the elementary grades. This kind of sentence is quite a departure from the noun-verb sentence structure that students have been learning since first grade. So it makes sense that they may not write this way naturally, even though they sometimes may be reading sentences in this format.

Although we could teach *ing* phrases as a single concept, there are more specific ways to name these descriptive phrases (see Table 5.9) when noticing them in student writing or when teaching whole-class lessons.

It is helpful to point out to students just how many opportunities there are to use an *ing* phrase to add an extra description. Because these phrases begin with a form of a verb, they imply ongoing action, whether it is a lively action like running or a more subtle action like wondering.

When teaching these *ing* phrases, it's important not only to teach the concept of adding these words, but also to tap into the thought process behind these kinds of multi-layered sentences. Before the words ever get written, a writer ideally takes time to carefully study the memory of whatever he or she is writing about. As Table 5.9 illustrates, *ing* phrases are commonly used in reference to a person. There is a greater chance that more than one verb can be used to describe a living being, whether they are verbs of being or action verbs.

Table 5.10 Different Places for *Ing* Phrases

IN THE BEGINNING	IN THE MIDDLE	AT THE END
Running as fast as her legs could carry her, Jessica flagged down the number 2 bus.	*Jessica, running as fast as her legs could carry her, flagged down the number 2 bus.*	*Jessica flagged down the number 2 bus, running as fast as her legs could carry her.*
Holding her new dress in front of her, Cheryl looked in the full-length mirror.	*Cheryl, holding her new dress in front of her, looked in the full-length mirror.*	*Cheryl looked in the full-length mirror, holding her new dress in front of her.*

So animals would also fall under this category of living beings. When Jeff Anderson illustrates the use of *ing* words in *Mechanically Inclined* (2005), he gives the following example from a lesson he taught:

> *Wagging its tail, the dog approached me.* (73)

He then shares other *ing* verbs that would also make sense in that sentence, such *barking, growling,* and *snarling.*

Ing phrases, of course, do not always fall at the beginning of a sentence as "openers." Sometimes they appear in the middle of a sentence, and sometimes at the end of a sentence. Jeff Anderson calls these two versions "interrupters" and "closers" (2005). One reason I like Jeff Anderson's terminology is that it reinforces the fact that sentences can have different layers that revolve around the main sentence and that these layers can occur in different places. The terms *opener, interrupter,* and *closer* reflect where the phrases fall in the sentence, making them easier for students to name when they talk about writing. These informal terms also make these craft techniques more approachable and perhaps less intimidating for students to use themselves.

The sentences in Table 5.10 demonstrate how the *ing* phrase can be placed in the beginning of, in the middle of, or at the end of a sentence. Because there was not a single word change from one column to the next, the overall image does not really change. But because the order of the words changes, so does the order of what appears in your mind. The different placement of the *ing* phrase also creates a different rhythm to each sentence. As with all other craft techniques, there are many times when I am not that aware of the reasons behind my decision to write certain sentences certain ways. Other times, I am more aware of sentences needing some variety and so I might more intentionally choose to put phrases in a different order.

Descriptive Phrases

Descriptive phrases are similar to *ing* phrases in that they also add an extra descriptive layer to a basic sentence. The only difference is that, rather than

---

Table 5.11 Descriptive Phrases

SPECIFIC CRAFT	EXAMPLE SENTENCE	WHY IS IT GOOD?
Phrase describing moods or feelings	*Exhausted and hungry, we finally stopped driving and looked for a motel for the night.*	Gives reader an extra description
Phrase describing thoughts	*Confused about whether he took the wrong exit, Luis pulled over to look at a map.*	Gives reader an extra description
Phrase describing clothes or appearance	*Dressed in a light blue uniform and top hat, the hotel manager appeared from behind the desk.*	Gives reader an extra description

---

using an *ing* form of a verb to add a description, these phrases use *ed* verb forms, as in Table 5.11, or regular adjectives, as in the sentences listed below. The examples in Table 5.11 describe people, but descriptive phrases can be used with things as well. Since we can't really comment on the feelings or thoughts of inanimate objects, descriptive phrases with objects tend to be primarily visual.

> *Full of flowers, the apple trees lined either side of the driveway.*
> *All red and shiny, the new tricycle sat in the middle of the store window.*
> *Covered with dust, her secret diary lay hidden on the top shelf of her closet.*

Again, putting a particular description at the front of the sentence highlights the description itself: it's what the reader is first introduced to before we even know what or who the description refers to. Also similar to *ing* phrases, many descriptive phrases can also be used as "interrupters" and "closers."

Ing phrases and descriptive phrases are not only similar in terms of how they can be moved around in sentences, but very often one can be substituted for the other. I could, for example, rewrite the above sentence about the apple tree as follows:

> *Bursting with flowers, the apple trees lined either side of the driveway.*

The version with the verb *bursting* might intensify the image just a bit, but the concept of highlighting the description first remains the same. These two examples of how to write about the apple trees support the idea that the more writing choices students (and adults) have at their disposal, the more they will develop sentence variety.

There are numerous ways commas can be used to craft writing. This chapter illustrates only a few of them. The point is not to teach everything there is to know about commas. The main purpose of the craft presented in this chapter is to help students move past two-dimensional sentences and become more comfortable with using commas to add layers to their sentences.

Integrating Punctuation Study into Writing Workshop

Similar to the specific craft charts in Chapter 4, the charts in this chapter are not meant to reflect a set sequence of teaching points. Since craft techniques within each table do follow the same pattern, however, teaching more than one within a unit of study can be beneficial. If I taught a lesson on starting a sentence with *As* (a reverse combination), for example, I might want to follow up with a lesson on starting a sentence with *Just as* or *Once* and have students talk about the difference the word choice makes. Because the specific craft in this chapter involves words and punctuation, it can be taught from either angle—the crafting of words or the use of mechanics. For example, several of the above combinations could be taught through the lens of sentence variety within a unit of study in memoir or nonfiction. But they could also be taught in a unit of study on punctuation or a unit just on commas. Regardless of what umbrella I teach them under, my actual instruction would not differ very much. Craft techniques presented in this chapter reflect the intersection of craft and punctuation.

Teachers can also support students' understanding of and interest in punctuation by setting aside times in the curriculum for students to study punctuation through exploration of text. Rather than tell students how punctuation affects writing, give them opportunities to discover this for themselves. Both Janet Angelillo in her book *A Fresh Approach to Teaching Punctuation* (2002) and Jeff Anderson in *Mechanically Inclined* (2005) discuss ways to support students in noticing punctuation themselves. Angelillo describes how she has had groups of students search through classroom library books to discuss and gather evidence on ways that authors use certain punctuation marks. She also supports an important school-life connection by encouraging them to look for punctuation outside of school—in magazines, on billboards, and even on tickets and sports cards.

My emphasis on teaching craft with punctuation does not mean I think there should not be accountability for proper punctuation use, whether it affects description or not. Students do need to feel responsible for properly using punctuation they have learned, whether they are writing in notebooks or getting writing up to publishing standards. This accountability tends to be more of a challenge during independent writing time, rather than during official editing times in the writing process. Teachers can support accountability during independent writing time in several ways. One option is to set aside several minutes at the end of independent writing time, before sharing time, when students have to put down their pencils and reread what they wrote that day. Sometimes I insist that they "read with their lips," meaning they silently mouth the words while they reread. Otherwise it can be very easy for eyes to scan the writing and still not really read what's on the paper.

Punctuation Beyond the Comma

There are, of course, punctuation marks that are more advanced than commas. Colons, semicolons, dashes, parentheses, and ellipses add tremendous variety to writing. Notice the different rhythms and intonations these marks bring to the memoir entry shown in Figure 5.4, written by middle school student Joannie Ortiz. The more advanced marks in this piece contribute greatly to the voice. The fact that this chapter does not spend time on this kind of punctuation is not reflective of its value, but rather of where I think the most energy around writing instruction should be spent, at least in elementary grades. The rules about when to use colons, semicolons, dashes, parentheses, and ellipses are a little obscure. Using them skillfully tends to come more from repeated exposure to this kind of writing than through direct instruction. Typically, it's not until students start reading on a fifth- or sixth-grade level and higher that these marks become more common in the books they read.

This is not to say these more advanced punctuation marks can't be taught in the upper elementary grades. Of course they can. And sometimes students like learning about unusual punctuation. The question is how much time we invest in these more advanced marks when students are not seeing them frequently in their own reading and when they are not yet using commas to their potential. Notice how Joannie, the student whose work is shown in Figure 5.4, crafts sentences with commas in a fluent and controlled manner, in addition to using the other punctuation.

FIGURE 5.4

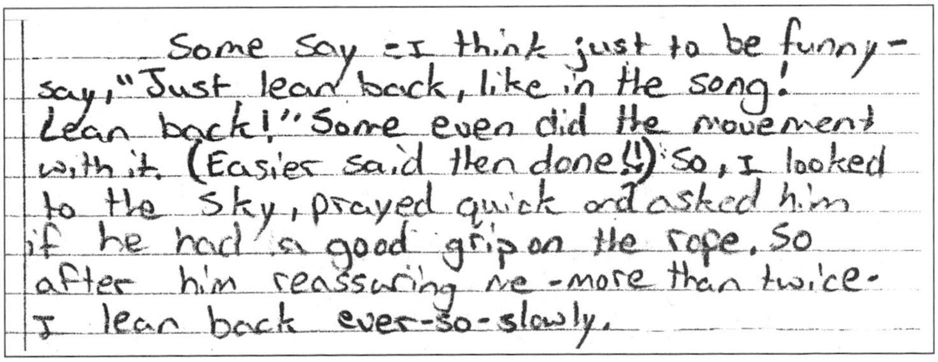

Some say —I think just to be funny— say, "Just lean back, like in the song! Lean back!" Some even did the movement with it. (Easier said then done!) So, I looked to the sky, prayed quick and asked him if he had a good grip on the rope. So after him reassuring me —more than twice— I lean back ever-so-slowly.

Supporting elementary students with the quality and variety of their comma usage rather than covering many different punctuation marks in the curriculum will, in my opinion, create a much more solid foundation for future instruction in the middle school grades. The next chapter looks at writing skills at the primary level that provide a similar foundation for writing at the middle- and upper-elementary level.

6

Primary Writing

During the month of November, Nikki began a personal narrative entry, shown in Figure 6.1, about her trip to Backyard Adventures. See if you can guess what grade she was in.

FIGURE 6.1

> I remember the 1st time
> I went to BackyardAdventure's.
> It's like a Place. on one Side is a Picnic
> Place and the Other Side is a
> Playgrond. At the Playgrond
> there is a MoonBawns

If you guessed first grade, you would be right! My assumption is that not many teachers would have guessed first grade, especially since it was written in the fall. I know it would not have been my answer. Every now and then we meet students like Nikki whose writing belies their age in a positive way. What occurs more frequently in many classrooms, however, is the opposite situation, when students' writing reflects an ability below what is expected at their age.

As any fourth-grade teacher knows, just because students are *in* the fourth grade doesn't mean they all *write* on what is considered to be a fourth-grade level. This gap between age and expected ability is especially common for special education students. English language learners, depending on their acquisition level, can also fall in this category. Their grade-level ability is not always a reflection of their ability to write with description and volume, but rather their development in learning how the English language works, both in terms of vocabulary and syntax.

Although *Crafting Writers* is geared toward teachers in middle- and upper-elementary grades, I felt it was important to take one chapter to look specifically at skills that can be seen in the primary grades. Considering the range of abilities in most classrooms, teachers of all grades would be somewhat limited if they were only familiar with grade-level skills, especially during conferences. The very nature of individual conferences is that we are meeting all students' needs at their instructional levels.

This chapter offers three main categories of specific craft that can occur in primary level writing.

✿ Drawing
✿ Writing Words
✿ Basic Craft

This is by no means an all-inclusive list. The development of writers, which can begin with oral storytelling and scribbling, is far too complex even to attempt to cover in one chapter. Similar to the craft skills in previous chapters, any specific skill, whether it pertains to drawing or writing, can be both a strength to notice in student writing as well as something to teach.

Drawing

Many primary teachers understand the important link between drawing and writing. This is especially true when teachers support students in using drawing as preparation for writing rather than as a nice accompanying visual to do after the fact. In their recent book, *Talking, Drawing, Writing* (2007), Martha Horn and Mary Ellen Giacobbe, discuss some of the work they have done in Boston around teaching drawing skills within the framework of writing workshop. Much of their work revolves around the idea that because drawing is important to the ability of young writers to make meaning and provide information, instruction on the craft of drawing should be taken just as seriously in these grades as instruction around writing skills. Horn and Giacobbe's work has changed many teachers' perceptions, including my own, of what we should teach in primary lessons and conferences. This validation of researching and teaching drawing skills reminds me of previous shifts in the teaching of craft: we no longer just hope for good drawings or praise those who show a natural artistic ability. We can also teach students some of the specific skills behind drawing.

Noticing strengths and specific skills in drawing, similar to writing, requires looking at the small parts. By knowing some of the finer skills that make up "good" drawings, we will be better prepared to explain to students what exactly they do well in their drawing and, when needed, offer them specific next steps to improve their drawings. Table 6.1 lists some of the smaller skills I have noticed through observations of student drawings. Since drawing is used as a preparation for writing, these craft techniques not only improve the drawing itself, but also provide more information students can draw upon when they write. You'll notice that the Why column in Table 6.1 suggests how each skill benefits both the "reader" of the drawing and the writer. Figures 6.2, 6.3, and 6.4 are examples of some of these drawing techniques.

FIGURE 6.2 Brand names in drawing

FIGURE 6.3 Brand names in writing

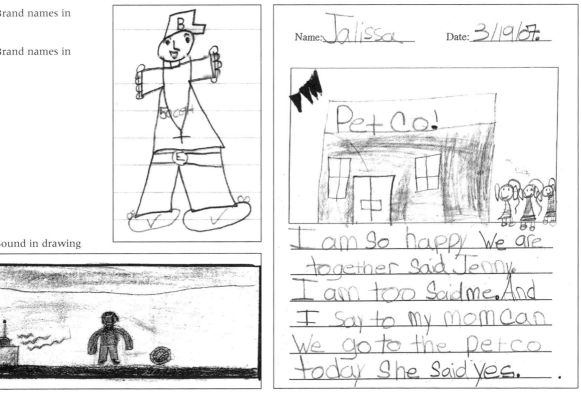

FIGURE 6.4 Sound in drawing

Table 6.1 Craft Techniques in Drawing

SPECIFIC CRAFT	WHAT DOES IT LOOK LIKE?	WHY IS IT GOOD?
Filling up the page	The picture is full; there is very little white space.	Offers a more full and detailed image; gives you lots of information that can help you think of many sentences to write
Small versus big objects	Rather than drawing only large objects such as a house, a car, or a tree, students are drawing smaller objects such as a purse, a seatbelt, or a mailbox flag.	Gives reader a more detailed image; gives student ideas for details to include when writing
Details of food	There are details in pictures of food, such as sprinkles on ice cream, lettuce on a sandwich, or pepperoni on pizza.	Gives reader a more detailed image; gives student ideas for details to include when writing about food
Details of clothes	There are details on people's clothes, such as a pattern, belt buckles, or pockets.	Gives reader a more detailed image; gives student ideas for details when writing about clothes
Drawing sound	The representation of sound usually includes music notes or lines coming from objects or people.	Sound helps to bring picture to life; sets a foundation for including sound in writing
Drawing action	Lines coming from objects or people show motion.	Movement helps to bring picture to life; sets a foundation for describing action
Drawing brand names	Symbols of clothes, stores, and other brand names are represented in drawing.	Creates a specific image and sometimes a personal connection; sets a foundation for including brand names in sentences
Writing brand names	Brand names are spelled out in the picture.	Creates a specific image and sometimes a personal connection; sets a foundation for including brand names in sentences
Speech bubble or dialogue	Dialogue is written in the drawing.	Adds an actual sound to the picture; sets a foundation for writing with dialogue
Showing the weather	The weather is shown in the picture by including rain, clouds, snow, etc. (Students usually draw suns almost automatically.)	Brings drawing to life through sense of touch; can indicate time of year and/or temperature
Drawing the background outdoors	There are objects in the background that are not central to the action of the picture.	Gives a fuller picture; sets a foundation for describing the background when writing
Drawing the background indoors	There are details of a room, such as wallpaper, small objects on tables, or pictures on a wall.	Gives a fuller picture; sets a foundation for describing the background when writing

Drawing Strategies

It is sometimes useful to teach general drawing strategies before getting into a lot of specific ways to draw. Many of the craft techniques in Table 6.1 reflect more detailed drawing, and some drawings are not as conducive as others to adding smaller details. I've seen many primary drawings that have four main ingredients: a house, one big flower, grass, and a sun. Sometimes the sun is in the corner and sometimes it's in the middle of the picture. There are variations of this (sometimes there's a bird too), but the important point is that these drawings indicate that students think they always have to show "the whole scene" in a drawing. But when the whole scene is shown, then there is less room for details. This is somewhat similar to upper elementary students telling the "whole story." They are so busy explaining everything that happened that there is very little time to mention any details.

One day this past year, I was planning to model a lesson on drawing small objects in a first-grade classroom, something the teacher and I had discussed in a previous inquiry meeting. But when I went around the classroom that morning to see the most current entries, I saw all these house-sun-flower pictures. I visualized the lesson in my head and suddenly it didn't seem to fit with what these first graders were doing. How could I ask them to add in details when there wasn't really any room on the page to squeeze in anything? I decided to transfer the zoom-in technique that students were doing with writing in the elementary grades to drawing. During the lesson, I modeled my own "zoom-in" drawings. First I showed them a drawing of my sister and me at the beach. There was an ocean, a few small stick figures, a huge sky, and a sun in the corner. I then showed them my zoom-in picture, which depicted the same beach but without a lot of white space. I had zoomed in on just the red buckets and our hands making a sand castle. I pointed out that because I didn't try to draw the whole scene, I could draw the sand castle and the shells, even the buckets with their white, plastic braided handle, with much more detail.

Zooming in, whether in drawing or writing, works best after an original version has been created that attempts to tell the whole story or show the whole scene. After students get the whole story or the whole picture on paper, it's easier to then choose and zoom in on one part. This is true even when adults write. One of the first personal narrative entries I wrote in graduate school was about the day my twin sister burned her knee at the beach when we were eight years old. I first wrote an entry that started with arriving at the beach for dinner and ended with rushing to the car to get ice and bandages after she burned her knee. It wasn't until I went back and wrote about isolated events—feeding bread to seagulls, the moment my sister actually burned her knee—that I was able to write with much more detail and dig underneath to the significance of this memory. Even now when I write about a memory, it is almost as if I have to get the whole story down before I can figure out which parts might have more significance. Any time I write, of course, I might naturally zoom in on certain parts, which is what we want students eventually to do. Zooming in, whether it's with writing or drawing, ideally is not left only for official revision times. In the beginning, however, it's important to validate that there has to be some scaffolding before this happens naturally.

Another craft strategy to consider in the primary grades, particularly second grade, is to have students draw pictures in the margin of their notebook entries, rather than complete scenes. This idea came from conversations with several second-grade teachers at the Tobin School in Boston who felt that many of their students were ready to spend writing workshop just writing rather than writing and drawing. They wanted students to build up the writing stamina they would need in third grade, but they also knew how important drawing was for writing. They also weren't sure it would be wise to make a cold-turkey switch in the middle of the year from drawing to no drawing. So, rather than decide between "all or nothing," we showed students how to draw smaller pictures in the margin. Students could still draw pictures and details to support their writing, but there wouldn't be a lot of time taken up with drawing the whole scene. Figure 6.5 is an example of this technique.

FIGURE 6.5

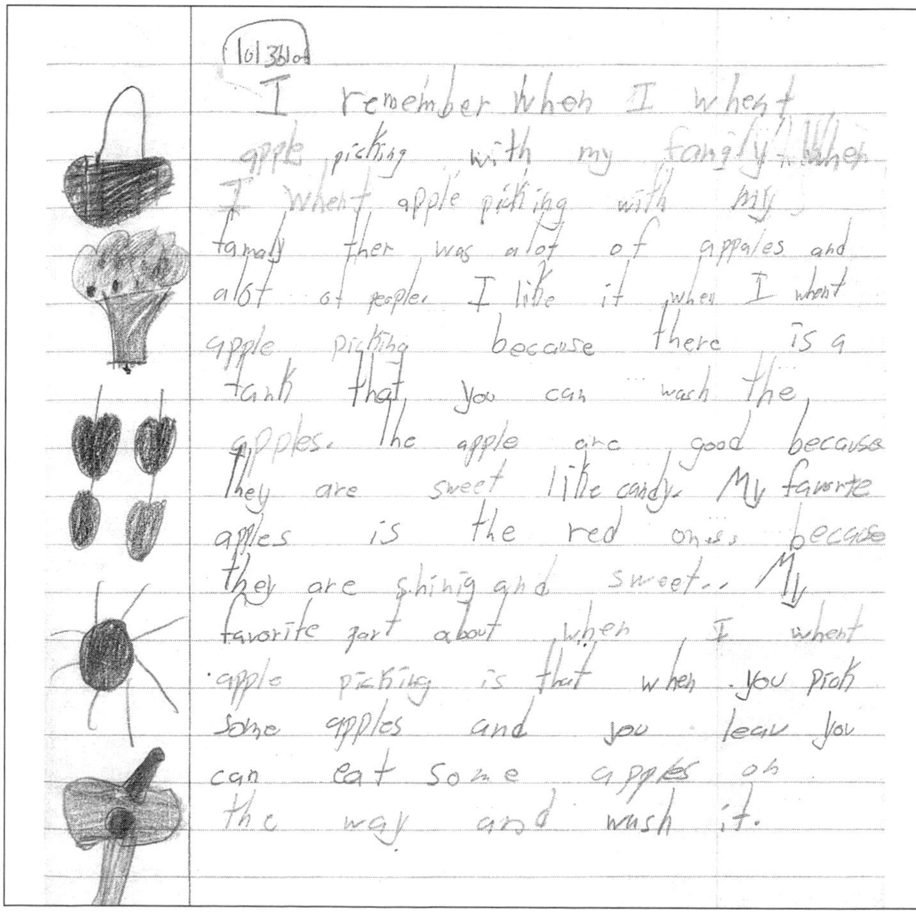
I remember when I whent apple picking with my family. When I whent apple picking with my famaly ther was alot of appales and alot of peple. I like it when I whent apple picking because there is a tank that you can wash the apples. The apple are good because they are sweet like candy. My favorte apples is the red ones because they are shining and sweet. My favorite part about when I whent apple picking is that when you pick some apples and you leav you can eat some apples on the way and wash it.

Rosa Verdu, a teacher of a combined class of first- and second-grade English language learners, found the margin drawing technique particularly helpful because of the large range of abilities in her classroom. Her first graders continued drawing larger pictures while she taught the new drawing strategy in several group conferences to her second graders. The students loved it! So did we. Students were writing more, but we had not asked them to let go of drawing either. Drawing in the margin also allowed students to highlight objects and people at different parts of their memoir stories. They did not have to choose just one moment from their stories to capture in their drawings. Because there was no scale in terms of size, it was easy for them to draw objects with more detail. These small drawings in the margins also gave a colorful, inviting tone to the writing and the notebook in general. I've since thought about teaching this to some of the older grades as well. If I were a fourth or fifth grader, I would feel even more attached to my writer's notebook if there were a few colorful pictures in the margins reflecting the content of my stories and memories.

Writing Words

As most teachers know, crafting writing sometimes has a different meaning at the primary level. Students not only are crafting meaning but also are crafting letters, words, and sentences. This section on writing words focuses on not so much word choice and description, but the more fundamental skills of shaping and spelling words. It's not that primary teachers aren't aware of most, if not all, of the skills listed in Table 6.2, but it might be helpful to see them all together with the adjoining Why column that can support instruction.

Although the use of capitals is also about writing words correctly, it moves into a slightly different realm where the "correctness" of words is determined by meaning. Just about every proper noun requires a capital letter, but I find students remember to use capital letters more often when they are taught within specific contexts. (See Table 6.3.)

Word Walls

One of the balancing acts in teaching primary writing is supporting students' use of inventive spelling while also creating a sense of accountability for learning the correct spelling of grade-level words. Many teachers use a word wall to assist students with correct spelling by publicly displaying high-frequency words or words that have been taught in lessons. As most primary teachers know, the more students interact with word walls, the more they will actually use them independently. As a result, teachers sometimes do activities such as bingo or word searches with word wall words in addition to using the word wall as an instructional tool during shared reading or interactive writing.

Table 6.2 Shaping and Spelling Words

SPECIFIC CRAFT	WHAT DOES IT LOOK LIKE?	WHY IS IT GOOD?
Sounding words out loud	Students say words out loud to themselves rather than trying to figure out a word in their mind only.	Allows writer to hear the sounds without asking the teacher; supports independence
Taking risks	Students write words even when they are not sure how to spell them.	Reaching for bigger words is how writers get better
Using alphabet chart	Students use alphabet charts on their desk to help them think of what letters to write.	Sounding out words helps student become an independent writer
Using the word wall	Students use the word wall to correctly spell words they have studied.	Using a resource for correct spelling helps student become an independent writer
Spacing	There are spaces in between words.	Keeps the reader from being confused; reader know where one word starts and ends
Writing on the line	If lined paper is used, the letters sit on the line rather than hanging in mid air.	Keeps the reader from being confused

Table 6.3 Using Capital Letters

SPECIFIC CRAFT	WHAT DOES IT LOOK LIKE?	WHY IS IT GOOD?
People's names	Names start with capital letters.	Shows it's one particular person
Writing the word *I* as a capital	*I*, when it's by itself, is capitalized.	Even though we are referring to ourselves, we are also a unique person
Places	Cities and states start with capital letters.	Shows it's a specific place
Stores	Names of stores start with capital letters.	Shows it's a specific place

Although frequent exposure to these words in any way is beneficial, it is helpful to have activities that isolate as much as possible the skill you actually want students to use during independent writing time. We certainly don't want students to look up at the word wall every single time they write a word. We want students to be immersed in remembering their stories so they can draw and write about their stories to the best of their ability.

The ideal word wall scenario would look something like this: Kalil is writing about the birthday party he had last month, with all that blank space ahead of him. After writing "I saw my . . . ," he is about to write the word *friend* when something in his mind reminds him that the word *friend* is on the word wall. He glances up from his seat, where he can easily read the words on the word wall, writes *f-r-i-e-n-d*, and then continues on with his sentence. Perhaps some teachers might notice there is one skill in that scenario that is the least likely to occur on its own. Most students write sentences, and most students can look at a board and copy words. The skill that is not as much of a given is when Kalil, without being reminded about using the word wall and without having it in his immediate line of vision, realizes that the word he is about to write is on the word wall. Kalil is so familiar with which words are on the word wall that the words themselves act as a trigger to look up and use this spelling resource.

One way to support the use of the word wall during independent writing time is not through direct instruction but through consistent practice of this very small skill in almost a game-like way.

Word-Wall Game

This quick game begins with giving a pointer to a student and asking him or her to find a certain word on the word wall:

> *Where is the word . . .* when?

After that student points to the word *when,* he or she chooses the next person to get the pointer for the next word-find challenge. After modeling the game a few times, students can take over the role of telling the other student which word to find. The game can then be run independently, with the teacher as facilitator. Other students can be involved by either whispering to each other if they know where the given word is or by giving a thumbs-up when the correct word is found.

Word-Wall Quiz

Another way to reinforce students' memory of the word wall is simply to quiz students:

> *Teacher: Is* friend *on the word wall?*
> *Students: Yes!*
> *Teacher: Is . . .* cousin *on the word wall?*
> *Students: No!*

At first some students scan the board to come to an answer. Some students may just pick up on what other students are saying. But that's okay, because it's the repetition and reinforcement of what is there and what isn't there that is important.

Both activities may seem quite simple—and they are—but their simplicity is due to the fact that attention is given to such an isolated skill. The best part about these kinds of activities is that they can be done in a matter of minutes whenever there is a small amount of time—after a morning meeting, before lunch, or during those last few minutes before buses are called. They can also be done as a transition, especially before writing workshop, when students ideally are putting this skill to use the most.

Basic Craft

Basic Craft relates closely to some of the specific craft presented in Chapter 4. Rather than listing skills that range from basic to more advanced, I have pulled together basic craft techniques from some of the different categories in Chapter 4: the five senses, show not tell, dialogue, sentence variety, and word choice. Although there is a slight overlap with Chapter 4 here, I find it helpful to consider many different kinds of basic craft all together. When I confer with students who write on a primary level, basic skills such as those listed in Table 6.4 are foremost in my mind, whether the students are actually in a primary grade or not.

Table 6.4 Basic Craft Skills for Primary-Level Writers

SPECIFIC CRAFT	WHAT DOES IT LOOK LIKE?	WHY IS IT GOOD?
Colors	*My shirt was blue.*	Creates a better picture for the reader
Inside sentences	*I was sad.*	Reader can understand how the author feels
Feelings	*I cried a lot.*	Gives reader a picture and a feeling at the same time
Basic dialogue	*Then I said Let's go.* (Initial dialogue usually does not have quotation marks)	Helps bring the memory alive and adds sound to writing
People's names	*I saw my friend Michelle.*	Makes the person seem real
Proper nouns and brand names	*We went to CVS.*	Gives reader a very specific image
Kinds of food	*We ate pizza.*	Gives reader more specific image than "food"
Weather	*It was snowing.*	Reader can picture the background

I made a point to write sentences on a more primary level than some of the basic craft in Chapter 4, which further emphasizes the fact that even the most simple use of basic craft can be a strength to notice. Many of these craft techniques also correlate with strengths that can be found in drawing. This connection is important for teachers to explicitly model. The more students understand how to look at their own picture for ideas for what to write next, the more independent they will be in writing with description.

Writing Materials

Because of the dual emphasis on drawing and writing in the early grades, there tends to be much more variation in what primary students write *on* compared with upper elementary students, who write mostly in notebooks. In some primary classrooms you might find sketch books, pads of blank paper, booklets with lines at the bottom, as well as different kinds of paper with squares for drawing and different-sized lines for writing. This variation is essential to support the different ability levels that invariably fill primary classrooms. As Calkins, Hartman, and White describe in *One to One: The Art of Conferring with Young Writers* (2005), "The goals we envision and the instruction we provide need to be multileveled. The good news for a primary writing workshop: It is not hard to provide for multileveled work. The secret lies in differentiated materials. Once we discern what is within the grasp of each child, we set each child up to write on paper that is 'just right' for him" (19).

Unlike notebooks in the elementary grades, where there is always room to write more, the paper we give out at the primary level will often dictate how little or how much students can write. This can hinder the writing development of some students. Several years ago, I experienced firsthand the expectations that materials bring. I had been working with a first-grade teacher during a memoir unit of study. We were focusing on building up the volume of student writing by showing students specific ways to include details in their pictures and how to use their pictures to get ideas for sentences. By the time of our writing celebration, students had final drafts with three or four pages of writing along with a final illustration. The following year, around November, I happened to stop by a second-grade classroom that had many of these same children. Because the teacher had been giving all students the same paper that had a box for a picture with about five lines underneath, five lines is as much as any of them wrote. What surprised me the most was that these children were completely fine with that! My first thought, although perhaps somewhat unrealistic, was, "Don't the students themselves realize they could do so much more? Don't they remember all that writing we did last year?" Then I realized that unless writing less was uncomfortable, why would they care? They were still enjoying themselves and telling their stories, and they were still making finished products. What was there to feel uncomfortable about? It may take more planning, teaching, modeling, and even more photocopying to provide differentiated materials to students, but this up-front investment will greatly support young students in developing their writing to their full potential.

As I mentioned at the start of this chapter, some students who write at a primary level are not necessarily in a primary grade. And for students in higher grades, the standard writing material for the class at this point likely is a notebook. There is little variation in materials, because the idea is that by third, fourth or fifth grade, differences in abilities have to do with vocabulary, description, and stamina. Writing notebooks support this ability range because they allow students to write at their own pace and level. For some students below grade level who are writing very basic sentences and need support with basic craft, the writing notebook can work just fine.

Other students who write below grade level, however, are still in the process of working on beginning skills in word and sentence formation. Asking these students to work in primary-like folders, although it is an option, can be met with resistance. But just expecting them to grow into the notebooks everyone else is using may not be the right answer either. We can make accommodations to avoid either scenario. For some students, teachers can demonstrate in a conference how students can write on every other line to give themselves more room. This little bit of extra space keeps sentences from getting cramped. Students can also fill a page twice as fast, which is also advantageous because if a student is behind in word formation or has an occupational therapy need, chances are this student is also behind his or her peers in terms of volume and even stamina.

Another option is to give students such as these a different kind of notebook that has fewer lines and bigger spaces. If the covers of notebooks are decorated in September, then the differences between notebooks will be less glaring. Looking for small ways for these students not to feel discouraged or overly focused on comparing themselves to others is important. It's not that we want to disregard reality, but as many teachers know, emotions and self perception can impact positively or negatively a student's willingness to take risks and invest themselves in writing.

An additional accommodation for below-level writers is to have them draw a picture before they start an entry, which is something I did when I was working with a combined fourth- and fifth-grade special education class several years ago. All the students in the class had writing notebooks, but the students varied tremendously in ability. One girl did write at the third-grade level and looked forward to writing workshop time. On the other end of the spectrum were two fourth-grade boys who wrote at about a first-grade level. If they wrote at all, they always wrote brief entries, partially because they saw writing as a chore and avoided putting much effort into it, and partially because they knew they were the farthest behind in ability. After the teacher taught his students strategies for coming up with their own ideas for topics versus giving them a prompt, their investment changed somewhat. But I could tell that both these boys still could use the support of drawing before writing. Given that they were ten years old, however, and already concerned about their tough exterior, I knew it would probably not be wise to have them write in folders while their peers continued in notebooks. They were already prone to resentment of work and school in general when it reminded them that they were not where they were supposed to be. So, in a small-group conference, I showed both of them how they could draw a box in their notebook by counting twelve lines down for the bottom line and tracing over the margins for the sides. Because drawing was such a doable, enjoyable step before writing, they no longer resisted beginning an entry. Not only did this give the teacher and me strengths to point out before they even wrote, but, like primary students, they could use the information in the pictures to come up with ideas for sentences.

Whether students are in the primary grades or just writing on a primary level, supporting students in both drawing and sentence-building skills can create a solid groundwork for descriptive writing. Knowing how to write letters and words, of course, has to become somewhat automatic before young writers have room to think about how to craft their sentences. By drawing, students get used to providing a visual image for someone besides themselves. Supporting both skill sets—drawing and writing—will prepare students as they move on to their next job of creating images for the reader with only their words.

Teaching Craft Lessons

The Columbia swimming pool was not only the place I had my first lesson about teaching, it's also where I had my very first teaching job. After many months of learning about proper swimming techniques from Chris and many more hours of practicing on my own, I was ready to teach a few beginners. The first lesson I gave happened by accident.

Every Monday when I was lifeguarding, my friend Brett, who was also on the Columbia swim team, came to the pool to give a swim lesson to a young boy named Nate. One Monday, Brett didn't show up. I watched as Nate's mother kept glancing at her watch while Nate sat next to her on a bench, his feet swinging and his goggles already on. Since my shift was just about over, I walked over and offered to give a swim lesson. A week later, I got a phone call from the mother. She wanted to find out if I would teach her son from now on instead of Brett. She said Nate enjoyed me as a teacher but that he also seemed to learn quite a lot in just one lesson. I imagine the factor of getting stood up played a part as well. Looking back on this surprising job offer (Brett and I laughed about it afterwards), I realized that the fact that I so recently had been learning about swimming myself was perhaps my biggest asset. There was no question that Brett was a much better swimmer than I was. He was a top backstroker on the swim team and had probably been on a swim team since he was six years old. Like most swimmers on a college team, he swam in a way that had become almost second nature to him. But I had just learned all these techniques from Chris and was fresh from thinking about information from the *receiving* end of instruction.

Expertise in a subject matter is not always the key to giving good lessons. You do have to know *something* about the subject you're teaching. You just don't have to know everything. Especially in the elementary grades, teachers don't have to be writers themselves, neither in the published sense nor even the "I like to curl up with my writing notebook on weekends" sense of the word. But teaching writing well does not happen on its own either: you do have to know something about writing. The first six chapters of *Crafting Writers* were dedicated to the first part of the equation—the content. From here on, *Crafting Writers* looks at the instruction of specific craft and how to transfer knowledge about craft into clear and useful next steps for students.

Types of Mini-Lessons

There have always been, and always will be, different schools of thought about how to best teach reading and writing. I do find, however, that writing workshop and the structure of a mini-lesson support the teaching of specific craft. The time frame of a mini-lesson, which is about seven to ten minutes, honors the fact that teaching just one concept each day will more likely lead to student ownership of skills.

Throughout the year, regardless of the genre being studied, you can teach different types of writing mini-lessons. Craft is only one type of lesson that should be considered when planning for instruction. Table 7.1 gives some other possible categories to consider.

Additional categories might include illustrating, especially in the primary grades, and management, which can include transition time and how to get materials such as paper, pencils, and notebooks.

Thinking in terms of categories helps keep instruction balanced when you plan lessons. There are other books that might suggest similar categories by different names. Regardless of what we call them, being aware of categories helps teachers support students in a variety of ways.

Most writing workshop periods tend to have the following structure:

MINI-LESSON
TRY-IT
INDEPENDENT WRITING
SHARE

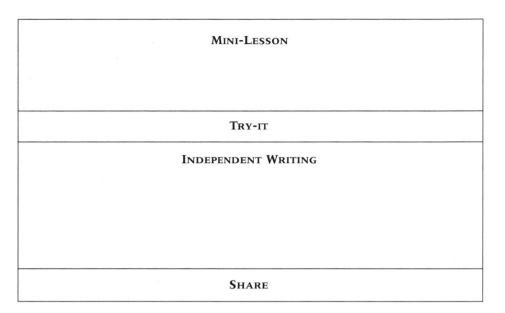

Table 7.1 Mini-Lessons Categories

CRAFT	MECHANICS	WRITING STRATEGY	TEXT FEATURES
Most often, craft skills affect the sound and rhythm of writing or help create an image for the reader. Craft lessons can also focus on craft strategies that affect the overall organization or tone of a piece of writing.	While mechanics can be considered craft, it is helpful to think of them in a separate category. Mechanics include punctuation, grammar, and capitalization.	Writing strategy lessons are ones that affect the writer but are not directly about the words and marks on the page. The steps in the writing process would fall under this category.	Text feature lessons focus on features that are particular to a certain genre being studied. Although they can overlap with craft lessons (because different genres are crafted different ways), students should understand what it means to write in a certain genre.

CRAFT

EXAMPLES
- Writing both short and long sentences
- Using *ly* adverbs after *said*
- Writing a nonfiction entry in the second person (*you* voice)

In the primary grades:
- Using colors to describe

MECHANICS

EXAMPLES
- Using quotation marks around dialogue
- Ending sentences with periods
- Using commas in a series

In the primary grades:
- Writing spaces between words

WRITING STRATEGY

EXAMPLES
- Coming up with memoir ideas on your own
- Writing a letter as a way to revise
- Taking risks with bigger words you are not sure how to spell

In the primary grades:
- Using your picture to give you ideas for sentences

TEXT FEATURES

EXAMPLES
- Writing asides with parenthesis (in a scriptwriting genre)
- The purpose of a glossary (in nonfiction writing)
- Line breaks in poems

In the primary grades:
- Writing a dedication page

The writing workshop period typically begins with a teacher-directed lesson about one concept in writing. A brief connection at the start of the lesson lets students know how this lesson connects with previous instruction or with what a teacher has noticed about his or her students' writing. The try-it, which will be discussed in more depth later in this chapter, gives students a few minutes to process the lesson. During independent writing, students write in notebooks, folders, or on draft paper while the teacher conducts one-on-one conferences. At the end of the period, there is time for a few students to share what they worked on that day. There are times when the structure of a writing workshop period looks a little bit different. But, any time I veer from the typical mini-lesson, either in structure or time, I always have a reason for doing so.

The Mini-Lesson

Most teachers would probably agree that in a lesson, something is taught. But sometimes what gets called a lesson is really more of an activity or a review of material that was already taught. I'm certainly not saying activities and review aren't important aspects of a school day—they are. But I do think that reserving the label of *lesson* for those times when we teach new material or skills will help teachers keep themselves accountable for teaching lessons that are aimed at growing students' independent skill sets in writing. Sometimes my college students describe a "lesson," either one they wrote or one they observed in a classroom, that has many positive aspects—it's engaging, it's related to the topic being studied, and it clearly took some preparation. But very often my question is, "What exactly is being taught?"

Talking about or demonstrating the concept of details or adding exciting words may feel like teaching, because this kind of activity is reinforcing an important aspect of writing. And again, reinforcing and reviewing what it means to write with detail can be beneficial. But teaching a writing lesson should mean you are teaching a skill or technique, no matter how small, that students are able to take away with them and independently apply in their own writing. It doesn't mean that every student *will* use that skill in their writing. The goal is just to make that one skill as accessible as possible. Perhaps some people might argue that presenting the concept of "adding details" *is* teaching something, that it *is* teaching "one thing." But the idea of specific craft challenges the notion that you can teach students how to add details in one lesson. You can review the concept, but there are so many ways to add details, that many separate lessons really are needed.

In recent years, the phrase "teacher directed" has sometimes gotten a bad reputation, primarily because it emphasizes the teacher as the giver of information. Recent shifts in education value the fact that students learn best when they have a chance to actively process information, not just constantly listen to information the teacher provides. It is true that when entire subjects are taught just by the teacher talking, students are less likely to retain information as well as they otherwise could. When it comes to smaller pieces of information, however, teacher directed can be a good thing. In fact, it can be a very good thing. Lucy Calkins points out that one reason mini-lessons tend to go on longer than they need to is because we have been taught that there is something wrong with "lecturing" to students (1994). Some teachers who think they should avoid lecturing altogether end up giving a "mini-lesson" that is so conversational, it keeps the instruction from being clear. Embracing the fact that the role of teacher is no longer the almighty knower and provider of information doesn't mean we should forget that our job is still to teach. The key to being comfortable with direct instruction in a mini-lesson is knowing that what you are teaching is specific and useful and that, as will be discussed later in this chapter, there is time right after the lesson when all students can process the lesson in a meaningful way.

Whenever I teach a craft lesson, or any writing lesson for that matter, there are two main questions that guide my teaching and support direct and clear instruction:

What exactly am I teaching?
Why am I teaching this? How will it help my students as writers?

As you might notice, these two points (which I sometimes call the What and the Why) are directly related to the two main steps in gathering craft, as illustrated in the first part of this book. The What relates to naming craft, and the Why relates to the purpose or benefit of certain craft techniques.

The What and the Why are a consistent part of my instruction because these two concepts are focused on the receiving end of instruction—students. My own measure of a successful craft lesson is not how interesting my lesson was or how engaged my students were, although these are certainly important aspects of instruction. My true test of a craft lesson is how well my students can hold on to what I teach them and bring what they learned into their writing independently. The What and the Why are not necessarily steps to follow in a lesson, but rather information I want to make sure my students understand by the end of the lesson.

Ways to Model Writing

Though it's important to be clear about what you are teaching and why, instruction around craft has to go beyond explanation. Writing is a physical and visual act: it is absolutely essential that modeling is part of the lesson. Following are some of the different ways teachers can model writing in a craft lesson.

Modeling with Published Literature

As most teachers know, children's literature is an invaluable resource when it comes to offering examples of craft. One way to enhance the use of literature in craft lessons is to make the text more visible for students. You can photocopy text onto a transparency and display it on an overhead projector. Another option is to copy text in your own handwriting, either on chart paper or on the overhead, prior to the lesson. Some teachers make copies of short text (excerpts from chapter books or short stories) at the start of a genre study and have students keep these in their folders. Similar to picture books, short text can be used for many different craft lessons. Regardless of how literature is used, it should be familiar to students. When a story, or even part of a story, is new, students are caught up in all those comprehension skills we encourage them to use during reading—making personal connections, wondering, and predicting what might happen next. When a book is nonfiction, students' minds should be absorbed in receiving new information as well as wondering and making predictions. When text used in a lesson is familiar, the novelty of the actual story or the information is not as strong, and this allows students to concentrate more on the *way* the text is written.

When teaching a craft lesson, teachers ideally should use literature in a very practical, focused way: it is not a time to read pages and pages of a book out loud. It doesn't matter how wonderful the writing is—if you are truly teaching a craft lesson, then the text should be used as a tool, not a read-aloud. As long as the craft technique you are teaching is specific, then it makes sense to read just a small portion of text or to read sentences from different pages that are all examples of your teaching point.

Suggesting that literature should be used this way in craft lessons does not mean reading literature is not an important part of teaching writing in general. The first few days of a genre study, for example, can include read-alouds from that genre. Teachers should choose books they know very well and that they can use several times for different lessons. Any book that was taken through the gathering craft process will automatically be an incredible resource for lessons and should be at the top of the list for read-alouds those first few days of a genre study. There also may be days when your lesson is about noticing craft in writing, in which case reading a page or two *would* support your lesson. The same would be true if you wanted to demonstrate a craft technique such as using a flashback or circular endings that can only be demonstrated by reading a certain amount of text. The point is not to make a rigid rule about how much literature to read during a mini-lesson, but to emphasize that any literature used in a lesson should directly support the teaching point. If you are teaching a specific craft technique, you want to be sure that the specific craft remains the focus.

Student Writing

Using student writing is a wonderful way to demonstrate a craft technique. If you have a conference with a student who uses a craft skill well, you can make a transparency copy of it and use it on the overhead during a lesson. I usually use this as a second example after I have modeled it myself on the overhead or read an excerpt from literature. Making a student's writing public in this way is not only quite powerful for that particular student, but it also reinforces for the rest of the class how doable a craft technique really is.

As will be discussed in upcoming chapters, purposefully teaching strengths in conferences makes you much more aware of craft that students are using and increases the chances that you will be able to use student writing in lessons.

Live Writing

Live writing is the term I use when I am actually writing in front of the students with the use of an overhead. The benefit of live writing is that it allows teachers to make public the thought process behind writing. This kind of modeling is the equivalent to a "think-aloud" in reading. If I were demonstrating using sound in writing, for example, I would verbalize the thinking I wanted my students to do as they write. On the overhead I might write the following:

One morning this summer Chrissy and I went to the beach. Only a few other people were there.

After writing those first few sentences, I would say things such as, "Hmmm, what sounds did I hear? Oh yeah. There were all these seagulls making noise in the air." And then I would add that sentence:

One morning this summer Chrissy and I went to the beach. Only a few other people were there. Seagulls were crying out to each other as they flew above us.

Then, a few sentences later, I would think aloud about another sound sentence. Whenever I do any kind of writing myself during a craft lesson, I make a point not to write only sentences that use the craft I am teaching. I write at least a paragraph in which I use the craft technique several times, because this is what I want my students to do. I don't want them to get good at writing isolated sentences or a list of sentences that use sound. I want it to be one kind of detail they include in their writing every now and then. As I write on the overhead I may use other types of craft in addition to the technique I'm teaching. In order to keep the teaching focused, however, I only think out loud in relation to the skill I am teaching that day.

At some point I realized there was a reason I kept saying "Hmmm" every now and then when I used live writing in a lesson. Since I am trying to teach the thinking process behind writing as much as possible, I have to put into words the way I think when I write. Much of writing involves making choices, and *Hmmm* demonstrates this kind of stop-and-go thinking. I don't think up everything I write as fluently as it appears on paper after the fact. I want to make this reflective thinking as transparent as possible as I model any writing for students.

Sometimes when I talk about live writing, teachers say they are not really comfortable writing in front of other people, even their students. Although I validate this feeling, I still encourage any teacher to at least try it. There really is no other way to do an authentic think-aloud and tap into the thinking process behind craft and mechanics than to write yourself. Using literature in lessons offers a wonderful connection between reading and writing, but there is no way for students to see the *creating* of writing if published literature is the only medium used to demonstrate writing. And, if students have to write and share their thoughts and life stories, it does make a difference when their teachers do the same thing—even if it's just a short paragraph.

My hope is that some of the tables of specific craft in the first part of this book will encourage any teacher who might be hesitant to use live writing in lessons. Demonstrating specific craft is not about modeling "amazing writing with compelling voice." Just as specific craft techniques are easier than general writing suggestions for students to imitate and bring into their own writing, so are specific craft techniques easier for teachers to model. And you can certainly plan out, generally, what you are going to write. You would not want to have a prewritten paragraph right next to you and glance over at each sentence as you write it on the overhead. The thinking has to appear natural, but it doesn't really matter if you are actually coming up with the ideas for sentences during the lesson or not.

Exaggerated Writing

Exaggerated writing could also be considered "before and after" modeling. Sometimes I find it helpful to get students to recognize what it looks like to *not* use a certain skill before I actually teach the lesson. For example, when I do a lesson on ending sentences with periods as a result of seeing an abundance of run-on sentences, I write a paragraph on the overhead filled with *and then*'s. With the overhead off, I tell students that I wrote something that uses a lot of the same words. I ask them to see if they can tell what those repeated words are. Then I flip on the overhead light and read what I wrote. I wouldn't need a think-aloud for this before version since I am showing them the opposite of what I am about to teach. Because the writing behavior is so exaggerated, students always notice what I am doing (or not doing). Every time I do this lesson and ask if they notice the overused words, students immediately raise their hands and start whispering to each other. I encourage a quick turn-and-talk and then ask someone to share. A more detailed version of this lesson can be found at the end of this chapter.

✿ ✿ ✿

There is no one right way to model writing, and it is good to use a variety of ways throughout the year, but I do favor methods that use an overhead. Not only is it easier to write on an overhead compared to chart paper, but overheads also seem to entrance students in some way. There's something about the light and the primitive (technologically speaking) yet magical quality of seeing large writing appear on the wall. Especially in classrooms that do not have a rug area of any kind, writing projected on a screen or a wall is almost always easier for all students to see than anything written on chart paper. Because it is such an asset to the teaching of writing, it's important that the overhead is easily accessible with the needed materials (pens, spray bottle of cleaner, and paper towels) all ready to go.

Sometimes I use two different methods of modeling in the same lesson. I mentioned earlier that I might model a craft technique myself and also show a student example. If I were starting a lesson using published literature to demonstrate a craft technique, I might also model it myself on the overhead.

Whenever I finish modeling a craft technique, regardless of the method I use, I usually restate what I am teaching and why it's good before moving on to the try-it.

The Try-It

I have mentioned the importance of lessons being clear and practical. It's also important that all students are looking at you during a lesson. Although these absolutely are *prerequisites* to learning, they do not yet hold any *expectations* for learning. As most teachers know, just because students are paying attention and looking at you, it doesn't mean they are absorbing information to their potential. As Lucy Calkins says, "The fact that we, as teachers, say something has very little to do with whether our children learn it. Telling is not teaching" (2001, 29). The try-it not only creates an opportunity for all students to actively process the lesson, but it also supports accountability. When students know they are going to have to either talk about or try out the skill you are teaching, their internal motivation to listen while you are teaching naturally increases. It's an important expectation and a fair one. It reflects the idea that if I am going to spend ten minutes teaching just "one thing," then I should expect my students to know that "one thing" well enough that they can talk about it or try it out themselves.

Some people might argue that students can actively listen. While this is true, active listening often relies heavily on a person's internal motivation. As adults, we are active listeners in school-like situations, either because we are interested in a subject or because we feel a need to understand. If Olympic athlete Michael Phelps came to Boston and talked about swimming, you can be sure it would not take much for me to listen actively and absorb everything he said. Likewise, if I went to a workshop on teaching reading in the content areas, I also would listen to the best of my ability because I want to learn more about this particular area of literacy. And, although I am not all that interested in real estate taxes, I am a much more active listener than I used to be when someone talks about this topic because now I have a mortgage.

In a sense, our students attend lectures and workshops all day for 180 days of the year. There is no way they can actively listen the whole time. On top of that, we can't assume or expect all children to come to our mini-lessons with an internal motivation to learn more about writing. It is certainly my *hope* that I eventually instill in my students a motivation to write well. But if I see it as their job to always want to take in the information I give them, then I am going against the nature of children as well as the reality that students come to our classrooms with different motivations to learn and different perceptions of school. Rather than just expect or hope that listening will lead to learning, we can set up structures that support active learning. The mini-lesson alone does not do this. Only the try-it, in combination with direct instruction, provides that structure.

The try-it is the reason my lessons can be teacher directed. I don't have to worry about throwing in time for several question-and-answers sessions, which can keep my lesson from staying on track. The compartmentalizing of teaching and student involvement keeps both aspects from being diluted by the other.

Types of Try-Its

Regardless of what kind of lesson I teach, whether it is about management, craft, or a writing strategy, a try-it is always part of my instruction. What differs is the way I ask my students to process the lesson. When it comes to craft and mechanics lessons, there are two kinds of try-its I tend to use most often: turn and talk, where students process the lesson orally, and writing try-its, where students have a short period of time to try out a skill in writing.

Turn and Talk

Turn and talk is a common teaching technique used across all content areas. The teacher usually asks a question or gives a prompt, and then students discuss amongst themselves for a few minutes before any one person offers an idea to the whole class. It is a very simple yet surprisingly powerful way to support student learning. Some teachers I've worked with have students in assigned pairs or groups. Other teachers use a more informal turn and talk where students just turn and talk to whomever is next to them. Fourth-grade teacher Iris Escoto developed an interesting way to have her students turn and talk in her rug area, where her students sit in a U-shaped circle made of chairs. She had previously noticed that when she said, "Turn and talk," there were sometimes people inadvertently left out. When this happened, it was hard for them to go talk to anyone else without getting up because they were sitting in chairs. So, Iris taught her students how to turn and talk in a domino pattern. The two people on one end turn to each other, then the next two, and so on. This way of getting the try-it started not only looks neat and keeps anyone from being left out, but it also gives each pair a visual cue to start talking.

One of the most important aspects of turn and talk is that *all* students are expected to talk. Calling on one or two students is not sufficient, because then only those two students actively process the lesson. If, for example, I call on Shane and Marie and they offer a terrific answer, the only students in my class I can be sure understood the lesson are . . . Shane and Marie. Although I would set the expectation that students are listening to their classmates, I can't assume they are. There was a time when I judged my lessons on the way they sounded. If a lesson sounded great—if I stayed on topic and gave an engaging presentation—and a few students gave some great answers, I considered my lesson a success. Perhaps I assumed that if all students heard my teaching and heard what their classmates said, then the lesson would stick. Now I have different criteria. It may sound a little odd, but when I think of the end goal of my instruction, I visualize twenty-five brains (or however many students are in my classroom at the time) absorbing the information. The words that fill a classroom are a critical conduit for learning, but my priority must be ensuring that my students' minds are receiving and processing the information or I am missing my goal.

To make the try-it as productive as possible, it is helpful to give students a directive of what they should turn and talk about. The directive I give aligns with the underlying goals of my instruction—the What and the Why. For example, if I were teaching a lesson to a fifth-grade class on using the word *as* with dialogue, I would probably have them try it out in writing, but first I would say one of the following turn-and-talk prompts right after I taught and modeled the skill:

❧ Turn to the person next to you and tell them one way you can add description to dialogue.

❧ Turn to the person next to you and tell them why it's good to sometimes use the word *as* with dialogue. What does it do to your writing?

Each prompt asks students to process my lesson in a different way. I tend to favor prompts that relate to the Why, as demonstated in the second example, simply because it pushes students' thinking a little bit more and it naturally incorporates the What. There are also times when I will have students talk about both the What and the Why, because each one only takes about thirty seconds. The turn and talk is not a time to ask a tricky question but rather a way to reinforce students' understanding of the lesson.

As students begin talking, I lean in (if it's a small rug area) or walk around to hear what they are saying. Because the prompts I give are so targeted, it sometimes takes just ten or twenty seconds for students to discuss an answer. I don't check to make sure each pair is getting the answers "right." Not only would this take too much time, but the emphasis of the turn and talk is on accountability and processing the lesson through talking. Once in a while during a turn and talk, enough students are off track that I realize they are interpreting my question the wrong way. In that case, I stop everybody and either clarify the prompt or ask the question in a different way.

After students talk, it's good to have one or two students offer a brief answer to the whole class, simply so others have something to check their answer against. One of my favorite things about this part of the try-it is that students often give different versions of the same answer. When students repeat information in their own words, it illustrates how much the try-it encourages ownership of understanding.

Writing Try-Its

The writing try-it is one of the most powerful ways for craft instruction to lead to student ownership. Using writing to try out a craft or mechanics skill means students are "trying out" the skill in the purest sense of the term. The most important benefit of these try-its is that they isolate a skill before students attempt to use it in their independent writing. This isolation of a skill in order to strengthen it occurs in sports when athletes do drills. I mentioned in Chapter 3 that swimmers move their arms in an S-curve under water. One drill that strengthens this not-so-natural movement is swimming with one arm. Some people hold one arm out straight or hold on to a kickboard while the other arm does all the work. There are drills for just about any sport, from running to basketball to soccer. And they are not just for beginners. Whether athletes are in Little League or in the American League, there is an understanding that the best way to strengthen small skills is to practice them separately where they can have undivided attention. Writing is no different. When students have a chance to actually try out a new skill with focused attention, it will have a much better chance of lasting when they go back to the varied act of writing a whole piece.

Students can have a section in their notebooks just for these writing try-its. Recently I have been encouraging teachers to have students create this sec-

Figure 7.1

tion with a tab in their notebooks in September (see Figure 7.1). I usually have students count twenty or thirty pages from the back to create the writing try-it section. Having the try-it section separate from their independent writing keeps the try-its from interrupting entries.

Below are some suggested steps for a writing try-it after a craft lesson.

- ❀ Students write the date and the name of the skill
- ❀ Give a quick prompt
- ❀ Say, "Ready, go" and give students a few minutes to write
- ❀ Have a few students quickly share

Students Write the Date and the Name of the Skill

One of the benefits of writing try-its is that students are literally recording your instruction. If they are going to be learning a skill, why not reinforce this learning by having them write down the name of the craft technique you are teaching? At the top of a third grader's try-it pages, you might see headings such as "Writing Sounds," "Ending Sentences with Periods," and "Inside Sentences." At the top of a fifth grader's try-it pages, you might see "Writing Sounds Without 'I Heard,'" "Dialogue with *As*," and "*Ing* Openers." Having these try-its all in one place can also support student accountability for knowing what was taught recently in writing workshop. Every student may not be ready to bring certain craft techniques into their writing, but shouldn't they have a general understanding of what lessons have been taught in the last few weeks? One year, fourth-grade teacher Michelle Gulla decided to give students quizzes based on what they had recorded in their try-it sections. And it was not a trick quiz in any way. Students studied from their try-it section and could quiz each other in pairs before we handed out the quiz. In keeping with the pattern of our instruction, students knew they were expected to know the What and the Why of skills that had been taught.

Another benefit of having a separate place for try-its is that teachers can more easily refer to previous lessons during conferences. Giving students a place in their notebooks where they can hang on to successful examples is a tremendous asset for skills you need to reteach in a conference. And we have to expect that we'll need to reteach some skills. Not every student who successfully uses a skill in a try-it will bring it into their independent writing. When conferences are used to revisit craft or mechanics skills already taught, it is quite a powerful thing to refer back to the student's try-it section where he or she has already modeled the teaching point.

Give a Quick Prompt

The greatest benefit to giving a prompt for the try-it versus encouraging students to come up with their own topic is that it emphasizes the skill I am teaching and nothing more. Students are already coming up with their own topics during independent writing. That is when student independence is important. The try-it is not about exploring ideas or life stories; it is about instruction. A prompt also helps students get started. Efficiency is important when it comes to the lesson and the try-it. The longer this part of writing workshop takes, the less time there is for independent writing.

The try-it prompt should give students two main criteria:

1. What they will write about
2. Expectations for using the specific craft you're teaching

When it comes to the topic of the prompt, there is one subject I frequently use: the lunchroom. A prompt, of course, has to be about a topic that is accessible to all students. I would not say, for example, "Write about a time you went on an airplane." The lunchroom, on the other hand, is clearly accessible to all students. In addition, the lunchroom works with many different categories of craft lessons. Just about every lunchroom memory has sounds, visuals, smells, tastes, dialogue, and feelings. The other topic I sometimes use is going to the dentist or doctor's office. Like the lunchroom, it is a familiar topic and lends itself to writing with many different senses and emotions. Using the same topic makes planning easier, but more importantly, using the same topic over and over takes attention away from *what* students are writing about, and lets them concentrate on *how* they are writing.

In addition to providing a topic, it also helps to give clear expectations of how frequently students should use the skill in their try-it. Expectations should be consistent with the modeling. If I made a point to use a craft technique once or twice within a paragraph of writing, then I would want my students to do the same thing.

Table 7.2 offers some examples of how writing try-it prompts might sound.

Table 7.2 Writing Try-It Prompts

IF I TAUGHT A LESSON ON:	A WRITING TRY-IT PROMPT MIGHT SOUND LIKE THIS:
Writing with sounds	Write about the lunchroom, and see if every few sentences you can describe a sound.
Using *as if* to give a visual description (comparing)	Write about the lunchroom. See if you can use *as if* at least once to describe something.
Sharing an inside thought	Write about going to the dentist or the doctor. See if you can include at least two inside sentences that show what you were thinking.
Using quotation marks around dialogue	Write about the lunchroom. Write at least two sentences that include what someone says. See if you can put the quotation marks around only what was said.

You might notice that I usually use the phrase *see if you can* when giving a prompt. This phrase validates that students are just trying out this skill for the first time. But there's another reason why I don't just say:

Write about the lunchroom, and include two sentences that have sound.

I realized that although there is nothing terribly wrong with this kind of prompt, it is more of a direction. I assign, you do. It's not that assigning work should not be part of the school day at times. But a direction doesn't really fit with the skills students use when they write. Because writing descriptively is somewhat of an art, we can't *make* students use certain craft skills when they go back to write on their own. Sentences are not "wrong" if they don't include descriptive details. Unlike our expectations of punctuation and other mechanics that have rules, we can't have concrete expectations of exactly which craft techniques students should use and when. They have to own these decisions themselves. *See if you can* invites students into the writing process, which more closely aligns to the fact that writing is about making individual choices. Clearly, how the prompt is said is a small detail, but because we can't *make* students write certain ways, every small teaching move that supports student ownership helps.

Say, "Ready, Go"

The try-it is not meant to take up a lot of time. After the prompt is given, there should be an expectation that students start right away. I find myself often saying "Okay, ready? Go ahead," I am always amused by how much this phrase makes a difference. But it does help bring a sense of efficiency to the time I give them, which is about three to five minutes. My sister, who is a professional organizer, once told me about putting on an egg timer for cleaning up the house. When I tried this, it gave me this same "Ready, go" feeling and made me aware there was a finite amount of time. I was amazed by how much more efficient I was when I knew I was being timed (by no one but myself). Even more amazing was that cleaning seemed to take less effort. Try-its are similar. When there's limited time to write, it's just much easier for students to get going. It's important to mention that it wasn't until I started giving students specific craft techniques that I truly had an expectation that they could start right away without individual help or encouragement from me.

Although I go around to see how students are doing, the try-it is not a time to make sure everyone does a skill perfectly. If I notice someone is misinterpreting the prompt or the lesson, I will nudge them back on course. But I will not stop to have anything that resembles a conference. Not only is individual teaching not the purpose of the try-it, but also I need that time to get a sense of how students are doing in general as well as decide whom I might call on to share. Similar to the turn and talk, if enough students are off track, there is nothing wrong with stopping everybody to clarify or change your prompt.

As I am going around the room, I keep an eye out for good examples. Usually after I have announced my one-minute warning, I quietly whisper to two students, "Would you mind sharing this?" Deciding myself ahead of time who will share makes the try-it go much more smoothly, because there is no public display of my choosing. The real reason for this behind-the-scenes choosing, however, has to do with instruction. The try-it time should not be confused with the official share at the end of writing workshop, when students share what they wrote independently that day. This quick try-it share is still part of my lesson. I need to have examples that support what I am trying to teach. And not every single student will do the try-it well. One of the best parts about teaching specific craft, however, is that when it comes to picking who will share, I rarely have to rely on the "top writers" in the class. Specific craft, because it is so precise, can be done by students at many different levels. I am looking for who exemplifies the lesson, not who wrote a "beautiful" piece of writing.

It's important not to get in the habit of giving students a lot of extra time for the writing try-it, even if they ask for it. They are not writing a full notebook entry, so they don't need to be "done." All that matters is that they attempt the craft technique that was taught. If a teacher keeps giving students more time for the try-it, it is out of good intentions, but it can decrease the impact of the "Ready, go" feeling. If students know you'll always give them more time, why rush to get started?

After students have been writing for a few minutes, I like to let them know when they have about a minute or so left. Giving them a heads-up not only emphasizes the finite amount of time, but, from the writer's point of view, it's just nice not to be stopped all of a sudden. Figures 7.2a and 7.2b show two examples of writing try-its that were part of a lesson on starting sentences with different words. Because this lesson was part of a nonfiction unit of study, I asked them to write facts about snow.

FIGURES 7.2A AND 7.2B

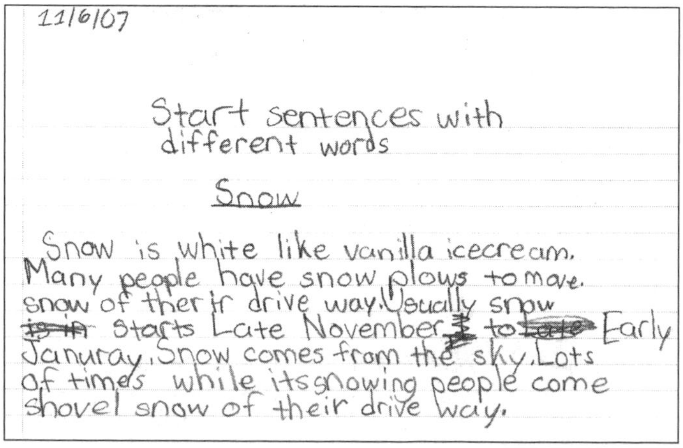

11/6/07

Start sentences with different words

Snow

Snow is white like vanilla icecream. Many people have snow plows to move snow of ther jr drive way. Usually snow ~~is in~~ starts Late November ~~to late~~ Early Januray. Snow comes from the sky. Lots of times while its gnowing people come shovel snow of their drive way.

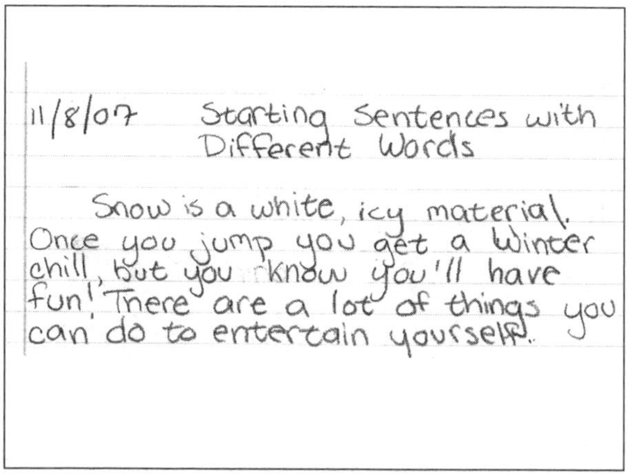

11/8/07   Starting Sentences with Different Words

Snow is a white, icy material. Once you jump you get a winter chill, but you rknow you'll have fun! There are a lot of things you can do to entertain yourself.

Have a Few Students Quickly Share

After students put down their pencils, I almost always ask one or two students to share what they wrote for their try-it. It would be a missed opportunity to just move on to independent writing. Having a few students share at this point is like having an extra modeling session for your craft lesson. And, similar to using student writing in a lesson, there is tremendous value in having examples that are written not by the teacher or a published author, but by the students themselves.

After a student shares his or her writing, I tend to ask the rest of the class to comment on the writing. Because this is still part of my lesson, I encourage comments that align with my instruction. For example, after a student shares a try-it in a lesson about writing with sounds I might ask, "What sounds did she include in her writing?" In a lesson about using *as if*, my question would be, "What did he describe using *as if*?"

Having other students offer brief comments not only helps students actively listen for craft that is embedded in the writing try-its, but it also serves as a model for how I want students to comment during the share at the end of the writing workshop period or even during publishing celebrations. Students at the elementary age are very capable of commenting on the craft that other students use, but only if we encourage them to. Sometimes students will say, "I like your writing," which certainly is a compliment. Teaching students how to be specific with their compliments will mean much more to the person they compliment, and it will support students' ability to notice craft themselves.

Writing Try-Its for Primary Grades

When teaching lessons in the primary grades, I don't use writing try-its as often. The main reason is time. It just takes longer for younger students to write a certain number of sentences. At earlier ages, oral language is the most accessible form of processing information. So turn and talk works very well for these grades. There are times, however, when it is beneficial to use a writing try-it with some of the more basic craft lessons.

In order to keep these try-its from taking up large amounts of time, teachers can ask primary students to write a few sentences rather than a paragraph. For example, I once taught a lesson on using inside sentences to a second-grade class and my prompt was, "Write two sentences about going to the dentist or doctor's office and see if one sentence can be an inside sentence about how you felt." It's worth the extra few minutes of having them write a few sentences rather than just the one inside sentence on its own. Having them just write one sentence about how they felt, although it would still be helpful in some way, is farther away from the act of writing and closer to just responding to a direction. Figure 7.3 shows one second grader's try-it for this lesson.

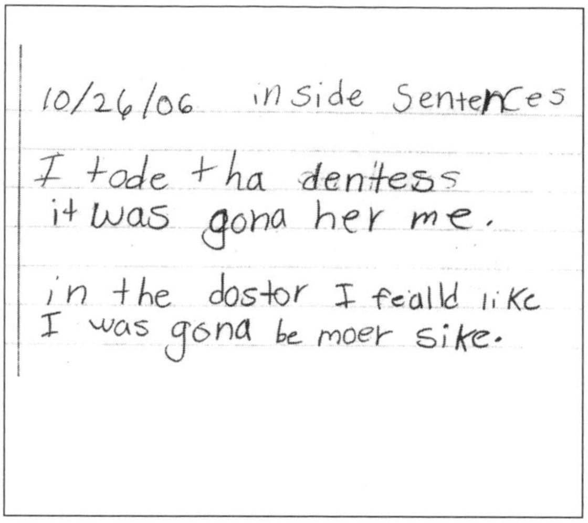
10/26/06 inside Sentences
I tode tha dentess it was gona her me.
in the dostor I feald like I was gona be moer sike.

FIGURE 7.3

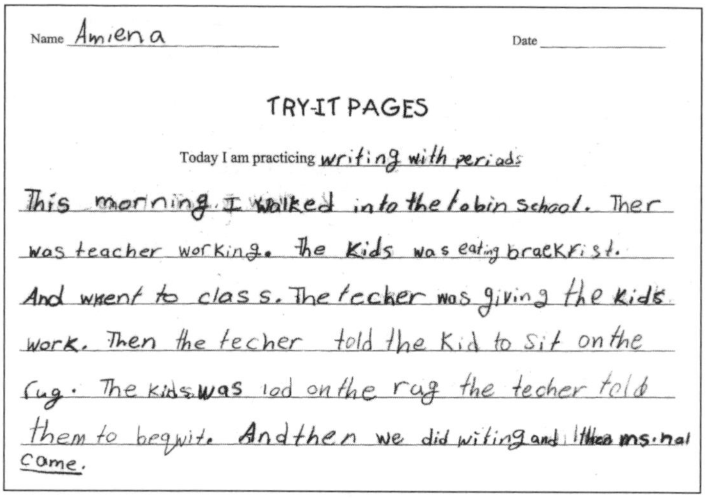
Name Amiena Date

TRY-IT PAGES

Today I am practicing writing with periods

This morning I walked into the tobin school. Ther was teacher working. the Kids was eating braekrist. And whent to class. The techer was giving the kids work. Then the techer told the Kid to sit on the rug. The kids was lod on the rag the techer told them to beqwit. And then we did witing and then ms. nal came.

FIGURE 7.4

If students are working with folders rather than notebooks, teachers can create try-it pages. Figure 7.4 is an example of a try-it page from a lesson on ending sentences with periods that I taught to a second-grade class. As you can see in Figure 7.4, there is still an expectation that students are aware of what they are learning. The fill-in-the-blank style title saves time yet still emphasizes that students are writing with a purpose. These try-it papers can be kept in folders, both for students to review and for reference during conferences.

Mini-Lesson Examples

The following mini-lessons relate to some of the craft presented in Chapters 4 and 5. A primary lesson titled "Inventive Spelling: Taking Risks with Words" and a more advanced punctuation lesson, "Starting a Sentence with an *Ing* Phrase," can be found in Appendix A. The text in italics in these sample mini-lessons offers my commentary about that part of the lesson. The regular text is what I say to students during the lesson.

Mini-Lesson: Sentence Variety: Starting Sentences with Different Words

The following lesson works well with both personal narrative and nonfiction. I usually present this lesson when I notice students starting many of their sentences with the same word. I use exaggerated writing as a way to demonstrate what I am seeing.

I have the beginning of an entry on the overhead. There is one word I use a lot. When I turn on the overhead, see if you can tell what that word is. Ready? Here it is.

Swimming is a sport people of all ages can do. Swimmers can practice on their own or train with a team. Swimmers need goggles to see underwater. Swimmers learn different kinds of strokes. Swimmers also learn how to do flip turns.

Turn to the person next to you. What word do I use a lot?

Connection Right, I used the word *swimmers* at the beginning of almost every sentence. This is something I sometimes see in your writing—you start a lot of your sentences with whatever your topic is about. If you're writing about dogs, it's kind of like, "Dogs do this . . . Dogs do that . . ."

Mini-Lesson If the topic you are writing about is dogs , then it might make sense that every sentence start with that word. But what do you think is wrong if every sentence starts with the same word? *I usually read my sentences on the overhead in a slightly monotone voice accenting the word* **swimmers.** *Every time I do this, students usually say, "It's boring" or "All the sentences sound the same."* Right, it's the same sound over and over. When it comes to the sound of writing, it's important to have variety, to not have sentences that all sound the same. It's like if you went to Dunkin Donuts and there was only one kind of doughnut. That's no fun! All doughnuts are great, but you want variety: some with frosting, some with jelly, some with chocolate—there are so many kinds. Writing is the same way—you want your sentences to have variety. So one way to have sentence variety is to   are you ready? . . . This one is easy. . . . You just start your sentences with different words

So *(as I erase the before version),* now I am going to write about the same topic, except this time, I am going to try to start my sentences with different words. *Keeping the same first sentence, I model my thinking before I write each new sentence, usually accenting the first word. I like using the same first sentence as in the before version: it further illustrates that you can write about the same exact topic and, because of choices you make as a writer, come out with a completely different piece of writing. I definitely do a lot of hmms here, just about at every sentence, because it does take a little thinking to start each sentence a different way. When I reread the writing in its entirety, I sometimes circle the first word in each sentence, just to highlight the point of my lesson.*

Swimming is a sport people of all ages can do. Some people swim on their own while others train with a team. In order to see underwater, swimmers usually wear goggles that cover their eyes. Without goggles it would be hard to see the wall and do flip turns. Goggles are also important because pool water has chlorine in it. If your eyes aren't protected, the chlorine can irritate your eyes.

Figure 7.5

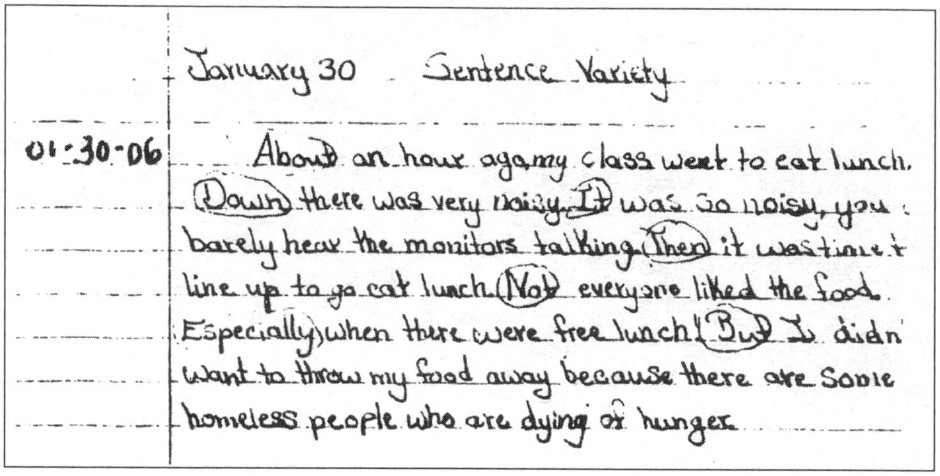

> January 30   Sentence Variety
>
> 01·30·06   About an hour ago my class went to eat lunch.
> (Down) there was very noisy. It was so noisy, you
> barely hear the monitors talking. (Then) it was time t
> line up to go eat lunch. (No) everyone liked the food.
> (Especially) when there were free lunch! (But) I didn'
> want to throw my food away because there are some
> homeless people who are dying of hunger.

See how different my sentences sound from each other? I had some variety to my sentences this time because I started my sentences with different words.

Turn-and-Talk Try-It   So, turn to the person next to you and tell them one thing you can do to give your sentences variety. *With lessons like these where the answer to the turn and talk is so obvious because I just said it, and because I'm about to do a writing try-it, I don't need to do a whole-class share. These kinds of turn and talks rarely take more than twenty or thirty seconds.*

Writing Try-It   Okay, so now it's your turn to try this. Everybody turn to your try-it section. At the top write the date and "Starting sentences with different words."

Write about five or six sentences that describe the lunchroom and see if you can start your sentences with different words. It's okay to start a sentence with "The lunchroom" once in a while, just not all the time. *See Figure 7.5 for a student example of this try-it.*

Several students share their try-its.

Okay, it's time for independent writing. Today as you write about your different topics, see if you can start sentences with different words.

- -

Mini-Lesson: Inside Sentences: What Were You Thinking?

Connection   You all seem to be enjoying telling your memoir stories, which is great. But it's important to start moving beyond just telling the story, beyond just saying—this happened, then this happened, then this happened *(I usually do a hand motion that implies jumping from one thing to the next.)* Yes, you do want to tell your story, but your real job as a writer is to make your memory or your story come alive for the reader as much as possible.

Mini-Lesson   Using inside sentences is one way to make a story come alive for the reader. A few weeks ago we looked at inside sentences that show how you feel. They are not about the action of the story, but about your experience—your inside feelings. You can also write inside sentences that have to do with what you were thinking. The things we think are often very private and you can't tell what someone is thinking just by looking at them. So, in addition to writing about what *happened* in your story, you can also write sentences about what you were *thinking*.

On the overhead I'm going to write about a time it was raining at the beach. Every now and then I'm going to try to remember what I was thinking—what was going through my mind. *I make a point after I write the first few sentences to pause and think out loud. I might say to myself, "Hmm. What was I thinking at that point?" and then proceed to write it down.*

One day this summer my family and I were having a picnic dinner on the beach. Then it started to rain. I thought all the food would get ruined, but my mom quickly packed it all up. We ran back to the car. I wondered why we didn't think to check the forecast.

I didn't just tell the story. Every now and then I wrote a sentence about what I was thinking.

Writing Try-It   Open up to your try-it sections. At the top, write the date and "Inside Sentences." When you're done, look up at me. Now, write about a time you went to the doctor or the dentist and see if you can include one or two sentences about what you were thinking. *Figure 7.6 shows a student's try-it from this lesson.*

Several students share their try-it.

Okay, it's time for independent writing. Today as you work on your drafts, see if you can include some inside sentences about what you were thinking.

FIGURE 7.6

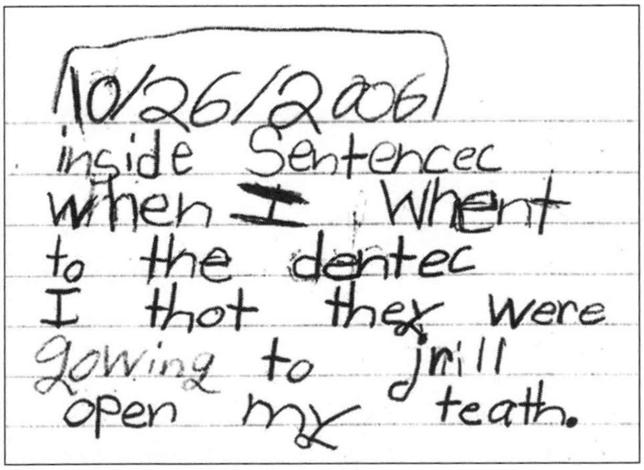

10/26/2006
inside Sentencec
when I Whent
to the dentec
I thot they were
gowing to jrill
open my teath.

Mini-Lesson: **Ending Sentences with Periods**

On the overhead I display a before version of an entry, with lots of and then's.

> I remember when Olivia and I made a sand castle this summer and then we got hot so we went in the water and it felt great and then we had lunch and then we went back to our sand castle and then . . .

I have an entry on the overhead, and there are one or two words I use a lot. See if you can tell what they are. *I turn the overhead light on. As mentioned previously, students can always spot the inordinate amount of* **and then's.** Can anyone tell me what words I use a lot?

Connection   Right! This is something I see in many of your entries. A lot of "This happened . . . and then this happened . . . and then this happened." In a way this makes sense, because sometimes this is the way we talk. But writing and talking are different.

Mini-Lesson   When you write, you have to write one sentence—one thought—at a time. You write a sentence . . . *(I make my voice imitate the rhythmic sound that basic sentences sometimes have.)* . . . then you stop and write a period. *(I make a period in the air.)* You write a sentence . . . then you stop. If you don't stop and write a period between thoughts, you will have sentences like this *(I point to the overhead)* that run on and on. Run-ons are no fun to read. The reader can't keep up with what you're saying. But today I want to show you how ending sentences with a period can help you as a writer. When you end each complete thought with a period, you can think about what else you want to describe before moving on to the next event or the next thing that happened.

So now I'm going to write about the same memory, but after I write about one thing, I'm going to stop and think about what else I want to write.

I erase everything except the first sentence. As I write new sentences, I make a very obvious period motion with the overhead marker. Sometimes I even make a sound effect. Children usually find this funny, but more importantly, it brings to life the use of the period just a bit more. After I write each sentence, I kind of tilt my head and look up pensively while I say, "Hmmm, what else do I want to say about building the sand castle? Oh yeah . . ." I do this "Hmmm, what else can I say?" or "What else could I describe?" think-aloud a few more times, continuing to accent the sound of a complete thought as well as a good, hearty period. The end product might look something like this:

> I remember when Olivia and I made a sand castle this summer. We used our plastic buckets and bright yellow shovels. I could feel the hot sun on

my back as we leaned over our buckets. When they were full I said to Olivia, "Okay, you go first!" We counted to three and laughed as she flipped over her bucket.

Sometimes when I reread what I wrote in its entirety, I invite students to make the period along with me, using their index finger on their desk. It seems game-like, but it is absolutely the motion I want them to start getting used to—lifting their hand and making a dot.

So ending my sentences with periods helped me think of other details I could add before I ran on to the next thing that happened.

Turn-and-Talk Try-It   Turn to the person next to you and tell them why it's good, as a *writer*, to use periods at the end of your sentences.

Writing Try-It   All right, everybody turn to your try-it section. At the top write the date and "Ending sentences with periods." Okay, write about coming to school today or yesterday, but for now, only write your first sentence. *I wait about 30 seconds and then continue.* All right, now you can write two more sentences. Just two. And what are you putting at the end of each one? Right—a period. You're going to write a sentence . . . then stop and write a period. *I walk around to see how students are doing. Then, I usually make one more announcement that they can write a few more sentences. When I have a few students share, I make a point to have them accent the pause when they get to their periods so the rest of the class can hear the punctuation.*

One important aspect of this particular lesson is the gradual release aspect. Writing without periods becomes such a habit that I know that if I did not have students write only a few sentences at a time, they might not write as many complete sentences. But I know they are capable of doing it. The short assignment of writing a few sentences at a time makes less room for the habit to take over.

When it comes to the topic of writing with periods, I find it very important to put structures in place that help students avoid slipping back into the habit of run-ons. I wouldn't wait for conferences to follow up, but would set a whole-class expectation about avoiding run-ons the very next day. This means the topic of the next day's lesson would not be about run-ons themselves (because I just did that lesson) but on the expectation that they don't slip back into the habit of run-ons. It's not that I expect perfect, complete sentences, but I do expect run-ons to not be such a habit. One way to support students with writing complete sentences after this initial lesson is to use a gradual release model over the next week. For example, the day after this lesson, I might tell my students they are going to write for five minutes followed by a quick break when they can reread their work on their own or with a partner to see whether or not they used a lot of run-ons. On the third day, my mini-lesson may not be about periods, but I would still have them check their own writing or their partner's sentences after ten minutes of writing, and on the fourth day, after fifteen minutes of writing. This gradual release structure gives this habit of writing without periods less air to breath and gives students time to get used to the change.

Planning Mini-Lessons

Trial and error is an implicit part of writing workshop, both with mini-lessons and conferences. Most of the time when I take a risk with a new lesson, meaning I haven't done it before and am making assumptions about what students can do, I am not certain how it will turn out. I remember feeling a little nervous when I first did a lesson on how to freewrite during a poetry unit of study in a second-grade classroom. I had a feeling students could do it, but it was the first time I was not giving students a formula for writing a poem. I knew there was a chance it might be too difficult. What the students wrote that day was amazing! If I hadn't taken the risk, I never would have seen just what these second graders were capable of writing. But there were also a few times during that unit when a lesson I planned went over their heads or it just didn't work. Writing workshop gives teachers room to grow as professionals. As with anything in life, growth only happens when you can accept that there will be mistakes along the way. We will never feel that all of our mini-lessons are perfect, either in planning or in delivery. Embracing this reality will make it easier to take risks and try out new ideas in lessons.

Researching Strengths in a Conference

I met Jonathan during my second year of teaching in Boston. He was taller than most of his third-grade classmates and had energy that came in waves. Every Monday and Wednesday at 10:35, Jonathan would reluctantly enter my room. I was now "the writing teacher" of the school. When Boston was first adopting writing workshop, my principal decided to introduce it to our school by having me teach it as a specialist to the different grades. Over the next few years, writing workshop was gradually integrated into all teachers' regular classrooms. Jonathan reminded me he didn't like being in my room for writing workshop by his scowl and the occasional roll of his eyes. During independent writing time in September, Jonathan didn't write much at all. He only wrote a few words in between talking or making a joke at the expense of someone's mother, which had a 50 percent chance of ending in a fight.

No matter how I approached Jonathan during independent writing time, he never wrote more than a few sentences. I tried rewards. I tried the "I'm going to call home" warning. I told his teacher. Nothing seemed to work. Then in the beginning of October, when we started memoir writing, I had my first conference with Jonathan. Over a period of four days he had written half a page. There were no other entries to read. The first thing I noticed was the slightly awkward shape of his letters, as if just writing them down was an effort. Much of his spelling was still inventive. He was clearly far below the rest of his third-grade class. I tried to talk to him about how his writing was going, but I did not get very far. As I slid his notebook over to read it, I looked at his face, which was already prepared, already filling up with something in between embarrassment and anger. I started to read the paragraph Jonathan had written about the time he and his cousin went to Franklin Park. Then I asked him questions. "Oh—does your cousin live here in Boston?" My questions were, for the moment, just about hearing his story. The tense look on Jonathan's face lightened just a little bit. He didn't look as closed, but still skeptical, as if wondering when I was going to start talking about all the things that were wrong with his writing.

Around the time of this conference I had learned to use literature as a resource for learning about craft. Because I had taken time to notice specific craft, I began to see strengths embedded within writing that, as a whole, might not be judged as "good writing." So when I read Jonathan's entry, I noticed a specific writing technique I might not have seen before. He was using people's names. Rather than move right into what he needed to work on, I spent some time on this particular strength. This is what I said:

> So Jonathan, one thing I notice that you do really well in your writing is you use people's names. Like here . . . when you say "My cousin Monica" and then also here when you wrote "My friend Shane." That's so great, because when you use people's names, it makes the person seem real for the reader. If I were writing a memory about my family, I could just write "My aunt." But if I wrote "My Aunt Penelope," see how she seems more like a real person? You're doing the same thing. I mean, some kids keep writing "my friend" or "my cousin" and I have to teach them to add people's names. But you don't have to work on that, do you?

When I looked at Jonathan for a response, I noticed his eyes had suddenly softened and the tension had left his face. He almost looked like a different person. Then he looked down at his writing, still looking quietly surprised, and nodded his head with the faintest hint of a smile. He did see what he was doing right. The very next class, Jonathan still talked and tried to throw a few balls of paper at his friends during independent writing, but not as much. As the weeks went by and I had several more conferences with Jonathan, I spent less and less time reminding him to write.

A few months later, Jonathan's regular classroom teacher, Mrs. Cooper, stopped by my classroom after dismissal. At first we were just talking about the fire drill that happened that morning in the thirty-degree weather. Then she said, "Oh, I meant to tell you something. The other day when buses were being called I was listening to this group of kids argue about which subject was the best. Most of them were saying gym was their favorite and one was talking about science. Then Jonathan shouted, 'No way, man. Writing's the best!'" She even showed me how he said it several times, swinging one fist for emphasis. "I couldn't believe it," Mrs. Cooper said, shaking her head and laughing. "I don't know what you did. But he loves writing."

Needless to say, that was one of those days I drove home smiling the whole way. Mrs. Cooper's comment, however, affected much more than that one day—it changed my understanding about how important it was to teach students, *all* students, their strengths in a conference. I still taught Jonathan what he could work on as a writer during his conferences, but there was no doubt in my mind that Jonathan's changed outlook on writing had everything to do with how much time I spent teaching him specifically what he was doing well as a writer and that I took his strengths seriously. As his attitude about writing changed, he not only spent more time writing, he also became more open to hearing what he could do to improve his writing.

Very often the urge is to jump right into "helping" students such as Jonathan so they can hurry up and improve their writing. In these cases, our intentions are good. The thinking is that, by getting right to what they need to work on, students will more quickly get to where they are supposed to be. At first glance, this thinking certainly seems logical. However, taking time to focus on students' legitimate strengths, even though it may seem counterintuitive, is one of the most powerful ways to help "struggling writers" improve. Believing in our students and caring about them, of course, are extremely important. But conferences give us a unique opportunity to directly affect one of the most influential factors for improvement—our students' academic self-perception.

Conferences should still leave students with a next step that relates to craft, mechanics, or a writing strategy. Consistently teaching students their strengths is in no way meant to dilute the teaching point that focuses on next steps. In fact, when teachers notice specific strengths in student writing and point them out in conferences, many students become more open to the next step teaching point. In his book *Do You Know Enough About Me To Teach Me?* (2006), Stephen Peters discusses the concept of "capture, inspire, teach," which points to the fact that relationships, and addressing the human element of motivation, will create a far more fertile ground for learning than just instruction alone. There are countless ways to capture and inspire students, both in and out of the classroom. Teaching students their strengths in a conference is one way to do so in an academic setting. For students who move on to each grade bringing negative labels of themselves as students and negative perceptions of school, the biggest impediment to learning is that their internal motivation has been shut down. Stephen Peters pinpoints what I think is the reason why teaching can be so challenging and yet so rewarding: "At heart we know that no one can educate another person, that all of us educate ourselves" (2006, 53). Trying to will someone else's internal motivation to change is almost paradoxical. It always has to come from within. Although I do want students to know what they do well as writers, the bigger benefit of teaching strengths in my experience is that it can sometimes be the key to affecting the way a student sees himself or herself as a student, which can in turn affect the student's internal motivation.

Similar to those of many writing workshop teachers and authors, my student writing conferences follow a research-decide-teach model. In this model, "teach" tends to apply to giving students a next step that is initiated by students talking about their writing plans or through the teacher's observations, or both. After I started teaching strengths to all students, my conferences began following this research-decide-teach model twice, once with strengths and once with next steps. This structure is presented in Table 8.1.

It's important to remind readers at this point that one of the main purposes of this book is to support teachers in using student writing to its potential during a conference. We do want students to help steer the teaching, and there are other aspects of writing to teach besides specific craft techniques. For now the researching of strengths and next steps refers only to what can be seen when reading student writing.

There are certainly times when I am reading student writing during a conference and I notice strengths and next steps at the same time. Thinking is rarely linear and orderly, and because students are also part of this process, I can't have rigid assumptions about how a conference will go. But after an initial conversation with students, I do find that compartmentalizing my attention and my teaching into one area at a time gives my conferences a dependable structure, both for me and for my students. I also find this dual structure keeps me faithful to my intentions of teaching all students their strengths, regardless of their ability level.

In order to develop an ability to consistently notice strengths in writing during the research phase, it's important to put the actual teaching point on hold. Agreeing that it's important to teach all students their strengths is one thing—it is another to do it during an actual conference. For many teachers, there is such a natural tendency to get to the phase of the conference that

---

Table 8.1 A Possible Structure for a Writing Conference

TEACHING A STRENGTH	TEACHING A NEXT STEP
Research Strengths through conversation and reading student's writing	*Research Next Steps* through conversation and reading student's writing
Decide which strength or strengths to make public in the conference	*Decide* which next step to teach
Teach by naming the strength and explaining why it is good	*Teach* by naming the next step and explaining why it is good
Record by writing down the strength that was taught	*Record* by writing down the next step that was taught

---

focuses on students' next steps that the teaching of strengths is usually absent or diluted. Sometimes teachers point out "good" sentences in a student's writing at the start of the conference. While this is certainly better than not addressing strengths at all, merely complimenting students is a missed opportunity. The key to powerful conferring is teaching all students their strengths, regardless of their ability, with the same seriousness we give their next steps.

The Research Phase

During a conference, there are several sources that can contribute to your research.

- ❁ Conversations with students
- ❁ Observations of students
- ❁ Students' writing

Conversations with Students

Conversations with students are an important part of the research phase, both for learning students' intentions for their writing and for gathering possible teaching points. One way to support the way students talk about their writing and the writing process is to be aware of the types of questions we ask students at the start of the conference. In his book *How's It Going? A Practical Guide to Conferring with Student Writers* (2000), Carl Anderson presents six categories of questions as well as "conversational strategies" to consider during the research phase of a writing conference. Anderson explains: "Each of these kinds of questions helps us gather information about the writing work students are doing, either by nudging students to say more about the work they told us at the beginning of the conference, or by eliciting information that they didn't tell us" (41). The questions we end up asking should depend on the student in front of us and our awareness of what missing information might help us better understand and help this student.

Conferring is more efficient and productive when students are supported with this conversation phase of the conference. Sometimes when teachers try to initiate a conversation with, "So how has your writing been going?" the response is a monotone, "Good," which is sometimes then followed with fishing questions from the teacher: "Why 'good'? What do you mean by 'good'?" Part of our job is to help students be more reflective about their writing. As Carl Anderson reminds us, "Good writers use strategies and techniques *thoughtfully* because they've learned to step back from their writing and reflect on what they're doing" (2000, 9). And we don't have to wait for students to become steeped in the philosophy of writing workshop to raise our expectations of their role in this conversation.

Michelle Gulla, a fourth-grade teacher at the Tobin School in Boston, noticed she was going through this fishing routine at the start of her conferences. So, she gave a mini-lesson on what students could talk about at the start of a writing conference. She explained to her students that the purpose of the lesson was not just to make conferences more efficient, although that was important, but it was also about helping them to be more reflective and independent in talking about themselves as writers. She created a list of things they could talk about in a writing conference. Knowing that students might need more support than just one lesson, she also made copies of this list that students kept in their folders. For the next month or so, when students had a conference with Ms. Gulla, she allowed them to take out this list before she asked, "So, how's your writing been going?" Students began taking more ownership of the conversation, which meant that Michelle could spend time on more meaningful questions. Gradually, as students became accustomed to contributing reflections about their writing and their writing process, they no longer needed to refer to their lists.

Students may also demonstrate an ability to understand their own strengths, whether it has to do with craft or another aspect of writing. For example, a student once told me at the start of a conference that she had decided to write about her birthday party in two different ways. I pointed out to her that not only did she understand she could write about the same event from more than one perspective, but also she was aware of something she tried as a writer.

In addition to being a forum for instruction, a conference is also a conversation between two people in which one person is sharing parts of his or her life, whether it is in the form of ideas, feelings, or a memory. We certainly need to be aware of responding as humans, especially with material that is more sensitive. We can learn a lot about our students in conferences, and it will make a big difference how we react to what is happening and has happened in their lives.

Observations of Students

Some writing behaviors may not come up in conversation or be visible on paper, but are noticeable in our observations of students. Here are some strengths I have brought up in conferences that were based on writing behaviors I had previously noticed.

- ✿ Saying words *out loud* to hear letter sounds
- ✿ Rereading writing from the day before
- ✿ Reminding a peer about a mini-lesson or a craft technique
- ✿ Being brave—writing about a difficult topic that happened in your life

Although talking with students and observing them as writers are important sources for research, the rest of this chapter focuses on how best to use the writing itself as a resource. Student writing is not the only resource, but it is by far the most underutilized.

Students' Writing

Conferring is all about seeing choices. This is true in any deciding we have to do. There have been several times when I have been out to dinner, ordered a salad, and had the waitress ask me, "What kind of dressing would you like with that?" After a few seconds of looking at her, wondering if she'll say anything further, I ask, "Well, what do you have?" I wait until she finishes listing all of the choices before deciding which one to choose. It's just much easier to make a decision when you start with a concrete list of specific choices. The same is true in conferring.

If you were to watch me confer, this might not be apparent. To an outside viewer, it may seem as if, after I read students' writing, I can "just tell" what strength I should make public or I can "just tell" what to teach. What a viewer would not see when I am researching strengths is a brief but critical period when, as I read the writing, I notice as many specific craft and mechanics skills as I can. Just temporarily, I hold off on judging which strength is the best choice to discuss in the conference.

Most teachers already do this kind of noticing with mechanics. Think about a time you read an entry or maybe a draft of student writing during a conference. Your eyes are very capable of scanning the writing for mechanics. You don't need to take the writing back to your desk for an in-depth study: you very quickly know which mechanics skills are there and which ones are absent as you read. When you know many types of specific craft, you can do the same thing with craft. Although craft is embedded in writing, not separate, and it is less about right versus wrong, it can still be noticeable.

Reading Student Writing

After a student has had a chance to talk about his or her writing, I usually prefer to read students' writing myself, as opposed to having the students read it out loud to me. There are always exceptions—poems are better read out loud, for example—and if a student wants to read the writing out loud to me because he or she is so proud of what he or she wrote, of course I would agree. For the most part, however, I find that having students read their writing out loud, while in itself is a nice thing, does not really benefit my conferring in any way. When students read their own writing out loud, it just takes a lot more time. Beyond expanding how many minutes you can devote to writing workshop, the only way to improve how often you can confer with students is to be more efficient, both in teaching the mini-lesson and conferring.

As I read students' writing, I might ask small questions or make comments along the way in reaction to the story, such as, "Oh, do you see your cousin a lot?" or "Do you know I still have not been to Chuck E. Cheese yet?" The purpose of these questions is not so much about research but simply to honor the fact that they are sharing the stories of their lives with me. If I just read in total silence, students would try to read my face, wondering what I was thinking. I might also ask some research questions as well if I am confused about something or want to know more about their thought process or writing plans. The whole time, the wheels in my mind are turning as I try to notice as many specific strengths as I can. In conferences with primary writers, students' drawings should be considered as one of the main sources of research: "Not only can we learn a tremendous amount about our students' interests, processes, and development by examining their pictures, but the teaching we do [related to] drawing work is easily transferred to their writing work later" (Calkins, Hartman, and White 2005, 107).

During a conference, there are two different ways I tend to notice craft techniques in writing—either I see familiar craft techniques or I see new craft techniques that, at least for me, don't yet have a name.

Seeing Familiar Craft Techniques

When I read student writing, I almost always see specific craft techniques I have noticed in previous writing or have taught in previous conferences. The more craft I have gathered from literature and other student writing, the more I can see in student writing. Following is an excerpt of a memoir entry by a fifth grader I knew when I worked as a literacy coach in Boston. She wrote about the day she had her first communion. Her original spelling has been retained in the excerpt below.

The silent ruffles of my dress were what I herd. I felt my heart beat faster than the speed of light, or that's what I thought. And at the end I saw the priest waiting. Waiting for him to do his job. Waiting for me!

When I first read this piece years ago, I could tell it had lots of craft in the general sense. I loved it—and I would certainly be able to say this piece had voice and some great descriptions. I asked the student if I could make a copy of it, which she allowed me to do. At some point my copy of this piece ended up in one of my boxes of student writing. About a year ago I was moving to a new apartment and cleaning up all my papers and files when I came across this piece. I remember sitting down on the floor amongst piles of white paper and loose overheads to read it again. I enjoyed it just as much as I did the first time. But there was one big difference. A few years prior, I had attended a workshop with Katie Wood Ray and had read her book *Wondrous Words* (1999). In one of her chapters about craft, she presents a technique called "close-echo effect." The example she gives is a line from *The Whales* by Cynthia Rylant (1996):

Someone is on the shore and his heart is filling up. Filling up and ready to burst. (1996)

In the same paragraph, Katie Wood Ray named the close-echo effect for her readers and also gave the Why: "A writer will often repeat words or phrases very close together when it is not necessary to do so, creating an echo effect in the text. . . . This lets the writer both call attention to words and repeat text rhythms" (1999, 164).

I hadn't committed this page of Katie's book to memory, but when I reread this student's writing there on my living room floor, I instantly noticed it—a close-echo effect—in her writing: "And at the end I saw the priest waiting. Waiting for him to do his job. Waiting for me!"

I also noticed that I had been using this technique in my own writing. This technique that Katie talked about in her book was just something that "came out" in my writing as it did in this student's. No one taught it to me, and I am guessing no one taught it to her either. We had just been exposed to lots of different books with that kind of rhythm. Had I learned about this specific craft technique earlier, however, I could have helped this student understand what she was doing as a writer. By learning where she did this close-echo effect, she might have been more intentional in using it again. I know that once I learned what it was, I was more aware of it in my own writing, both when it just "came out" and when I used it more intentionally.

Although the close-echo is a wonderful craft technique, it's not something I would expect to see in a majority of student writing. The key to researching strengths is being familiar with a wide range of skills, which is

FIGURE 8.1

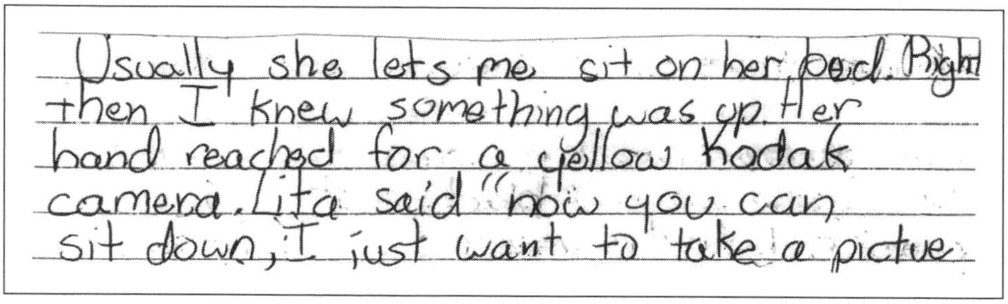

> Usually she lets me sit on her bed. Right then I knew something was up. Her hand reached for a yellow Kodak camera. Lita said "now you can sit down, I just want to take a picture.

FIGURE 8.2

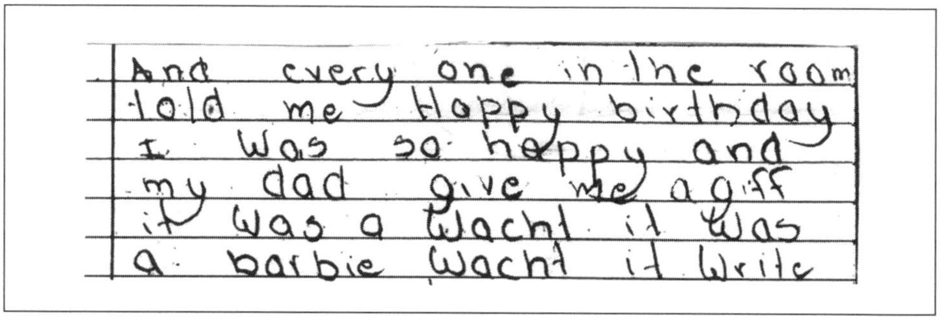

> And every one in the room told me Happy birthday I was so happy and my dad give me a gift it was a wachi it was a barbie wachi it write

why the specific craft charts in Chapters 4 and 5 run the gamut from simple to complex, and why a chapter on primary level writing is included.

When the craft you know is specific, the easier it will be to see, just as I could see the close-echo effect in this student's writing. For example, after I realized how brand names could be a specific kind of detail, brand names started to pop out at me. Figures 8.1 and 8.2 are notebook entries in which I noticed students using brand names. Because I had "harnessed" the craft behind the words, I didn't need a student to write about a Band-Aid tin, as Patricia Polacco did, for me to recognize this specific kind of detail. It's not that my students weren't using brand names before I studied Patricia Polacco's writing—I just didn't specifically notice that they were. But now I see brand names all the time. And, because I have already been through the process of thinking about why this kind of detail is good, I have my teaching all ready to go.

Table 8.2 shows another example of how the process of naming specific craft and building up familiarity with different craft techniques helps you see craft that is embedded in writing. It wasn't until I gathered the craft technique in Table 8.2 that involves repeating words and slowed down my reaction as a reader, that I was able to capture it as a craft technique I could either see in writing or teach.

After I had collected this as a craft technique, it became much easier to recognize later in student writing, as in Figure 8.3. I also noticed that this repeating of verbs is a more craftlike alternative to using the phrase "a lot."

Coming to conferences with certain skills you can recognize easily—and already know how to teach—should add a confidence to your conferring. There are, fortunately, certain craft points that occur frequently in certain

Table 8.2 Gathering a Craft Technique			
EXAMPLE SENTENCE	**NARROWING DOWN TO THE CRAFT**	**NAMING THE SPECIFIC CRAFT**	**WHY IS IT GOOD?**
Even when I finished singing, the people just kept laughing and laughing.	*laughing and laughing*	Repeating a verb with *and* in the middle	Gives the reader an image of an action going on for a long time

FIGURE 8.3

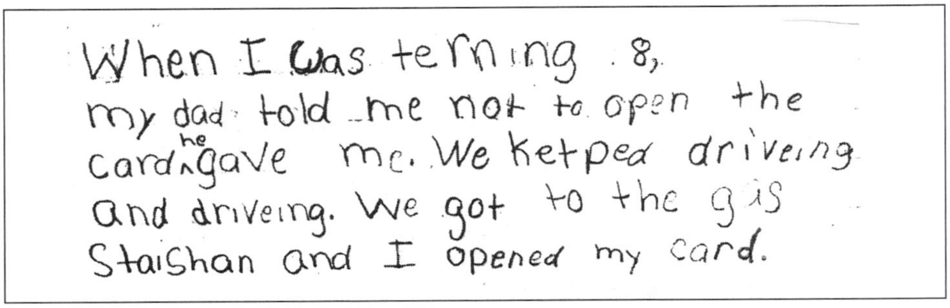

> When I was terning 8, my dad told me not to open the card he gave me. We ketped driveing and driveing. We got to the gis Staishan and I opened my card.

grades. For example, when I confer with students who write on a first-grade level, whether they are actually first graders or not, I keep an eye out for the use of colors and simple inside sentences ("I was sad"). When I confer with students who write on a fourth-grade level, my lens changes, and I keep an eye out for skills such as using sound for description and showing a feeling instead of telling it. And if I don't see evidence of these skills at their respective grade levels, then I often consider them as possible choices for teaching next steps. Although I always keep my eyes open for different and new craft techniques, I know that if nothing else, there is a good chance I will either see some of these grade-level craft techniques or see an opportunity to teach them. The thought of "What if I can't find anything to teach?" makes some teachers feel uneasy about conferring. Having a few stand-bys to look for is what makes me come to conferences feeling somewhat relaxed, which in turn makes it easier to look for and notice different kinds of craft.

Noticing familiar craft is essential to feeling comfortable with conferring. In order to get better at conferring, however, you also have to be open to seeing and gathering new craft that you didn't necessarily "bring with you" to the conference.

Seeing Related Craft Techniques

In addition to seeing familiar craft as I read student writing during a conference, I will also see craft that I have not taught or studied before. At first I don't really know what "it" is—I just know I like it. Sometimes a phrase I like is somewhat similar to a craft technique I already know. For example, being familiar with repeating verbs like "driving and driving" in Figure 8.3 helped

Table 8.3

EXAMPLE PHRASE	SPECIFIC CRAFT	WHY IS IT GOOD?
Taller and taller	Repeating an *er* adjective	Shows a gradual increase of something

FIGURE 8.4

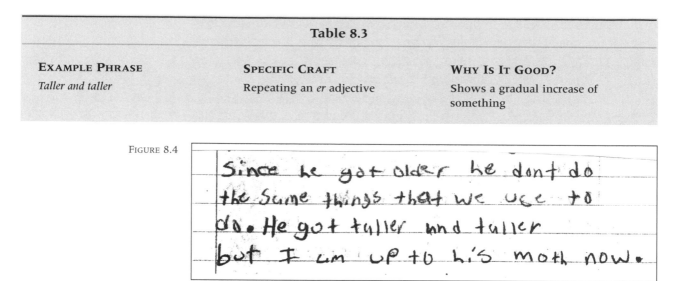

Since he got older he dont do the same things that we use to do. He got taller and taller but I am up to his moth now.

me notice other words that repeated but weren't exactly the same, such as the adjectives in Figure 8.4. A word is repeated in Figure 8.4, but it's not a verb. So in my mind I just went back to the process of gathering craft to capture it as yet another craft point. (See Table 8.3.)

Very often after gathering craft like this, I think about how this craft technique could be used in other contexts. For example, I thought of the sentence "His face just got redder and redder." This example does the same thing: it gives the reader a growing image. What is neat about this craft is that it gives a visual image but one that moves. I am told the color of someone's face, but I can see it turning from pink to really red. Once I go through this gathering process and teach the student what he or she is doing, I can also take this somewhat new craft technique and "put it in my pocket" along with all the other, more familiar, craft techniques I know.

Seeing New Craft Techniques

There are also times when a phrase or word catches my eye but does not really remind me of any other craft technique I've taught before. If I think it has the potential of being the strength I choose to make public in the conference, then I quickly go through the same process in my mind so it can be tangible enough to teach: After I try my best to name it, I try to verbalize why it's good.

The student writing in Figure 8.5 is from a conference in which I noticed a completely new craft technique. Table 8.4 shows the craft gathering process that I went through during the actual conference.

Once again naming this craft and saying why it was good not only helped me teach this student in that conference, but allowed me to gather another craft technique. It doesn't necessarily matter if I use it again. After all, the way she crafted her sentence was unusual and is not something I typically see in

Table 8.4 Gathered Craft from Student Writing in Figure 8.4

EXAMPLE SENTENCE	SPECIFIC CRAFT	WHY IS IT GOOD?
We did it big, wide, huge, deep.	Listing several adjectives in a row (without using *and*)	Gives several visuals but gives the sentence an unusual, lyrical sound, almost like a poem

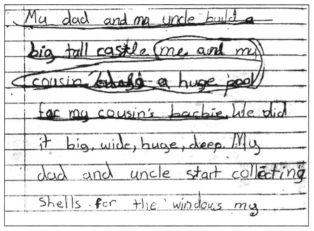

FIGURE 8.5

elementary writing. It is also probably not something I would teach in a mini-lesson during the memoir unit of study when it was written, although I might save it for a poetry unit. Being open to noticing what students are doing with their writing, beyond what craft you already know, keeps students' unique use of words at the forefront, as opposed to just matching what you see with craft you already know.

As you might imagine, conferring about new craft techniques you notice during a conference requires a lot more quick thinking and is more challenging than recognizing familiar craft. The more you confer, however, and the more you practice noticing craft in student writing with colleagues, the easier this "on the spot" thinking can become.

When Strengths Are Hard to Find

Have I read student writing and had a hard time finding any type of strength? Absolutely. The two entries in Figure 8.6 are from the notebook of a third grader. Years ago I might have jumped right into a next step in order to help him. But now I have conditioned myself to notice and teach a strength, no matter how far behind a student is. When I first looked at this writing, I could see at least one craft skill—he was using colors ("A red rose"). Even if a student uses a craft once, it can be a legitimate strength to point out. As I continued to look for more choices, I had to pull back from looking for craft points typical at his grade level and consider other skills. I realized another one of his strengths was using inventive spelling for "bigger" words: *elergick* for *allergic*, and *buitiful* for *beautiful*. He could have written *sick* instead of *allergic* or *pretty* instead of *beautiful*, but he didn't. He took a risk and reached for a bigger word. I also realized that he was coming up with ideas for entries on his own. I had previously taught my students strategies for coming up with memoir ideas independently and wrote those strategies on an anchor chart for support. So, yes, my expectation was that everyone was coming up with their own ideas

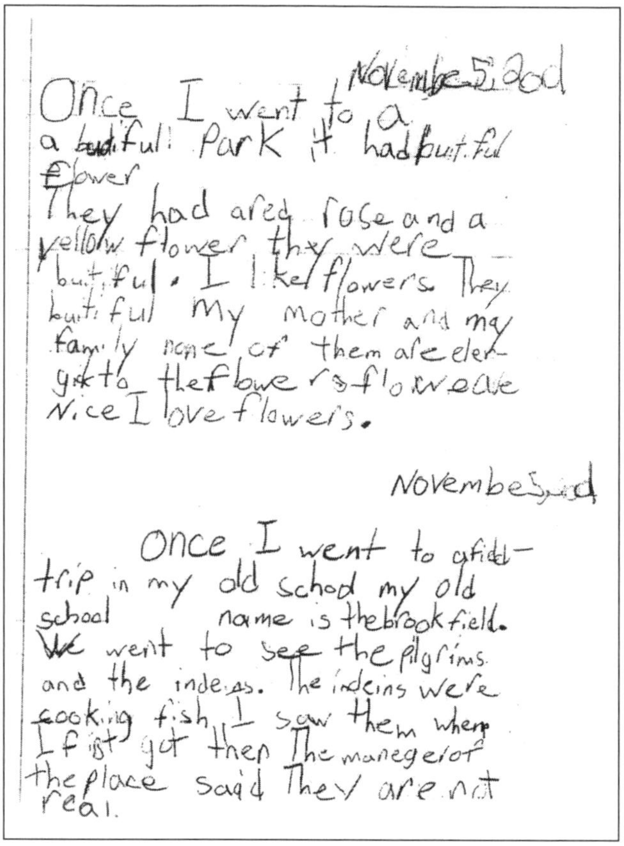

November 5, 200d

Once I went to a
a butiful Park it had butiful
flower
They had a red rose and a
yellow flower they were
butiful. I liked flowers. They
butiful My mother and my
family none of them are eler-
gik to the flowers flowers are
Nice I love flowers.

Novembe 5, 2od

Once I went to a fidd-
trip in my old school my old
school name is the brookfield.
We went to see the pilgrims
and the indeas. The indeins were
cooking fish. I saw them when
I fist got then The manegerof
the place said They are not
real.

FIGURE 8.6

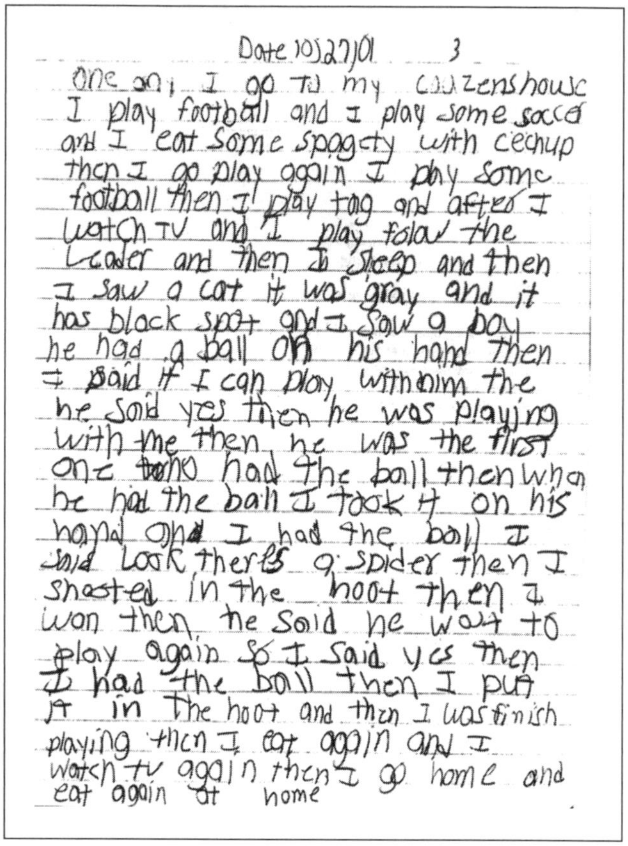

Date 10/27/01 3

One day I go to my couzens house
I play football and I play some socce
and I eat some spagety with cechup
then I go play again I play some
football then I play tag and after I
watch TV and I play folow the
Leader and then I sleep and then
I saw a cat it was gray and it
has black spot and I saw a boy
he had a ball on his hand then
I said if I can play with him the
he said yes then he was playing
with me then he was the first
one who had the ball then when
he had the ball I took it on his
hand and I had the ball I
said look there's a spider then I
shooted in the hoot then I
won then he said he want to
play again so I said yes then
I had the ball then I put
it in the hoot and then I was finish
playing then I eat again and I
watch tv again then I go home and
eat again at home

FIGURE 8.7

anyway. But in times when I am reaching for a strength to teach, it is still a legitimate skill to consider.

Figure 8.7 is an entry by a fourth-grade boy from a Haitian Creole bilingual class that had me stuck for what to say during a conference. There really wasn't anything craft-like about his writing. I didn't know what I could say about mechanics either. It was one of those conferences that went on too long with questions because I really could not see any strengths. However, I had recently committed myself to giving a positive point to every student, so I didn't give in to the urge of just moving on to the dearly needed teaching point of writing in complete sentences. I stopped searching for craft and pulled back to consider anything about his writing. When I got away from looking at just craft, I could see other aspects that support good writing, even if they might be considered givens at his grade. I decided the *amount* he wrote could be a valid strength. So, writing with volume became the strength I made public.

When researching strengths in student writing, I use these two lenses—one that notices familiar craft I already know and one that keeps an eye out for good writing that could become a new teaching point for me. The fact that it's easier to recognize familiar craft than it is to recognize new craft is the reason why I have three chapters dedicated to examples of specific craft. I hope to give teachers a head start, in a sense, in regard to noticing and teaching craft in conferences. I wanted the craft that is now familiar to me to be familiar to anyone who reads this book. Coming to conferences with a good amount of familiar craft in your pocket should not only make it easier to recognize different specific strengths, but your teaching of this craft (knowing a name for it and why it's good) is all ready to go.

Students, of course, can also show strengths in relation to craft that are not necessarily at the sentence level. So much of crafting a piece has to do with the way it is structured, how it moves in time, or how a student revised an entry. This book does not spend as much time on these larger concepts of craft but they are absolutely important to consider when researching student writing.

Putting It All Together

Now it's time to combine the researching of craft in a conference with the researching of mechanics. After all, this is what should really happen during a conference. All the attention on craft in this book is not meant to take away the importance of mechanics skills in writing or from any other skills affiliated with writing. It's just that the attention is needed, because many teachers are still trying to better understand and become more comfortable with craft. As demonstrated in Chapter 5, the mechanics of writing are also tools that help writers sculpt some aspects of craft. So mechanics, at least in this book, can refer to either the more conventional rules—sentences ending in periods, quotation marks, and the use of capital letters—or it can refer to craft techniques in which words and punctuation work together.

Figure 8.8 includes a sample of student writing by Liliana, a third grader whose first language is Spanish. Beside her writing is a chart of my notes about the strengths I saw in the writing sample. It is important to point out that researching strengths is not about filling out a conference sheet. My intention with this chart is to slow down the thinking process behind my conferring and make it more visible.

The chart has two columns—one for craft and one for mechanics. Although we may not think in columns as we confer, it is essential to practice looking for both mechanics and craft. When you can look at writing through two lenses, then any time you choose to point out a mechanics skill as a strength or a next step, you will do so because it is a wise choice—not because it is what is most familiar.

The lists reflect the fact that I notice as much as I can about the writing before I make a decision about what to discuss in the conference. Keep in mind that in just about all my conferences, I am reading the last few entries a student

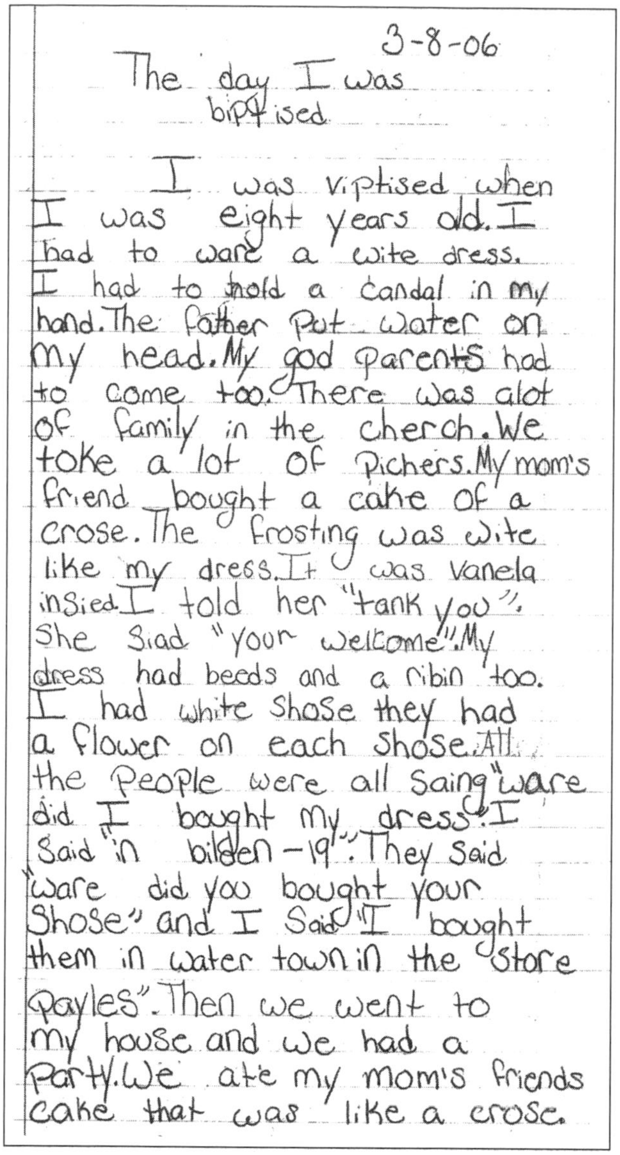

3-8-06

The day I was
biptised

I was viptised when I was eight years old. I had to ware a wite dress. I had to hold a candal in my hand. The father Put water on my head. My god parents had to come too. There was alot of family in the cherch. We toke a lot of Pichers. My mom's friend bought a cake of a crose. The frosting was wite like my dress. It was Vanela insied. I told her "tank you". She siad "your welcome". My dress had beeds and a ribin too. I had white shose they had a flower on each shose. All the People were all saing "ware did I bought my dress". I said "in bilden -19". They said "ware did you bought your shose" and I said "I bought them in water town in the store Payles". Then we went to my house and we had a Party. We ate my mom's friends cake that was like a crose.

FIGURE 8.8

Researching Strengths

CRAFT	MECHANICS
Gives her age—we know when this memory happened	Ends sentences with periods
Uses colors before words	Uses quotation marks in the right places
Gives the shape of the cake	
Gives flavor of the cake	
Compares color between cake and dress	
Uses dialogue	
Describes details on clothes	
Uses brand names/proper nouns	
Mentions the actual city	

---

wrote, not just one. Not only is it important to look for patterns in students' use of craft or mechanics skills, but researching more than one piece of writing keeps you faithful to "teaching the writer, not the writing."

Appendix F contains guided practice so that you can try researching strengths on your own. Samples of real student writing are included along with blank charts. On the next page in the appendix is a chart where I've noted the strengths I saw in the student writing sample. This guided practice appendix, which also includes practice on researching next steps, the topic of Chapter 9, is an important aspect of this book. Like any middle stage in a gradual release model, these practice sections are meant to support your movement toward ownership of teaching specific craft. You will have the space (literally and figuratively) to practice noticing craft on your own before looking at what I saw in the writing. The purpose of this is not to make a statement about what you are *supposed* to see, but to offer something to check your thinking against after you try the work on your own. You can either fill out the blank charts in Appendix F or use them as a mental guide as you read the student writing.

You don't need to see as many skills as I listed in some of these charts in order to have a good conference. Although one goal in conferring is to keep increasing the number of skills you can see in student writing, you can still go through this process of "noticing and deciding" even when you only see two or three strengths.

Deciding What Strength to Teach

After noticing as many specific strengths as you can, the next step is to decide which strength you actually want to make public to the student. Sometimes what you end up teaching will be based on your conversation with the student or your observations of the student's writing behaviors. Sometimes I teach two strengths rather than just one because I am not teaching students anything new: I am just helping them realize and take more ownership of skills they are already using.

In terms of choosing what strengths to teach, there is rarely one right answer. There are, however, some choices that are better than others. The following are some factors that might contribute to your decision.

Skills You Taught in Your Last Conference

If a skill you taught a student in your last conference is now apparent in his or her writing, then this strength should be a high priority on your list. You can take the opportunity to reinforce the use of this skill, whether it relates to craft or to mechanics. If you taught using colors as a way to describe, look for evidence of that skill, whether it occurs often or not. Making public the fact that what used to be a next step is now a strength can be empowering for a student. Since this kind of positive point is more about reinforcing what you taught in the last conference, it's a good time to look for an additional strength to teach.

Mini-Lessons You Have Recently Taught

If a student is using a craft or mechanics skill that you taught in the last few days, this is also a good strength to highlight. That being said, it's important that the topic of that day's or yesterday's lesson is not *automatically* what you look for or teach. Because reading and writing conferences are one-on-one conversations, they are opportunities for tailor-made instruction, whether it is in response to what a student says or what we observe in their writing. As part of our decision-making process, it's important to ask ourselves, "What could this student benefit from the most at this time?" If our conferences are responding to *only that student*, then that student's work and what he or she says should be the driving force of the conference.

Awareness of Where Your Students Are Coming From

One skill I sometimes see teachers point out as a strength, especially in second grade, is *sequence*. In conferences, they sometimes say this as, "You tell your story in the right order." But very often, I haven't seen this particular student write personal narrative *out of* chronological order. If it is a skill they have been displaying for a while, it may not be the best choice for the positive point. My guess is that many teachers choose a skill such as sequence for the same reasons many teachers want to point out mostly mechanics: sequence is recognizable and "correct," at least in the primary grades.

Craft Versus Mechanics

Unless a student has made a visible improvement in a mechanics skill they were previously having difficulty with or you notice a student using punctuation in a unique way, it is usually better to choose a craft skill over mechanics. Teaching students their strengths is an opportunity to show students what they are doing as writers that they might not otherwise notice on their own. If they are using quotation marks or a question mark correctly, then they already know what they are doing.

An Example of the Decision-Making Process

Although the process of narrowing down to a decision is unique for every conference, I can share how I might come to a decision if were conferring with Liliana who wrote the baptism memory in Figure 8.8, and why I would choose some skills over others. A few skills I would probably not choose to make public are using colors and using quotation marks. This student is writing with more advanced craft than using colors, and her use of quotation marks is an example of a mechanics skill that, if she is doing it correctly, doesn't really need reinforcing. Because I had conferred with Liliana in the past, I also knew it was not a skill that had previously needed attention.

Even if students are more advanced writers, I still notice more basic craft or mechanics as I read their writing. Noticing craft is not something you vary according to level. Either I notice everything I can about craft or nothing at all. Researching is easier when it is somewhat devoid of judgment. You might rank what you like in your mind as you research but ideally you still notice as much as you can.

One strength I might consider choosing from the baptism memory is the use of proper nouns for stores: "bilden-19" (Building 19) and "Payles" (Payless). Proper nouns—in this case the brand names of stores—create specific images and are not always used intentionally at this level of writing. Another strength I might choose is the use of details that relate to clothes.

These details clearly offer a specific image, and many students at this level of writing tend to not go any farther than mentioning the color of clothes. Also, writing about people's clothes is a somewhat common occurrence, so there is a good chance she will have another opportunity to use this craft technique again.

At this point, it is just a matter of making a decision. Although some choices are better than others, don't look for the *perfect* strength to choose. By now you've seen that conferring is about seeing and then choosing—not about "finding the right answer." For Liliana, I now have two good options— proper nouns and details about clothes. For no other reason than knowing I just have to make a decision, I would choose to teach proper nouns.

Sometimes this process of narrowing down to a decision happens in a matter of seconds and sometimes in a matter of minutes, depending on the student. Chapter 10 will describe how the teaching of the strength would actually sound.

Suggestions for Further Practice

Although reading books and watching videos on conferring is helpful, it is essential to practice conferring skills in order to do it well. Conferring is like any skill or muscle that needs to be used in order to become stronger. Earlier in this book I made an analogy between this kind of conferring and practicing guitar on stage. Each skill requires practice. And it is much better, and much easier, to practice "off stage."

The guided practice in Appendix F is a good place to start, but the best practice will involve your own students' writing. In Appendix E is a blank form titled "Researching Student Writing" that you can duplicate to practice the research phase with your own students' writing outside of class time. Of course, you can also just draw the same type of chart on regular paper. I highly recommend doing this research practice with a colleague or during grade-level meetings. Practicing with colleagues is much more enjoyable, and the nature of group discussion will be much more productive because it gives you another set of eyes and requires you to verbalize your thinking. Remember to practice researching strengths with all the different levels of writers that you teach. This will keep you from favoring, whether intentionally or not, your stronger writers when it comes to this part of the conference.

Practicing with student writing would not, of course, mimic an actual conference—there is no conversation with a student in a practice session. But isolating and strengthening your ability to gather information about students' strengths and needs by only looking at their writing will help you come to conferences with more confidence and allow you to use all of your resources to their potential.

9

Researching Next Steps in a Conference

During my first swimming lesson with Nate, I could see so many things he needed to work on. His arms splashed in every direction, but he barely moved. Because I had learned such specific swimming techniques from Chris, I could notice the presence and absence of the skills when I watched others swim. What I really wanted to say was, "Wow. All right, Nate. You need to work on keeping your hips up, don't keep your head up so much when you breathe, don't kick so wide, you need to pivot your shoulders, and you really need to breathe on each side. Okay?" I didn't know much about pedagogy at the time, but I instinctively knew telling him all these things at once would be counterproductive.

I knew that the best thing I could do for Nate was focus on one skill he was ready for and teach it as solidly as I could. So, instead of rattling off all the skills he needed to learn, I said, "Okay, Nate. The first thing we're going to work on is keeping your head in the water when you swim." I also told him why it was important. "Because if you keep your head out of the water, the rest of your body will sink like this," I explained as I made my hand flat and then tilted it down. "That makes it harder to swim. You have to use more energy to move in the water." Keeping your head in the water also provides a foundation for other skills. It's hard to put your arms in the water correctly or keep your hips up, for example, if your head is out of the water the whole time. So for the first part of the lesson, Nate focused just on keeping his head in the water. Then we moved on to another technique that would help his swimming.

Later that same year, I started teaching another beginning student named Leroy. He was about the same ability level as Nate: he could swim to stay afloat, but his arms went everywhere and he certainly didn't keep his head in the water. So, guess what Leroy started with in his first lesson? We went to the shallow end to practice blowing bubbles under water and turning his head to breathe. What was the biggest difference between Nate and Leroy? Leroy paid for lessons with his own money. He was thirty-six years old and getting his MBA at the Columbia Business School.

The reality of our classrooms is that, despite expectations about where our students are supposed to be at certain ages, they sometimes arrive in September reading and writing one, two, or even three years below grade level. Just like my swimming students, some students' abilities match their age and expectations of where they "should" be, while others' don't. The standard rule of conferences is that you "teach one thing." It's easy to understand why teachers might be tempted to teach more than "one thing" in a conference, especially with students who are behind grade level. After all, these students clearly need to obtain more skills than their peers in order to get up to grade level. It wasn't easy to stay true to teaching one thing when I first started conferring, because the gap in ability level in combination with district expectations for where my students were supposed to be made me feel like I should be "helping" them more.

Teaching Leroy, I did not feel the same pressure, so the idea of teaching him one next step was not at all problematic. Regardless of how big a gap I noticed between where he was and where he "should" be as a thirty-six-year-old adult, I just focused on teaching him one skill I knew he could maintain on his own. Even though I was completely aware of many skills Leroy needed in order to get up to the standards of a regular recreational swimmer, it didn't occupy a large space in my mind. I was aware, but not preoccupied. My energy was instead spent on narrowing down my decision of what next step would benefit Leroy the most at that time and then deciding how to help him learn that skill as solidly as possible. Later in that lesson I might move on to another small technique for him to learn. But how would it help him swim better if I told him five things at a time to work on? My teaching would be diluted because I would spend more time telling him what to work on than actually teaching him, and he would probably feel overwhelmed in the process.

Although I compare the teaching of swimming to the teaching of writing, one could easily argue that when teaching swimming, I did not have the pressure classroom teachers do. Nate was not going to take any bubble tests on swimming later on, no one was going to read in the newspaper how well Leroy had learned to swim compared with other thirty-six-year-olds in the state, and my one-hour lesson was not in competition with other subjects. While all this is true, it does not change the nature of learning.

Writing, like swimming, is not about learning information; it is about incorporating new skills into a preexisting, multifaceted skill set. If you try to teach too many things at the same time, the likelihood decreases that a student can incorporate the new skills into the already complex act of writing.

Teaching one thing, however, is not what tends to be the most challenging aspect of conferring. The most common question teachers ask about conferences is, "How do I know what to teach?" This is a fair question, because it may seem as if teachers on videos about writing workshop just magically know what to teach. There may be some exploratory questions and maybe a little visible thinking on the teacher's part in such videos, but very little sweat breaks out. It may seem like they just automatically see that one thing they could teach, but the internal thinking is much more complicated than that. Although I can't say for certain what that internal process is for all teachers who confer, I can share with you my thinking process when I am trying to decide what next step to teach students based on their writing.

The Research Phase

The initial conversation at the start of the conference is where teachers tend to get the most information about students' ideas and intentions about their writing. The research questions we ask can help us navigate through the important parts of a piece as well as better understand what path this student might be on as a writer. As discussed in Chapter 8, the more we invest in these initial conversations by teaching lessons on how students can talk about their writing, the more likely students will be able to help direct the conference in a meaningful way.

Although supporting students in talking about their writing is important, I am sure most teachers would agree that we will still have conferences with students who have very little to say about what they are doing as writers. This doesn't mean we can't ask more questions throughout the conference. Sometimes after I teach a strength and have shifted my attention to deciding what to teach next, I think of more research questions to ask. Regardless of the level of input each student is capable of offering, conferring will be far more productive (and comfortable) when teachers are prepared to notice possible next steps for a student just by reading their writing. Noticing possible next steps to teach in a conference is a slightly different process than noticing strengths. Although seeing some of the smaller craft that is embedded in children's writing may take some getting used to, it at least involves noticing what is already there! Even when the strengths we notice involve revising, editing, or the way a student talks about his or her writing, those strategies or behaviors are *there*—we just have to notice them. Deciding what to teach, on the other hand, is about the hypothetical. It's not about noticing what students *are* doing as writers, but what they *could* do.

Seeing Possible Next Steps in Writing

Deciding what next step to teach in a conference also involves noticing as many possible teaching points as you can before choosing one to make public. This may at first seem contradictory. If teaching next steps is about the hypothetical, then what is there to "notice" when you are reading the writing?

My answer is directly related to all the small parts of craft that have been presented in this book so far. In addition to gathering craft techniques that I know and can recognize, I have also accumulated what it looks like for sentences to have an absence or variation of these craft techniques. Being familiar with what sentences look like when students *don't* use a particular craft technique gives you something concrete to recognize in writing. Knowing variations of specific craft that are within the same category can also help you recognize alternatives to craft students are already using.

There are five main ways I tend to recognize possible next steps by looking at student writing.

- ✿ Seeing an absence of specific craft
- ✿ Seeing related craft techniques
- ✿ Seeing an opportunity for basic craft
- ✿ Seeing the need for a general writing strategy
- ✿ Seeing an absence of punctuation
- ✿ Seeing a need and responding with a new next step

Seeing an Absence of Specific Craft

In writing this book, I clearly spent a lot of time describing how to notice different kinds of craft techniques in writing. I even wonder if some readers might have seen the table of contents and wondered why I would spend only one chapter on "deciding what to teach"—at least in terms of next steps—in a conference if it's such a concern for teachers. Although gathering specific craft for the purpose of mini-lesson instruction and noticing small skills in student writing is beneficial in itself, it also is what creates the foundation for seeing possible teaching points.

Perhaps the most important part of the gathering process in terms of creating an ability to see possible next steps is the Why stage, when we ask why a certain craft or mechanics skill is good. As discussed in Chapter 3, one way to arrive at an answer is to compare the sentence or phrase in question to a more basic choice. By creating an alternative sentence (in your mind or on paper) that represents that more basic choice, you are able to see what it looks like to have an *absence* of a particular craft technique.

For example, after I gathered the idea of repeating adjectives from reading "old, old shoes" in *Cherries and Cherry Pits* by Vera B. Williams (1991), I compared it to a more basic choice and stored away what the *absence* of this skill looks like—writing "very old" or "really old." This gave me something tangible to recognize in other student writing. And when I did recognize an absence of a particular craft technique—in this case by noticing an overuse of the words *very* or *really*—I already had an adjoining craft skill all ready to teach.

Table 9.1 contains some other examples of craft and their more average alternatives.

I often point out these basic choices as examples when teaching students their strengths. After I name what they do well, I basically compare what a student did in his or her writing with what "some kids do," which is always a more average way of writing something. If you remember my conference with Jonathan, this is exactly what I did when I pointed out his strength of using people's names in his writing: "I mean, some kids keep writing 'my friend' or 'my cousin,' and I have to teach them to add people's names. But you don't

Table 9.1 The Presence and Absence of Specific Craft Techniques

SPECIFIC CRAFT	EXAMPLE SENTENCE	
	USING THE CRAFT	WITHOUT THE CRAFT
Using brand names	*Last night before we saw* Star Wars, *my sister and I bought Twizzlers and Junior Mints.*	*Last night before the movie, my sister and I bought some candy.*
Using *as* to connect a sound and a visual	*"It's getting too noisy in here!" my teacher shouted as she flicked the lights on and off.*	*"It's getting too noisy in here!" my teacher shouted.* **OR** *"It's getting too noisy in here!" my teacher shouted. She made the lights go on and off.*
Using people's names	*When we got to the park my friend Chuck and I saw my Aunt Marlene.*	*When we got to the park my friend and I saw my aunt.*

have to work on that, do you?" This kind of comment heightens students' awareness of what they did in their writing. I don't use this teaching move for the purpose of keeping the more basic choice fresh in my mind, but it does end up doing just that.

Some types of craft techniques presented in this book have more direct "opposites" than others. In the category of using specific words over general words, for example, each specific word, which in many cases is a proper noun, is directly related to a more basic choice. So, any time I see the words *food, candy,* or *store,* I see a possible next step teaching point. The same is true with words that tell rather than show. Any time I see words like *good, pretty,* or *fun,* the idea of adding one more sentence to show how something is good, pretty, or fun becomes a possible teaching point.

Unlike brand names and some of the examples above, not all craft techniques have such neat and tidy opposites. Writing would not be much of an art if that were the case. Very often, there is more than one possibility of what a sentence might look like without a particular craft skill.

Seeing Related Craft Techniques

A second way of finding possible craft teaching points by seeing related craft techniques in writing also relates to the charts presented in Chapter 4 and the fact that small craft skills can be related to each other. Very often when I am conferring, I will notice a craft technique that has several "cousins"—other craft techniques from the same category.

I most often use this strategy to spot teaching ideas when I see basic craft as presented in the charts in Chapter 4. The primary reason for including these more basic craft techniques in those charts was to emphasize that even though they are simple descriptions, they are still legitimate strengths. But, when looking through a teaching lens, these same basic craft skills can also serve as an important link to more advanced specific craft in the same category. Table 9.2 gives an example of a basic craft skill and its related craft techniques.

Table 9.2 Ways to Include Feelings in Writing

BASIC CRAFT SKILL	EXAMPLE SENTENCE
Including feelings in writing	*I was sad.*

RELATED SPECIFIC CRAFT	EXAMPLE SENTENCE
After telling a feeling, giving a reason (using the word *because*)	*I was so sad because I couldn't find my dog.*
Using *so . . . that* to describe a feeling	*I was so sad that I wanted to cry forever.*
Telling a feeling, then showing it	*I was so sad. Tears came streaming down my face.*
Showing a feeling instead of telling it.	*My heart sank and tears ran down my cheek.*

Any of the specific craft in Table 9.2 could be possible next steps if I saw a student writing sentences like "I was sad" or "I was mad." Teaching related craft is a great way to connect with students as a fellow writer. First you can acknowledge the craft they are using, sometimes even choosing it as a strength to teach, and then share this other "cool way" of using a similar craft.

Since a basic craft technique can be a strength but also a portal to a possible next step, how do you decide which one it is? The answer is that it is never one or the other. It is always both. The question to ask is: Considering a particular student's ability, would it be appropriate to choose it as a strength or next step? This is why it can be helpful during a conference to somewhat compartmentalize the reading of student writing, first looking at it through the lens of strengths and then through the lens of next steps.

During a recent conference, for example, I was reading an entry by a fifth grader who wrote somewhat near grade level. On one page I noticed she wrote, "I was so mad." Objectively I can recognize the inclusion of a feeling as a legitimate strength that can occur in writing. Remember that when noticing strengths, you're at first just noticing everything you can. You have to give yourself room to do this. If you start mixing in the decision-making too soon, the pressure will hamper the noticing. I still noticed "I was so mad" as a certain kind of craft skill, but as I got closer to deciding, this skill fell further down the list of strengths I saw. Relative to the work she was doing as a writer, there were too many other more advanced craft techniques that I'd rather bring to her attention. A minute later, when I went back to her writing more focused on what I might teach as a next step, the sentence "I was so mad" and its related craft skills became a top candidate.

When I confer with a first grader, however, and see the phrase *I was so mad*, its placement on my research list will probably be different. It will most likely rank high on the strength list, and even though I am *aware* I could teach other ways to write inside sentences, there would probably be other skills, either drawing, word development, or other basic craft, that are greater priorities.

Seeing an Opportunity for Basic Craft

There are also many times when student writing may not show a direct absence of or relation to any particular craft technique. When that happens, I start considering the basic craft techniques themselves for actual next step teaching points.

Earlier in this book I alluded to a conference I had with John, who was writing about a Celtics basketball game. Figure 9.1 shows his initial entry on this topic. Based on the research of his last few entries, including the one shown in Figure 9.1, I didn't see any particular craft that had a related next step. This is when I consider my trusty standbys of basic craft such as writing with sound, adding colors, and basic inside sentences. Because John's topic lent itself so well to adding sounds, this basic craft technique was high on my

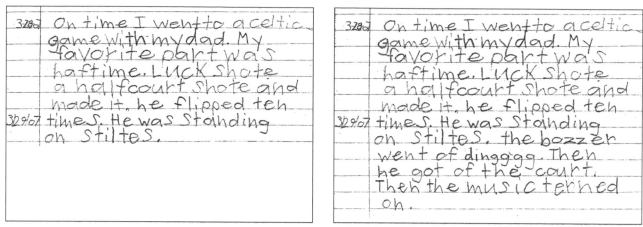

FIGURE 9.1   FIGURE 9.2

list of possible next steps and is what I actually ended up teaching. Figure 9.2 shows what John added to his entry after our conference on adding sounds.

Seeing the Need for a General Writing Strategy

Although this book is primarily dedicated to craft that is embedded at the sentence level, it's important to mention the concept of teaching more general writing strategies that deal with the structure of a piece of writing or the writing process itself. Very often, what can help students improve the development or description of their writing, rather than a specific craft technique, is a strategy that is not directly aimed at a particular choice of words. In Lucy Calkins's *Units of Study for Teaching Writing, Grades 3–5*, the lesson "Writing Small About Big Topics" is a great example of this (Calkins and Chiarella 2006). This writing strategy doesn't deal with the crafting of individual sentences and words, but when students use it, they can make room for more vivid details.

One time, I was conferring with a student who was writing about a visit to Six Flags. Like most students, he wrote about one thing after another, starting with when he put on his shoes at home. After I suggested he pick one part of his memory to focus on at a time, some details started coming out of the woodwork. He started writing about the Superman ride—what it looked like, things his cousin said, and how the cotton candy felt in his stomach mid-way through the ride. Because he wasn't explaining what happened at each part of the whole day, there was nothing left to do but describe in more detail the ride he chose to write about. The more students focus on smaller moments like this, the more room there is for using specific craft techniques because they are no longer just listing what happened. The key is finding a balance between these two types of craft instruction—general writing strategies and specific craft.

Seeing an Absence of Punctuation

There are two different ways to look at writing when considering possible next steps that involve punctuation. The first has to do with basic punctuation marks—periods, question marks, exclamation marks, and quotation marks. These stand out more because the absence of these marks is just as easy to notice as the presence of them. When students don't use these basic punctuation marks, it's not that they missed an opportunity to "craft sentences." They just didn't follow the standard rules of writing. Think about any time you have read writing where there were missing periods or missing quotation marks. Not a lot of hypothetical thinking is needed. The same is true for punctuation that is misplaced. It is easy to spot where students put quotation marks around the wrong words—a common and natural occurrence as students figure out the rules of dialogue.

The other way to notice possible next steps involving punctuation is less about noticing a rule that was not followed and more about thinking of different ways a student could have used punctuation to craft his or her sentences. Some craft techniques that involve commas also have more basic choices that can be noticed. If you recall, I also used "more basic choices" in Chapter 5 to determine the effectiveness of using commas in a series.

Using commas in a series	*In my oversized beach bag I put my sunglasses, a towel, two books, a chocolate bar, and my cell phone.*	Reader understands that words are separate items in a list

Although the commas in this example sentence help to keep these words in order, thinking about the Why also made me notice that this list was more desirable and descriptive than just writing "stuff" or "things." Because I pinpointed the more basic choice and have it in my mind as I confer, I don't have to wait for sentences that have to do with beach bags to see an opportunity to teach a student about writing a series with commas. I would only have to see the words *stuff* or *things* where a list of items could have been used to better describe all those *things*.

When it comes to dependent clauses that use commas to support description by allowing the writer to pack more than one description or idea into a sentence, the more basic choice is very often two or more sentences. Table 9.3 offers a few of the specific craft techniques from Chapter 5 and examples of the more basic choice that relates to each technique.

Students' use of *then* to describe two things that happened close together might be the trigger for teaching some of these comma craft techniques. In order for me to choose a comma craft technique in a conference, a student would have to be at a point where he or she is ready to write longer, more complex sentences. Many second graders write sentences that begin with *Then*, but this doesn't mean

Table 9.3 The Presence and Absence of Craft with Commas

SPECIFIC CRAFT	EXAMPLE SENTENCE	
	USING THE CRAFT	WITHOUT THE CRAFT
Starting a sentence with *Just as*	*Just as Keon was about to give Ameina her cupcake, he tripped and it went flying in the air.*	*Keon was going to give Ameina a cupcake. Then he tripped and it went flying in the air.*
Starting a sentence with *As soon as*	*As soon as he finished passing out all the cupcakes, his class sang "Happy Birthday" to him.*	*He finished passing out all the cupcakes. Then his class sang "Happy Birthday" to him.*
Starting a sentence with an *ing* phrase	*Wondering if everybody would laugh at her costume, Shannon walked slowly out on stage.*	*Shannon walked slowly on stage. She wondered if everyone would laugh at her costume.*

teaching them about combination sentences is necessarily an appropriate choice. Usually there are other skills that need attention or less advanced craft techniques that are more appropriate to teach for younger writers.

Seeing a Need and Responding with a New Next Step

Coming to conferences with teaching possibilities in your back pocket can make conferring a much more productive and comfortable process. But it is just as important to be open to coming up with ideas for new next steps on the spot. Since the reigning question in a conference is, What does this student need most at this time? a student's need, not what you already know, should be the most important. The hope is that by knowing some of the craft strategies that are presented in this book in addition to other writing strategies and teaching points you already know, you can offer many specific next steps that are familiar but also appropriate responses to students' needs. Of course this will not always be the case. Even though I have gathered a lot of craft and mechanics teaching points, I frequently have conferences where I see a need and try to think up a new way to respond. This is how I gathered so many teaching points in the first place! If, two or three years ago, I stuck with only what I already knew, not only would I not be responding as directly to some of my students' needs as I should, but also my store of what I could notice in writing today would be a lot smaller.

A conference that had a large impact on my teaching and that is an example of this kind of thinking took place several years ago in a third-grade classroom. I was working with Ms. Auerbach, a third-grade teacher who was doing a nonfiction unit of study with her students. During independent writing one day, I was conferring with Christopher, who had been working on an entry titled "Folding Laundry" (see Figure 9.3).

FIGURE 9.3

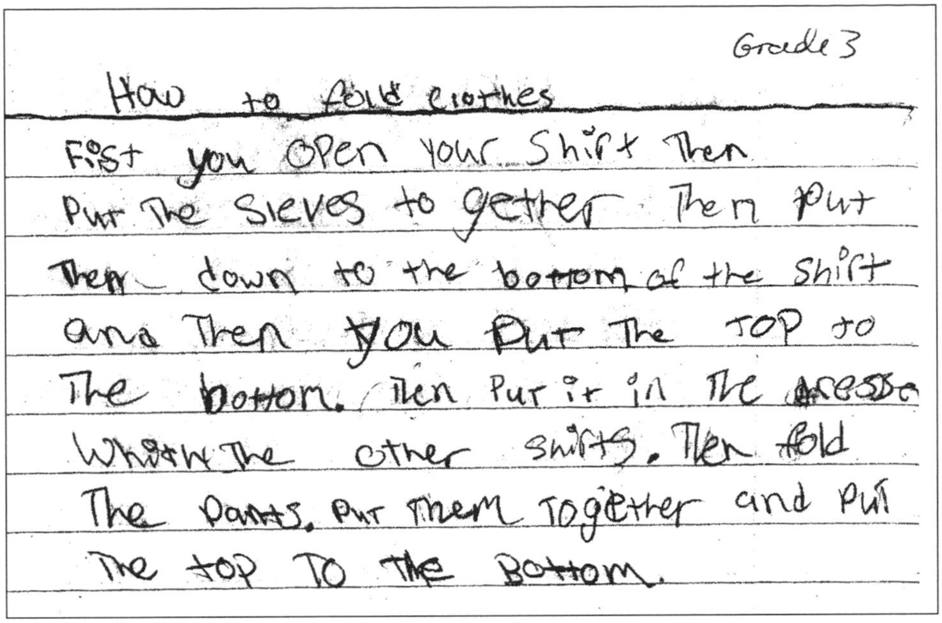

Grade 3

How to fold clothes
Fist you open your Shirt Then
Put The Sleves to gether Then Put
Then down to the bottom of the Shirt
and Then you put the TOP to
The bottom. Then Put it in The dresser
Whaw the other shirts. Then fold
The pants, Put Them Together and Put
The top To the Bottom.

Perhaps many teachers in my position would have also noticed how often Christopher started sentences with *Then* and how his sentences were very similar to each other. At the time, I didn't really have anything specific in my back pocket to offer him. I asked myself, "What is one thing I could teach him that he could keep doing tomorrow when I am nowhere to be seen?" I figured, instead of offering suggestions for sentence starters, why not just tell him to start his sentences with different words?

I asked Christopher if he had more to write about folding laundry. He said he was done and wanted to start a new entry about how to make paint out of crayons. Using some of the strategies that are presented in the next chapter, I taught him about not starting too many sentences with the same word. Twenty minutes later, after conferring with other students, I went back to Christopher's desk to see how he was doing. What I saw is what I hope happens in any conference: he had authentically taken ownership of what I taught (see Figure 9.4). Had I not thought of the next step from *his point of view*, that authentic ownership might not have happened.

That teaching point about starting sentences with different words from then on became one of my favorite mini-lessons and, as you might recall, is one of the lessons presented in Chapter 7. Because I had also gathered the "absence of craft," I could easily recognize in future conferences the opportunity to teach this very same thing. Whenever I see lots of sentences that start with the same word, "starting sentences with different words" is placed high on my list of possible next step teaching points.

I don't tell this story to illustrate how I came up with an absolutely original teaching point, because it's not original. I have since heard about similar

FIGURE 9.4

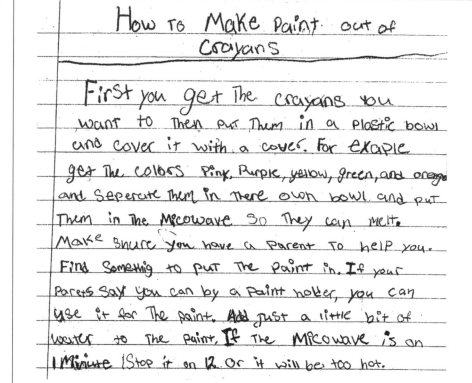

How To Make Paint out of Crayans

First you get The crayans you want to Then put Them in a plastic bowl and cover it with a cover. For exaple get The colors Pink, Purple, yellow, green, and orange and seperate them in there own bowl. and put Them in the Micowave so They can melt. Make shure you have a Parent To help you. Find Somethig to put The paint in. If your Parets say you can by a Paint holler, you can use it for The paint. Add just a little bit of water to The Paint. If The Micowave is on 1 Minute Stop it on 12. Or it will be too hot.

teaching points in a workshop and seen it mentioned in a book. But at the time it felt original. That's the thing about a conference—it's like improvisational theater in the sense that you're on stage and you don't have time to consult anyone for an idea. You have to respond right there. Ideally there are times in conferences when you do feel like you're coming up with original ideas (and they actually may be), because it means you are not relying on a fixed set of teaching points. The most important aspect of this kind of conferring is that identifying a general need moves along the conveyor belt toward thinking of a small next step.

Another example of this kind of conferring, which starts with seeing a need and ends with a new next step teaching point is my conference with Daniel, a fourth grader. During the research phase of our conference, I noticed that most of Daniel's entries barely reached the end of the page. Most teachers have seen entries like this one, in which there is a lot of telling; as soon as he lists an event, he moves right on to the next one and then suddenly the story is over (see Figure 9.5).

FIGURE 9.5

Daniel

In the weekends My cusin came. It was alot Of fun. I played Video-games With him. I always won. We played baseball, I beated him. Then we played tage

At the time of our conference, Daniel had just started writing about a time he went to the zoo. I could see that Daniel needed to work on developing his entries. As with my conference with Christopher, I didn't really have anything in my store of teaching points that came to mind as a possible next step. I knew I could help him make this particular entry longer and fuller by asking him questions. But I wanted to leave him with a skill he could hold on to so that his writing would not go back to the same kind of telling the next day. This was one of many times I learned to pull away from where his writing was supposed to be as a fourth grader, focus on where he was, and think about one small step he could own. I had a feeling that if I just gave him an expectation of writing one more sentence for each animal he visited before moving on to the next one, he could do it. I also knew I would have to link this technique to writing in general, not just to the topic of the zoo, if he was to continue to use it on his own.

This kind of instruction lessened my role of sparking ideas by asking questions. I could have asked, "So, what did the gorilla look like? Why don't you put that in?" Instead, I set an expectation that he add one more sentence about each animal. Not only did he understand that he didn't need me to help him come up with ideas of what to describe, but he came up with better descriptions than what I might have "fished" out of him. After all, he is the one who was there! As a teacher, I just helped him slow down the thought process behind his writing, so he could draw on his memory for descriptions.

One of the best indicators that I helped teach the writer and not just the writing is that Daniel was able to truly take ownership of this next step. Several days later when I came back to his classroom, Daniel was still working on his entry about the zoo. On his own he was continuing to write one or two sentences that described an animal or specific event before moving on to something else (see Figures 9.6a and 9.6b).

Once again I now had a new teaching point to put in my pocket alongside all the others I had so far. It's important to point out that not every teaching point that comes about this way affects a student's entire entry. Implicit in responding with a small, specific next step is that you are *not* trying to "fix" all of a student's needs at once.

Putting It All Together

Similar to the process of looking for strengths, researching possible next steps in student writing begins by noticing as many possible teaching points as you can before moving on to deciding what to teach. Let's look again at Liliana's entry about her baptism (Figure 9.7)—the same sample we saw in Chapter 8, Figure 8.8. This time I present some possible next steps. Once again there is a column for specific craft and a column for mechanics.

Appendix F, discussed in Chapter 8 in relation to researching strengths, also offers guided practice for noticing possible next steps in elementary

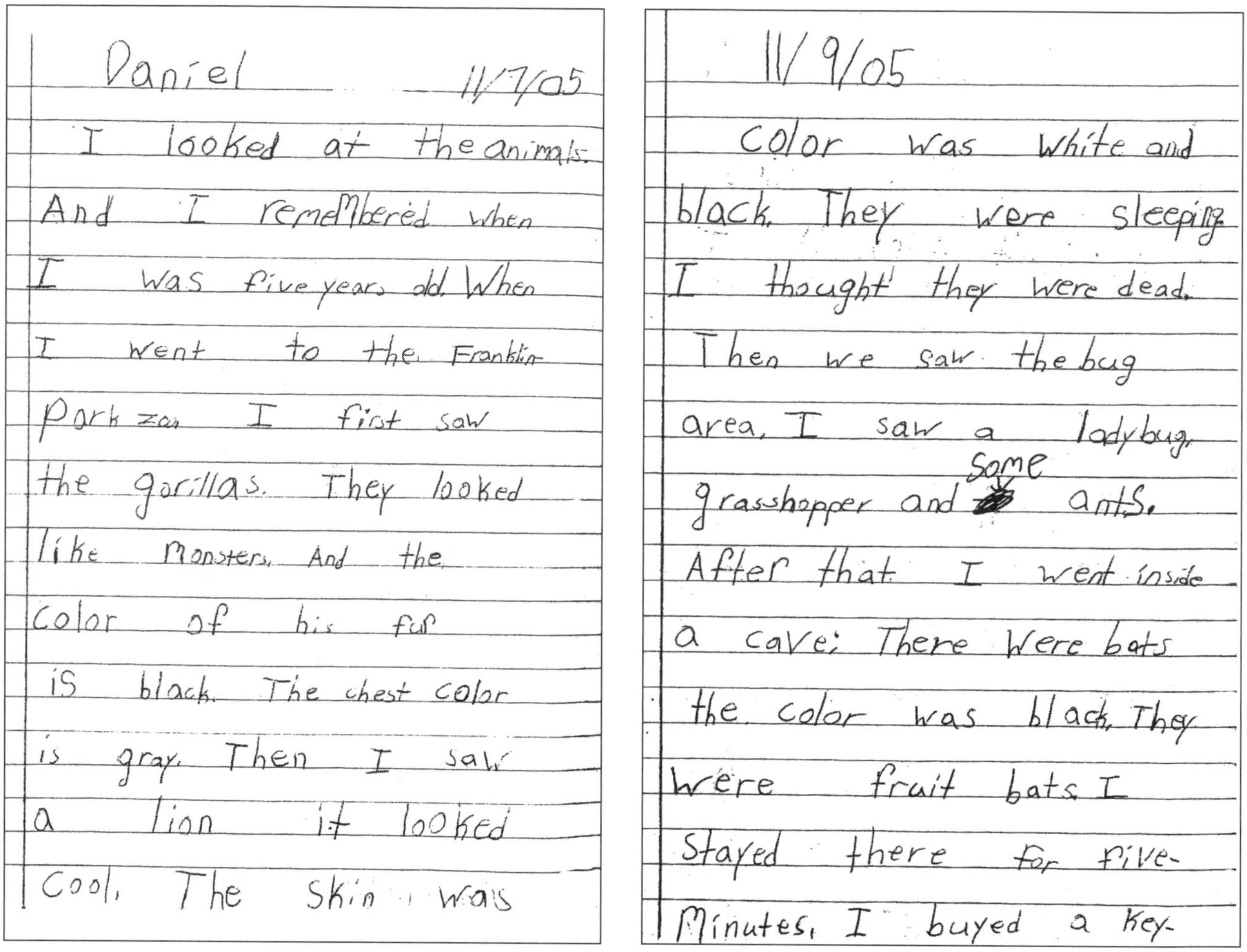

Daniel   11/7/05

I looked at the animals.
And I remembered when
I was five years old. When
I went to the Franklin
Park zoo. I first saw
the gorillas. They looked
like monsters. And the
color of his fur
is black. The chest color
is gray. Then I saw
a lion it looked
cool. The skin was

11/9/05

color was white and
black. They were sleeping
I thought they were dead.
Then we saw the bug
area. I saw a ladybug,
grasshopper and some ants.
After that I went inside
a cave: There were bats
the color was black. They
were fruit bats I
stayed there for five
minutes. I buyed a key-

FIGURE 9.6A AND B

writing. Using the same writing samples as the ones used for the practice of researching strengths more closely reflects an actual conference, when you look at the same entries through two different lenses—one that looks for strengths and one that looks for next steps. This balanced focus of craft and mechanics is especially important when looking for next steps, because so much of our own background in "helping," often inspired by how we were helped as children, sometimes favors mechanics more than necessary.

Deciding What to Teach

Conferring is not about *knowing* what to teach, it's about *deciding* what to teach. This difference in semantics may seem insignificant, but I do believe that the statement "knowing what to teach" can support a mind-set of "know or not know." If you are in a conference, and it's not exactly clear what should

3-8-06

The day I was
biptised

I was viptised when
I was eight years old. I
had to ware a wite dress.
I had to hold a candal in my
hand. The father put water on
my head. My god parents had
to come too. There was alot
of family in the cherch. We
toke a lot of pichers. My mom's
friend bought a cake of a
crose. The frosting was wite
like my dress. It was vanela
insied. I told her "tank you".
She siad "your welcome". My
dress had beeds and a ribin too.
I had white shose they had
a flower on each shose. All
the people were all saing "ware
did I bought my dress". I
said "in bilden-19". They said
"ware did you bought your
shose" and I said "I bought
them in water town in the store
payles". Then we went to
my house and we had a
party. We ate my mom's friends
cake that was like a crose.

FIGURE 9.7

Researching Next Steps	
CRAFT	**MECHANICS**
Writing different-sized sentences	Begin a resource for sight words (*where, saying . . .*)
Writing a longer sentence using *as*	Using a capital to start a quotation
Adding inside sentences	
Adding thoughts	

be taught, you will probably feel like you fall into the "not knowing" category. These are the times when a teacher might be tempted just to say to the student, "Okay, keep going" or might have a conversation with the student but not really teach anything. On the surface this seems like a fair next step, because how can you teach something if you don't know what to teach? I think it's important to validate that, especially for teachers who are new to conferring, there will be times when conferences don't feel so easy and when you may feel unsure of what to say. I hope this book in addition to other resources will help any teacher feel more comfortable conferring. And I do think it's important to validate that no one has excellent conferences all the time. But when you start letting yourself off the hook whenever you feel like you "don't know," you give yourself an easy out. In the long run, taking the easy out will slow down any growth in becoming more skilled and more comfortable with conferring. The mind-set of *deciding* what to teach, on the other hand, means you work with the options you have and choose one that seems the most appropriate.

The sections that follow describe some factors to consider when deciding what to teach in a conference based on observations of student writing.

Craft Versus Mechanics

Because words and punctuation work together to produce any desired aspect of writing, whether it's topic development, voice, or organization, it's important that there is a balance in the teaching of these two aspects of writing. How well you can maintain this balance rests almost entirely on the research stage in a conference. There is no real rule for which aspect of writing to teach when, because what each student could benefit from most is so unique to every single conference. The key to deciding is seeing as much as you can from each side before you make your choice. Ideally, any time you decide to teach about quotation marks or periods, for example, it is because it is truly what you think will help that student most at that time, not because mechanics skills are the only specific next step teaching points you can see.

The Student's Current Entry

Whether the teaching point in a conference ends up being about craft or punctuation, it's important to consider the entry or draft a student is working on at that time. Regardless of which entries gave you the most information during the research phase of your conference, the entry that has the blank space ahead is the one that will allow you to "teach forward" (this will be discussed further in the next chapter). There are some mechanics and craft techniques that can be tried out by students no matter what they are writing about. Ending sentences with periods and starting sentences with different words are two examples. Also, any next steps that relate to volume, such as writing past the end of the page or writing a certain amount during independent writing, can also be taught through any topic. But if the choices that are at the top of your list relate to certain types of images or details, you want your choice to work well with a student's current entry.

Mini-Lessons You Have Recently Taught

When deciding what to teach, you can also consider recent craft or punctuation skills you have taught in whole-class lessons. If a student used the try-it section in his or her notebook during the lesson, then all the better. You have a model created by that student all set to go.

As mentioned previously, recent mini-lessons can be a great resource for a next step in conferences, but they should not be an automatic response. Conferences are not meant to be a checking-up time to make sure students have used what you taught in a mini-lesson. Even though every student may have practiced a craft technique during the try-it, not every single student will be at the point where they are ready to incorporate the new skill into his or her independent writing.

Small Next Steps

Very often we will encounter students whose writing shows very little "need." The more this happens, the better, but the fact that a student is already writing with lots of voice and description does not mean their writing cannot be lifted up in small ways. Although students who write well may be more apt to be able to and want to direct their conferences, it's still important to be *prepared* to offer students like this specific next steps. It's important to remember that conferring is not always about helping students to improve their overall writing ability; a conference can also help students expand the number of choices they have at their disposal. This is when the strategy of noticing related craft is particularly useful. I can notice what craft techniques students are already using and then show them similar specific craft techniques to add to their repertoire.

An Example of the Decision-Making Process

I decide what to teach based on many factors, including my conversation with a student. But, based only on my reading of the writing, I can share what my decision process would be in deciding what to teach Liliana, who wrote the baptism memory in Figure 9.7. I would probably not choose next steps that have to do with sentence length, such as using *as* to connect two sentences or writing different-sized sentences. Although these may be good next step teaching points at some point soon, I would want to focus on other writing skills first.

I should take a moment here to address the topic of dealing with spelling in conferences. It is an issue that occurs frequently, especially with English language learners like Liliana. Correct spelling, especially with grade-level words, is an important part of writing. We might want students in the upper elementary grades to use inventive spelling for bigger, out-of-reach words, but we hope that the number and complexity of words students know how to spell correctly increases. If a conference is about teaching the writer and not about fixing a piece of writing, however, then a conference is not the place to work on how to spell certain words. It may be tempting, because helping students correct words can be satisfying: you are helping a child go from doing something "wrong" to doing something "right." But it's not supporting what they can do as writers the next day. This is as good as telling a student how to say a word during a reading conference as opposed to teaching a reading strategy a student can work on thereafter. Ideally, any teaching point about spelling in a writing conference focuses on a strategy. If a student is not taking advantage of the word wall or other spelling supports, for example, this can be a teaching point. Teachers who use the three-column spell-check method during editing, where students make several attempts at misspelled words before getting the correct spelling, can have students write the correct spelling of these words in a section of the writer's notebook. Students can then periodically get in pairs and quiz each other on their words so the memory of how to spell these words is automatic. Having a student find a partner who will quiz them on a regular basis could also be a strategy as a result of seeing a lot of grade-level misspellings.

Because Liliana shows a good amount of beginning craft, I would probably want to lift up the mechanics side of her writing. I know that she keeps a list of spell-check words in her notebook, so, I might focus on how often she reviews those words. Just by looking at her writing, however, I would probably choose to focus on another aspect of mechanics and teach her about starting dialogue with a capital letter.

Balancing Research

I do want students to drive their own conferences as much as possible, but not at the expense of lifting up students' writing skills. Carl Anderson (2000) mentions, "While I value ownership, I also value teaching, and sometimes these two values conflict. Each conference is such a precious teaching opportunity, and I want to be sure to use it to teach a child what I feel he most needs to learn at this point in time" (71). There are times when I can address what a student talks about in a conference in addition to a need I see in their writing. For example, if a student wants to talk about his plans for an entry he just started or wants to talk about his entry's beginning but I also see he has used no periods whatsoever, we can talk about both. First I would discuss his writing plans, probably asking questions more than teaching. Then when the student came to some sort of conclusion, I would move into a more formal teaching point about writing complete sentences. The first issue, writing plans, was part of our conversation, while the second issue of using periods was the official next step.

An example of balancing students' intentions with my own observations of their writing occurred when I was conferring with a student who said she wanted to work on her lead, but I also saw that she could really use some support around sentence variety. Almost every sentence started with the words *Then* or *We*. I knew that of the two possible next steps—her lead or sentence variety—her future writing would probably benefit much more from a teaching point about sentence beginnings than if we just talked about her first sentence. Granted, every entry and draft is better off with a great lead, but this first sentence is only a very small portion of the total piece of writing. Through our conversation, I helped this student to think out loud about possibilities for leads, reminding her of a few lessons I know her teacher gave several months ago about leads. Because she showed maturity in this brief discussion, her ability to reflect on her own writing became one of the two strengths I taught and wrote on my conference sheet. If she had needed a little support I would have offered it, just not in an official teaching way—I knew I wanted to save that precious "teach one thing" to support her with sentence variety.

Students' intentions and my own observations can very often go together. For example, students might talk about certain parts of their entry they want to describe more fully. I could then focus on that paragraph or section of the writing and possibly see a particular next step involving description that would work well there. Any time I take the lead in a writing conference, it's not because I don't want to honor students' voices; it's because I see an opportunity for a next step that will lift up the quality of their writing.

The decision-making process in a conference, especially when it comes to next steps, is a constant balancing act. I am balancing what students say with what I see in their writing. I try to keep a balanced lens between craft and mechanics. And even when it comes to teaching craft, I try to find a balance between teaching smaller specific craft skills and the more general writing strategies that are not at the sentence level. I don't think the answer lies in figuring out how to reach the *perfect* balance. What's important is being *aware* of the need for balance and supporting students in different ways as you are deciding what to teach. The next chapter looks at how the teaching of a conference might sound after you have reached a decision about what strength and what next step to teach.

Teaching the Conference

Imagine you are a first-year teacher. And you're struggling. When it's time for your formal observation, your reading lesson absolutely flops. Your explanations went on way too long, Jason and Gavin were running around the room during independent reading (again), and you spent all your time either getting them back to their seat or reminding Ashley and her friends to stop talking and start reading. Then Cedrick picked today to indulge in his rubber band flicking fetish.

The next day you dread going to your principal's office for feedback. But imagine that, before your principal goes into what could be improved about your teaching, she discusses the small strengths she sees embedded in your teaching. She says she likes the way you did a think-aloud to model the reading strategy you were teaching. It made the skill more visible for students. She points out that even though you got to only one conference, the fact that you had your conference notes organized in a binder meant you could easily and quickly find any student's conference sheet. Rather than judge your lesson as a whole, she talks about the small strengths embedded in your teaching before moving on to what needed work.

How would you feel? Would a principal pointing out strengths like this give you a false sense of your ability? Would you suddenly think you were fine and had no room to grow? Probably not. In fact, instead of being overly aware of your deficits, you might actually have a more balanced understanding of your strengths and weaknesses and no longer feel hopeless about your progress. I know how this feels, because this story is mine.

It wasn't until my second year in Boston that I was able to even get close to the teacher I knew I was capable of being. That first year, I wasn't all that great. I cared about my twenty-eight students very much and tried incredibly hard, but my lessons rarely went as planned and my class was not always under control. My principal, Cheryl Watson-Harris, not only saw small strengths embedded in my teaching, which if only judged as a whole was not so terrific, but also made a point to tell me what those small strengths were. When I first went into her office, I was sure all the feedback was going to be negative or "instructive." Or, because she was a nice person, I thought I would get a generic, "Okay, good effort" before she moved on to what needed work. But when the door was closed, Cheryl started our conversation by telling me the specific strengths she saw in my teaching. After a moment of disbelief—because I certainly hadn't noticed my strengths—I felt an overwhelming sense of relief, gratitude, and an immense desire to be better. I am still working with her today, partly because of her leadership, but also because of a dedication that stems from my experience that first year. She believed in me when I was at my worst and most vulnerable, which helped me to believe in my potential.

It's possible that some teachers might feel that although it might be interesting to be able to notice skills in different levels of writing, spending a lot of time teaching students their strengths might give them a false sense of their capabilities. Or perhaps there are some teachers who feel that the time used to teach strengths would be better spent on additional support of next steps, so students have a better chance of improving. When we put ourselves in the position of our students, however, it's easier to realize how greatly we can affect their attitude toward writing by pointing out their strengths, whether they are excelling overall at writing or not.

Powerful conferring requires us to let go of where we want our students to be. Am I advocating that it is okay if our third graders write on a first-grade level? Of course not. I *am* advocating that during a conference, we accept, without subconscious resentment *toward our students*, that this is where they are.

In their book *Teaching for Comprehension in Reading, Grades K–2* (2003), Gay Su Pinnell and Patricia Scharer discuss in depth how the emotional aspect of teaching can either impede learning or cause it to flourish. In one chapter they even offer scientific explanations for how the brain functions under stress. What I like so much about their attention to this topic is that they honor how important it is to look at the psychological and emotional aspects of learning. Reaching one's potential to learn depends so much on the relationships between the people involved, not so much the content of what is being taught. When you can change the way students view their own capability in a certain subject, it can greatly affect the investment of energy and a willingness to take risks. "Success builds emotional support, confidence, and the willingness to try" (Pinnell and Scharer 2003, 58).

While district- and school-wide efforts on closing the achievement gap are important, taking the time to teach students their strengths is often the key to affecting the motivation of low-achieving students. The difference between praise and academic praise is critical. At one point in their book, Pinnell and Scharer discuss a student named David who is behind his peers and is very aware of this fact: "Saying 'You can do it' is not enough. . . . Telling a child he is smart will not solve the problem; chances are, a child like David will not believe you anyway. David had to learn to act as a reader and writer, as one who mastered part of the process" (2003, 64). The use of the word *part* in this last sentence is extremely important. Students don't have to be told or have to think they are mastering a subject matter completely in order to feel capable. They just need to be shown a part, no matter how small, that is proof of their capability in this subject matter on some level. This is how my principal made me feel during that initial feedback session. Knowing there was something I was doing right, even if I was very aware of how far behind I was compared to other teachers in the building, gave me a reason not to give up and to keep trying.

Any teacher movie that has been made, typically based on a true story, is usually about that teacher's ability to change the way his or her students' see themselves and their capabilities. Examples that come to mind are *Stand and Deliver* (Menendez 1988), *Music of the Heart* (Craven 1999), and the *Freedom Writers* (LaGravanese 2007). The center figure of each movie may teach music, math, or English, but the content area is the vehicle for change, not the reason for change. Athletic coaches can have the same effect on students. Whether the arena is academics or sports, these stories are not about seeing raw, undiscovered talent in a future scholar or future NFL player, although that may indeed happen. These inspiring stories are about helping students see that despite where they are in the eyes of others, whether those others may be their community, society, numbers on a state test, or themselves, they are capable of success, and more importantly, they are capable right now. If you're too busy noticing the gap between what students are doing and where they

Table 10.1 A Possible Structure for a Writing Conference

TEACHING A STRENGTH	TEACHING A NEXT STEP
Research Strengths through conversation and reading student's writing	*Research Next Steps* through conversation and reading student's writing
Decide which strength or strengths to make public in the conference	*Decide* which next step to teach
Teach by naming the strength and explaining why it is good Ask the student, "Say back to me . . ."	*Teach* by naming the next step and explaining why it is good Ask the student, "Say back to me . . ."
Record by writing down the strength that was taught	*Record* by writing down the next step that was taught

are "supposed" to be, it will be harder to see strengths. It's only when you genuinely notice specific strengths yourself that students can detect true sincerity in what you say about their academic capability. Showing students what they do well, regardless of whether a strength is on grade level or not, can affect not just self-perception but motivation. When I take their strengths seriously in an academic way, students see that I take them seriously as writers. This sets the stage for students to receive instruction as a writer. When students understand how they are successful at one aspect of writing, no matter how small, it gives them a reason to try.

So, when it comes to teaching strengths in conferences, the structure I present is not about teaching strengths only when they are obvious and right there before your eyes. It's about setting an expectation that every student in every conference gets taught a strength, whether it takes a few seconds or a few minutes to find one. When you know many specific craft skills, the chances increase that you'll see many different strengths in students' writing as well as possible next steps.

The structure of my conferences, shown in Table 10.1, reflects this dual emphasis on teaching strengths as well as next steps.

I've said before that there is no one right way to confer, a statement that is important to bring up again at this point. One of the best parts of writing workshop for me is that it honors teachers as professionals and individuals. Although there are underlying philosophies that should be similar in any workshop classroom, the details can be different, conferring included. Being exposed to different styles of conferring means you will have more choices at your disposal when it comes to helping the varied levels of writers and personalities in your classroom.

As I discussed in Chapters 8 and 9, a good deal of the research about what to teach in a conference occurs up front when, ideally, there is an open conversation with a student. During this time, I listen to the student carefully in addition to reading the writing and looking for possible teaching points. How much I lead in the conference depends entirely on what I see while researching in combination with what each student has to offer at that time in terms of goals, requests, and writing plans. There are, of course, other times besides the beginning of the conference when the students will bring up a need or request in our conversation and it will make sense to follow this line of thinking.

Sometimes when I am reading students' writing, I might notice both a strength and a possible next step to teach. At other times I am not quite sure what I might teach in the first few minutes of research and so first just give my full attention to looking for and teaching strengths. After I have finished that part of the conference, I may need to do some additional research. Usually this means asking the student more questions as well as rereading some of the writing with an extra focused lens on possible next steps. Whether a majority of the research occurs mostly at the beginning or is interspersed throughout the conference, how I actually teach strengths or next steps does not change all that much. Whether teaching strengths or next steps, there are certain teaching moves that I find keep a conference productive and efficient:

❖ Transitions
❖ Naming the skill
❖ Saying why it's good
❖ Say back to me
❖ Record the teaching

Table 10.2 is an example of how these steps might sound if I were having a conference with Liliana, who wrote the baptism piece presented in Chapter 8, Figure 8.7. Remember, right now I am only discussing the delivery in a conference—the "teach" in research-decide-teach. As I explain and illustrate each step of a conference, you won't hear much of the student's voice, because the focus for now is on how it might sound to actually explain and teach specific craft. At the end of this chapter, I offer transcripts of entire conferences from start to finish in order to illustrate the true sound of an entire conference, which includes both the teacher's and student's voice.

Because all conferences are unique, they don't always follow this structure in a seamless way. These are fairly simple steps, though, so it is usually not too difficult to stay on this path. Conversations can get off track, so having these small steps within the teaching phase of a conference provides an anchor for my teaching. The following sections provide a more in-depth look at each of the steps.

Table 10.2 The Teaching Voice in a Writing Conference

TEACHING A STRENGTH

TRANSITION	Liliana, one thing I notice you do well as a writer is . . .
NAMING THE SKILL	. . . when you describe the details of your clothes. Like here when you mentioned how your dress had beads and ribbons on it. And then later you mentioned how your shoes had flowers on them. That sounds so pretty!
SAYING WHY IT'S GOOD	Some kids just mention the color of clothes when they describe them. It's great to talk about the color, but what you're doing—describing some of the details of clothes—gives me an even better picture. You can do this whenever you mention clothes, whether they are yours or someone else's. For example, if I were writing about my mother's apron when she was cooking, I could talk about the picture of a frog on the front and the little splotches of gravy stains. See how those little details give you such a good picture? That's what you did when you described your dress. So, giving several details about clothes is something you can do whenever you're describing what someone is wearing.
SAY BACK TO ME	Can you say back to me—what's one thing you do well as a writer?
RECORD THE STRENGTH	(On my conference sheet, I write down what was taught.)

TEACHING A NEXT STEP

TRANSITION	Okay, one thing you could work on is . . .
NAMING THE SKILL	. . . starting your dialogue with capital letters. You do an excellent job of putting the quotation marks where they go, which is the most important thing when it comes to dialogue. Because otherwise it can be confusing, right? I love that you add dialogue to your memory, and I am not confused at all about where it begins and where it ends. Now you're ready for some of the small rules of dialogue. And one of them is that whenever you start a quotation, you have to start with a capital letter.
SAYING WHY IT'S GOOD	Because what people say *is* the beginning of a sentence. See how in all your regular sentences, you do such a good job of starting with a capital? You've learned that even though you have a period, a capital is another way to show the reader "Hello, I am starting a new sentence now!" So even though you have quotation marks, you also need a capital. So here, when you wrote, "All the people were all saying 'where did I buy my dress.'" "Where did I buy my dress" is its own sentence. So what letter should be capitalized? . . . Right, the *W* in *Where*. All right, so here you're writing about the cake at the party . That's so neat it was in the shape of the cross. I guess since it was a party, there were lots of things that were said? Okay, I'm going to have you write a little bit more about the party, just a few sentences. See if you can add at least one line of dialogue. And what little rule are you going to try and remember as you write? . . . Yes, the capital letter at the beginning of the dialogue. Okay, go ahead.
SAY BACK TO ME	(after a minute or so) Can I see what you wrote? Great, look at that. You wrote about your brother asking for more cake and you started it with a capital letter. Great job. Can you say back to me . . . what is the new little rule about dialogue you just used in your writing? Right, and why is it important to put a capital at the beginning of dialogue? Yes, great.
RECORD THE NEXT STEP	(On my conference sheet, I write down what was taught.)

Transitions

After the initial research is over and I have decided what strength I want to teach, I usually start with one of a handful of phrases:

So one thing I notice that you do well as a writer is . . .
Okay, let me show you something really good you're doing as a writer . . .
One strength I notice about your writing is . . .

When it comes to teaching next steps, I use similar transitional phrases to let students know the conference is moving into the teaching realm again.

Okay, so one thing you could work on is . . .
One thing I think you're ready for as a writer is . . .
So, based on what you're saying, one thing you could try is . . .

Most people who confer consistently find that it becomes a natural practice to use similar phrases at different points in the conference. Carl Anderson, for example, frequently uses the phrase, "How's it going?" to begin his conversation with students (2000). Conferring requires enough thinking that we don't have to come up with ways to sound original in different conferences. Any transition phrase used regularly also offers a sense of predictability for students: they know when I am done researching and ready to teach.

Naming the Skill

Similar to the way the What and the Why offer a structure for mini-lesson instruction, so can these two instructional goals provide a dependable structure for teaching strengths and next steps in a conference. Sometimes when a student's strengths are mentioned, it comes in the form of a compliment or personal reaction. Positive feedback of any kind is a good thing. When we offer merely praise without giving the What and the Why, however, we make this stage of the conference reach only half its potential. Comments such as "Nice job" or "Good description" are positive but vague. A student may feel good about your praise, but you are not really helping them understand what they did well.

Sometimes positive feedback goes beyond a general comment and does focus on what a student is doing with his or her writing. In the example conference in Table 10.2, I could have said, "What a great sentence, Liliana. I really liked how you wrote about the beads and the ribbons. Those are such nice details!" This kind of reaction goes beyond a compliment because it points to something specific in her writing. She would certainly understand that this phrase is a nice one. And she would probably feel good about what I said. But it's still not taking advantage of the opportunity a conference presents, which is *teaching* a student what she did well in that sentence. When you *teach* strengths in a conference using the What and the Why, the words or phrases on the page are not the sole focus of your teaching; they become the vehicle for your teaching.

The What and the Why also offer an architecture for teaching next steps. Being aware of pinpointing a specific skill is important, because it's very possible to help a student in a conference without actually teaching anything in particular. For example, some conferences center around helping students with their plans—plans for how to go about an entry, plans for what they might write about, or plans for how they might structure a first draft. This kind of support is clearly helpful, because students usually come out of the conference with a better idea of what to do next. The act of simply discussing writing plans with another person, student, or teacher, is beneficial. But it only takes one extra step to then name that skill. Once a skill is named, the teaching moves closer to teaching the writer, not just the writing.

Even when naming non-craft skills, it's still important to try to be as specific as possible. Using a word wall, writing about a difficult topic, writing with volume, and peer conferring are all examples of skills that could be possible strengths or next steps to teach. If I notice Santiago does a great job peer conferring, for example, I would try to pinpoint what exactly was good about it. Does he use good suggestive phrases such as, "Maybe you could think about . . ."? Did he use a certain kind of question that was recently taught in a mini-lesson? Or, did he offer suggestions for how he and his partner could run their peer conference? Taking the time to analyze a strength so you can name a specific skill in the conference benefits not just the students but the teacher as well. Any time I have done this, the student can hold on to the skill and intentionally do it again, but so can I. After I pinpointed that one reason Santiago was good at peer conferring was that he used the phrase "Maybe you could think about . . . ," it became a specific skill I could teach. Had I not challenged myself to name a specific skill, I might not have thought to teach it to other students. It's not that I wouldn't have *heard* him say those words. But chances are, if I didn't take the time to look for a specific skill, those words would have remained a hazy part of my overall judgment that he was "good" at peer conferring.

Saying Why It's Good

Similar to its importance in mini-lesson instruction, explaining *why* a certain writing skill or craft technique is good can support understanding and student ownership in a conference. Although we are not introducing students to a new skill when teaching strengths, offering the Why is still important: it can help students understand the value of the craft or mechanics skill that already exists in their writing. Students might be aware of the words they choose but not aware of the craft behind the words, especially if the craft was not recently taught in a lesson.

Teaching Moves

One teaching move I often use to support students' understanding of the Why is to offer an example that is removed from the student's writing. In the example of using details with clothes in Table 10.2, I described my mother's apron to further illustrate the craft technique I saw in Liliana's writing. Rather than simply encouraging her to use this craft technique again, I created a more visible bridge between what Liliana wrote and other topics. Using this teaching move in a conference is one of the best ways to "teach the writer, not the writing."

When it comes to teaching next steps, providing this bridge is even more important, because I am teaching skills that are not yet part of a student's repertoire, at least not in a solid way. It's up to me to make that skill as tangible as possible. If I only help create an example in the student's entry or draft in front of us, it can be hard to get away from feeling as if I am mostly helping the student fix his or her writing. Giving an example outside the student's writing frees the craft from the writing in front of us.

"Some kids" is another teaching move illustrated in the example in Table 10.2. After I name a student's strength, I sometimes explain the Why by comparing what they did to "other students" or to what "some kids" do. The comparison can help students more easily understand their strength by giving them a more visible alternative. Very often, I already have this "opposite" skill in my mind from gathering craft and trying to figure out the value of a particular skill. "Some kids" is something I often use when I teach students who are below grade level, because the message underneath this move is, "You are doing something well that other students are not yet doing." This can be a powerful morale boost for a student who struggles with writing. It doesn't matter how simple the strength is or whether it's a grade-level skill or not. The point is not to compare a student to a particular person, of course, but to make a student aware that a namable, academic skill he or she possesses is not a given for all students. The way this is said matters. As Peter Johnston says in his book *Choice Words*, "Language . . . is not merely *representational*, (though it is that); it is also *constitutive*. It actually creates realities and invites identities" (2004, 9).

Students Try It Out

One way to strengthen student ownership of a teaching point that focuses on next steps, at least when it comes to specific craft, is to have them quickly try out what was just taught. In order for students to use a craft or mechanics skill as authentically as possible, it's important to "teach forward." This is a phrase I started using to emphasize the ideal forward movement when students try out a skill in a conference. During the research phase, the student and I may discuss sentences he or she has already written, but I usually don't ask students to fix anything they already wrote. As I mentioned in a previous chapter, writing entails thinking of and using certain craft and punctuation as you write new words. Changing or fixing something that is already written strengthens editing more than it does writing. If our energy is meant to be directed toward our students' skill sets, and not solely on products they produce, then it would also make sense that writing notebooks honestly and authentically reflect students' forward progress.

After I've discussed a next step, at least one that has to do with craft or mechanics, the student and I both look at the part of the entry he or she is currently working on. At this point, I usually ask what he or she might write about next to get a context in which to place the use of the craft technique. In the example in Table 10.2, it was clear where Liliana was in her story about the baptism. At other times, I ask students what their intentions are for the next part of the entry. Notice with Liliana I didn't have her talk out the exact sentences she was going to write. When I teach forward, I mostly assist students by getting their *thinking* ready. Although talking out sentence ideas can be productive and at times is needed in a conference, most students don't talk sentences out loud when they are writing on their own. Getting students ready to think a certain way before writing, rather than just getting them ready to copy down what they just said out loud to me, more closely supports an independent writing skill.

When a student begins to write, I let go. It's time for that student to be independent, and I make a point to be involved as little as possible as he or she tries out the new skill we've just discussed. Students know that after about a minute I'll be looking to see how they did, so the accountability factor is not lost. At first it was a little hard to abstain from looking over students' shoulders as they wrote their next few sentences, but resisting is important. This makes a public statement of trust that they can do it on their own, and it creates an opportunity for students to prove to *themselves* that they can do it on their own. It's important to point out that it was only when I started giving students specific teaching points related to description and other aspects of craft that I was confident they could be successful in these attempts without my help.

I sometimes make a point to make this independence as obvious to students as possible. Sometimes I let them know that while they write, I will start recording the conference and decide which student I will choose next. Sometimes I tell the student that I'll be right back and then take that opportunity to see how the rest of the class is doing—maybe giving a positive comment here or there or checking in with a student from a previous conference.

This quick check-in around the room also helps the teacher see how students are doing and maintains a sense of accountability for the rest of the class, and is especially important for teachers who confer in a stationary spot.

One of the best parts of having students try out the teaching point in conferences is that the teaching can end with positive feedback. After a minute or two when I ask to see how they've been doing, I get to react to their attempts at using this skill. Whenever a student is not successful at this independent attempt, I just offer more guidance as he or she tries again.

Say Back to Me

I always end a conference by having students say the teaching points—both the strength and the next step—back to me. This final step has not always been a consistent part of my conferring, and it is not an implicit part of the research-decide-teach model. I remember to the day when I started incorporating this step in all my conferences. It was my first year of teaching in Boston, and I was conferring with Erica, one of my third graders. I thought the conference was going great. She had been writing about a time she and her cousin were flower girls at a wedding. After I asked questions about the part when everybody was dancing, she told me a little bit more about this part. My teaching, which was not as specific at that time, had something to do with adding details so the reader could tell what kind of dancing it was. I ended the conference by saying, "So, maybe you can add some of those things we talked about to your writing." She smiled and nodded. "All right, great!" I said. Then, just as I was about to send her back to her desk, I had a sudden impulse to see if she could repeat what we just talked about.

"So Erica," I asked. "What are you going to work on now? Can you say back to me what we just talked about?" She looked around the room with a drawn out "Ummm . . ." and then suddenly smiled as if she had found a good answer. "Add periods?" she asked hopefully. I couldn't believe it! Here I was thinking my conference was so great, but if Erica couldn't even say what the conference was about literally five seconds after it ended, then what were the chances my teaching was going to have any kind of lasting impact? As I described in Chapter 7 in regard to the topic of mini-lessons, rather than just expecting or hoping that listening leads to learning, we can set up structures that support active listening. The try-it is the step that supports accountability for listening during whole-class instruction. In a conference, having a consistent expectation that a student should be able to repeat what you just taught provides a similar accountability. I no longer rely on questions such as, "Does that make sense?" or "Do you see what I mean?" to check for understanding. Rather than ask students if they understand, I ask students to *show* me they understand.

I still get a lot of students who, when I ask them what they could work on as a writer, say, "Add periods?" But they are almost always students who are new to this way of conferring and aren't used to the accountability factor at the end. It makes sense that this is what they think I want to hear. Students probably have been hearing teachers say, "Add periods" since the first grade. Based on probability alone, "Add periods" is a pretty good guess. But when students start to understand that conferences are tailor-made instruction that may or may not involve periods and that you will expect them to verbalize their next steps, they naturally become more present throughout the conference. When students are more verbal about what they would like to work on, this kind of accountability may not be quite as important. But even when they are more invested in conversation about their writing, it can still be helpful to have students recap their plans or what they learned at the end of a conference.

There are different ways to prompt students to say the teaching back to you. Sometimes my questions are general:

So, what's one thing you can work on as a writer?
What's one thing you can do now whenever you write?

My questions at other times are more specific to the skill I've taught:

So, if you want to add a sound to writing, what's one way you can write it now?
What's one thing you can do when you write an inside sentence?

Very often after a student answers me, I will also ask them a Why question. I want to strengthen their ownership and understanding of why they should use skills just as much as I want them to remember what the conference "was about":

And why is it good to sometimes write sounds like that?
And why is it good to start sentences with different kinds of words?

These prompts have several characteristics in common. First, they all focus on the writer. Even though some may be grounded in sentences a student just added, the wording of the prompt puts the student, not the entry, at the center. Second, these prompts emphasize that whatever was taught in that particular conference was "one thing" they can work on or bring into their writing, but not the *only* skill that could be used. Just as there is never only one thing that a student does well as a writer, there is also never only one thing we want our students to work on as writers. Even within a particular category of craft there is no one specific craft that is the best and only way. When I teach a student about adding *because* to an inside sentence, for example, I wouldn't want to give the

student the impression that any time he or she writes a feeling, it should be followed with *because*. There are other ways to write about feelings. I want to support students' decision-making skills as writers and help them understand that
adding *because* is "one thing you can do" when it comes to inside sentences.

At first I applied this accountability step only to the teaching point that
focused on students' next steps. But the more that teaching strengths became
part of my practice, the more I realized there was no reason not to apply this
to the teaching of strengths as well. Asking students to say their strengths out
loud increases the opportunity to positively affect their self-perceptions as
writers. I have seen this simple act affect writers at all levels, from the farthest
behind to the farthest ahead, to the point that it has become my favorite part
of the conference. It is particularly empowering for students who are *not* doing
well in writing. These students are used to being on one side of the comparison chart, where they are constantly aware of what they aren't doing well
compared to the rest of the class. This is not necessarily a reflection on teachers. Students can have the most caring, supportive teacher and still label
themselves incapable based on their grades and seeing the more advanced
writing and reading abilities that surround them every day. When students
verbalize their own strengths, they acknowledge their strengths in a way that
just listening to a teacher doesn't do.

Similar to prompts used with next steps, the wording for asking students
to "say back" their strengths is sometimes general:

> So, can you say back to me—what's one thing you are good at as a
> writer?
> What do you do well as a writer? . . . And why is that good?

Although my students may be doing many things well as writers, they
understand that I am asking them to restate what was just taught. Sometimes,
especially when students aren't used to being accountable for knowing what
was taught, I will streamline the prompt a little bit more:

> What is good about the way you wrote about the clothes? Right, and
> what does that do for the reader?
> What do you do well in terms of peer conferring?

Another benefit to making the "say back to me" a consistent step in both
parts of the conference is that it keeps *me* accountable for always clearly teaching both a strength and a next step. If I am going to expect my students to verbalize their strengths and next steps as a result of the conference, then I need
to do my part to make it as clear as possible what those two things are. Again,
you could probably see how specific teaching and this last step go hand in
hand. I would not be able to hold myself to this expectation had I also not
developed an ability to notice and teach smaller, more specific skills.

The following transcript is one more example of how the *teaching* part of a conference might sound using the steps presented in this chapter. You'll notice that the parts of the conference, which are labeled in the margin, sometimes overlap. This more closely reflects the flow of a real conference.

Teaching a Strength

TRANSITION AND NAMING THE SKILL

So Gaby, one thing I notice you do well as a writer is that you have different kinds of sound in your writing.

NAMING THE SKILL AND SAYING WHY IT'S GOOD

One way you write sound is here when you give a lyric from a song. That's so great, because rather than just say what kind of a song it is, I can actually hear the song. I can actually hear the music and the beat. Another way you use sound is when you write the actual sound, like here when you wrote, "The machine went pff every time it blew up a balloon." A lot of students think that a sound has to be a "real" word, like one you would find in the dictionary. But so many writers just write the sound something makes. Have you heard of the word *onomatopoeia*? That's what you're doing here. Sounds are great to have in writing and ideally writers learn to write sound in different ways, which is exactly what you are doing. So, not only are you including sounds, but you're also adding variety to your writing because you're writing sounds in different ways.

SAY BACK TO ME AND RECORD THE STRENGTH

So, I'm going to write on my conference sheet that you are writing sounds in different ways. Okay, can you say back to me what you are doing that's good in your writing? . . . Right. And why is that good?

Teaching a Next Step

TRANSITION

All right, one thing you can work on is adding some thoughts to your writing. I notice that you have a lot of feelings, like here when you talk about how excited you were about your birthday party and then later here when you write about being nervous before the first person came. And you gave the reason too. Remember how we said those are inside sentences?

NAMING THE SKILL AND SAYING WHY IT'S GOOD

Well, now I think you're ready to include the other kind of inside sentences, which are not about how you were feeling, but what you were thinking. It's just another way to connect with the reader when you explain what was going on in your mind. Because our thoughts are very private. Say I was writing about going to the dentist. If I was just writing about what happened, that would be one story. But if I included some of my thoughts, I might write sentences like, "When I heard a drill, I wanted to run out of the waiting room," or "I wondered if he was going to use any of those sharp instruments I saw." It's like you get to hear my personal story. Okay, so right here [pointing to the last few sentences he wrote] you've just finished writing about getting ready for the party and then the music and the dancing. What were you thinking of writing about next? . . . That's great. I'm sure you had lots of thoughts going on in your mind when you were opening presents. Or even before you opened them. Could you share one thing that was going through your mind before you opened them? . . . So that's maybe a thought you could include. Okay, I'm going to check to see how the class is doing. Why don't you just stay here for a few minutes and keep writing about your birthday party. And what kind of sentences are you going to try to add? . . . Yes, I'll be back in a few minutes.

(a few minutes later)

Okay, can I read what you wrote? . . . That's great. You have two inside thoughts. Now I know what was going on in your mind! Did you ever end up getting an iPod? . . . Oh, well, maybe next birthday.

SAY BACK TO ME AND RECORD THE NEXT STEP

All right, can you just say back to me what's one thing you can add to your writing sometimes that you just did?

Right. Let's write that down on our conference sheets. And this is something you can do now no matter what you write about, okay? Great job.

It's important to point out that whether I am teaching a skill as a strength or as a next step, the language I use is often similar, because whether a student *is* using a certain craft technique or *could* use a certain craft technique, the What and Why don't change. If I saw that a student was writing lots of inside sentences about what she was thinking, my explanation of what it is and why it helps the reader would probably sound very similar to what I said to Gaby. Any specific craft technique I've mentioned in this book just sits in my pocket and when I bring it out, there is only a slight difference between how it sounds as a strength versus a next step. The tone is either, "Hey, here's something you do" or, "Hey, here's something you could do."

Record the Teaching

Some teachers say, "I have conferences. I just don't write them down." It is certainly possible to conduct conferences without writing anything down, but the accountability factor—both for the teacher and the student—goes way down when we don't document what we've taught. It doesn't take any time at all to jot down the teaching points, because they should be just short phrases. If we don't record what was taught, then it's very easy to go through a conference without actually teaching anything. This is not so much about proof for administrators that you are conferring, but about effective instruction. If I know I have to write down a teaching point—not what was talked about in the conference, but a real teaching point—I'm not going to let myself off the hook when a conference is not simple. This is so important, especially for any teachers who are new at conferring. The only way to feel comfortable conferring is if you embrace the beginning stage when it may not feel all that easy. It is beneficial to practice any kind of conferring skill with colleagues during sessions when you can look at and discuss student writing behind the scenes, but it will still take some live practice in the classroom as well.

In addition to keeping us accountable for our teaching, recording conferences can also affect student follow-through. Even if our teaching is specific, there is no way to remember a week or two later what we taught if it's not written down. And students intrinsically know you will not remember. It's not that they are consciously trying to get away with something, it's just one of those human nature things. When the next step is documented on paper, there is reason for students to feel more accountable for working on or trying out what was taught.

How we organize the records of our conferences is one of those details that differs from teacher to teacher. I've known some teachers who record their conferences on index cards—one index card for each student—and keep the index cards in a box. Some teachers use notebooks. Other teachers use a full-page conference sheet for each student and keep the sheets on a clipboard. My personal preference is to keep conference sheets in a three-ring binder. I write students' names on the tabs for easy access, and the binder keeps the conference sheets from getting crumpled.

The conference sheets that I currently use have the student's name at the top and five columns below. Figure 10.1 is the record of my conference with Gaby about his entry on his birthday party.

This conference sheet shows the dual focus on teaching strengths and next steps. The column for "Maybe Next Time" is something I added in the last few years. This column is a place to write down other possible next step teaching points that I didn't choose that particular time. It helps during those conferences when I'm not sure about what I should teach. I may be torn between teaching a student a skill related to sentence variety or adding sounds. Writing

FIGURE 10.1

| | Name | GABY | | |

Date	Working on...	Strength	Next Step	Maybe next time...
10/22	birthday party / Memoir	Writing different kinds of sounds • lyrics • ker-plop	including thoughts	using paragraph spaces

one of these in the "Maybe Next Time" column doesn't mean that this is what I will definitely teach next time, because the student's current writing is always my main research. But it will give me a head start in terms of what to look for as I read the writing.

Student Conference Sheets

Several years ago, a group of fourth-grade teachers and I did a two-month inquiry around the question, "How can we get students to better verbalize their strengths and next steps?" We felt that although reading and writing workshop instruction was improving overall, there wasn't an accountability factor naturally built in for students. To address this, we started to give students quizzes based on their try-it sections and recent lessons. As I described in Chapter 7, the purpose was not to trick students but to solidify their knowledge. We then wanted to bring in the same expectation for one-on-one instruction. If we were offering tailor-made instruction with conferences, shouldn't students feel somewhat accountable for knowing what their strengths and current next steps were?

One strategy that resulted was the student conference sheet. Not only would students have a better chance of remembering the content of a conference if they also wrote down the teaching points, but they now had a written record of their own learning. We had students glue their conference sheet in the back of their writing notebook, where it was easy to access. As the teacher wrote down the teaching points in his or her record, so did the student.

Conference Examples

The following two transcripts of conferences in their entirety illustrate how the different teaching steps might sound with actual students when teaching specific craft. In these transcripts, unlike in the abridged one we saw earlier, the students' voices are fully included to reflect an actual conference. The following transcripts also differ from the preceding abridged ones in that the parts of the conference are not labeled here, because I wanted this transcript to read like an actual conference. Even so, you should still be able to identify transitions and teaching strategies, such as naming the skills, saying why the skills are good, teaching forward, and having students say the teaching back to me.

Tomás

Tomás, a fourth-grade English language learner, was writing personal narrative entries in his notebook when we met for a conference. Figures 10.2a and 10.2b are samples from Tomás's writing notebook.

FIGURE 10.2A

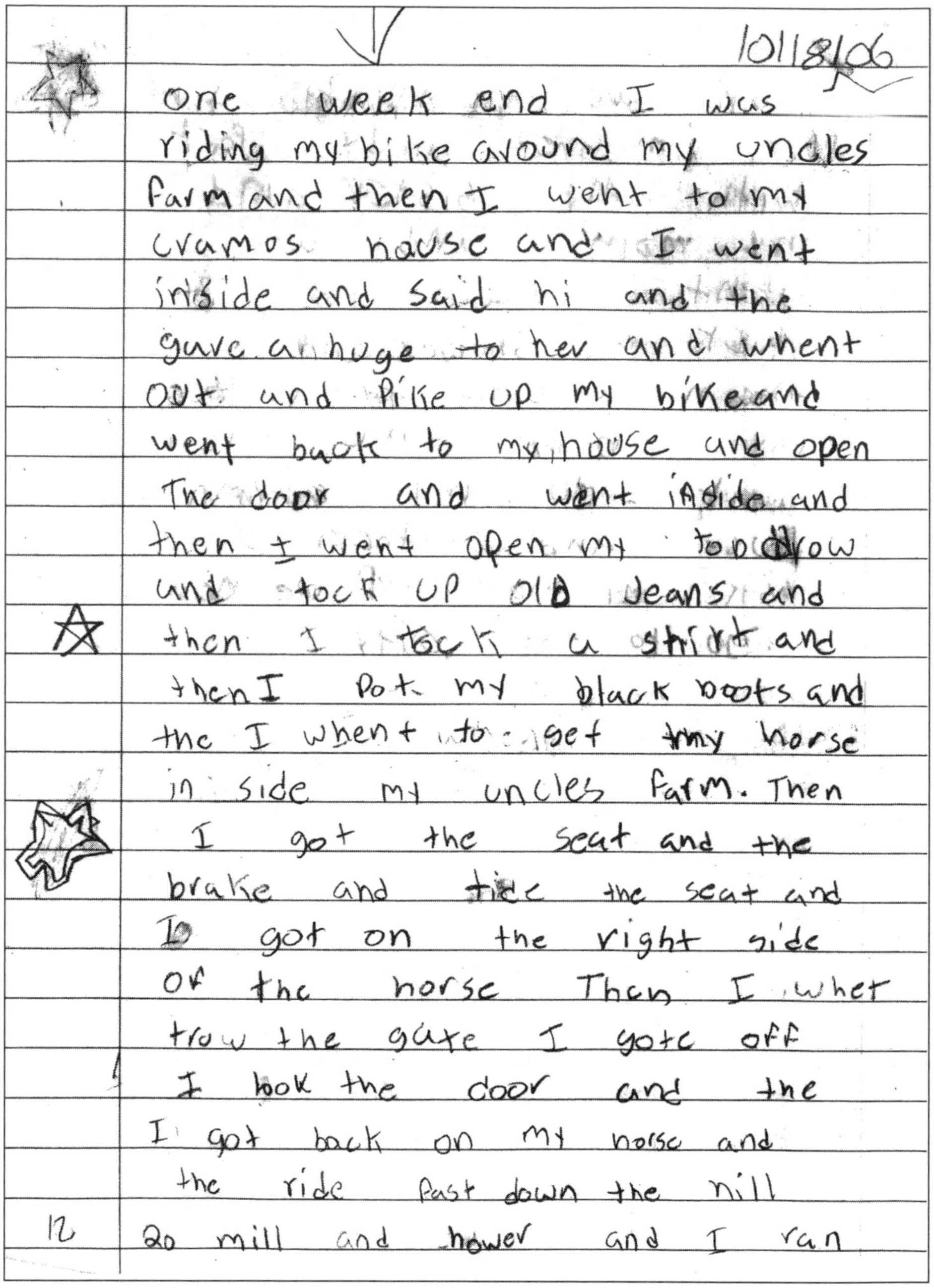

> 10/18/06
>
> one week end I was riding my bike around my uncles farm and then I went to my cramos house and I went inside and said hi and the gave a huge to her and whent out and pike up my bike and went back to my house and open The door and went inside and then I went open my to drow und tock up old Jeans and then I tock a shirt and then I Pot my black boots and the I whent to get my horse in side my uncles farm. Then I got the seat and the brake and tiec the seat and I got on the right side of the horse Then I wher trow the gate I gote off I took the door and the I got back on my horse and the ride fast down the hill
>
> 12   Qo mill and hower and I ran

"Play-by-play" is a writing strategy described in *Units of Study for Teaching Writing, Grades 3–5* (2006) by Lucy Calkins et al.

Liz: Hi Tomás. How has your writing been going?

Tomás: Pretty good.

Liz: Can you tell me a little bit about what you've been working on? It looks like you've been working hard today.

Tomás: I've written lots of pages. This here is what I did today. This one took me three pages. And then my teacher was teaching us "play-by-play."

FIGURE 10.2B

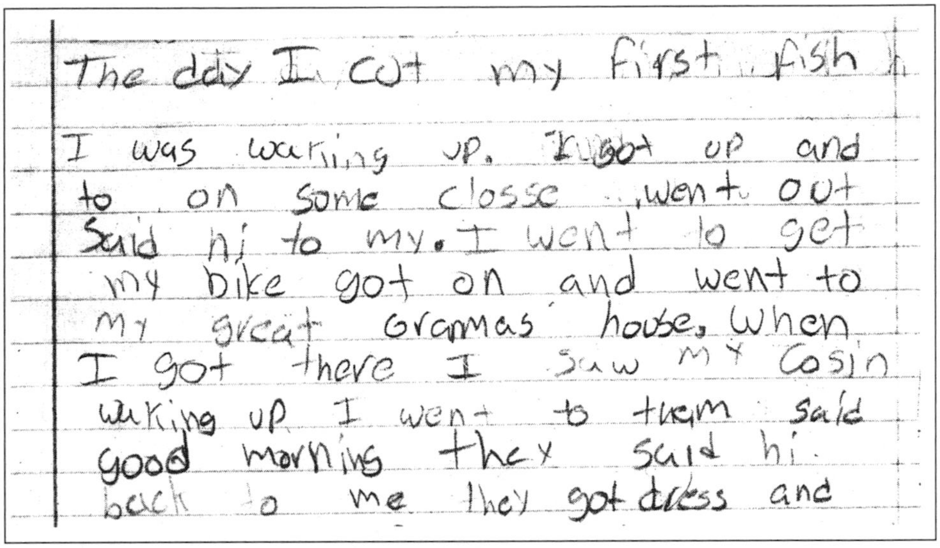

> The day I cut my first fish
>
> I was waking up. I got up and
> to on some closse ...went out
> Said hi to my. I went to get
> my bike got on and went to
> my great Grammas' house, when
> I got there I saw my Cosin
> waking up I went to them said
> good morning they said hi.
> back to me they got dress and

Liz: So, you took this idea and then when you did play-by-play you doubled the amount you wrote? (He nods.) That's great. Do you have any plans for how the rest of this entry is going to go?

Tomás: I don't know. I'm not sure yet.

I make these comments as I read. It's like I am researching out loud. Although I have not decided on which strength to actually teach, I do mention strengths along the way.

Liz: Okay. Can I read it? . . . Oh, now you're including what you were wearing. That's a great detail. . . . You know what, you do something that I was just doing in my last conference. When you wrote, "I went in the water deeper and deeper," that's kind of a craft thing when you repeat words. That's nice. Instead of just saying the water was deeper. There's something about repeating words. . . . I like how you say "mango tree." It gives me a good image in my head. And this is still the same entry right? (He nods his head as we look at the second page.)

Liz: Now is this is a different memory here? (I point to a third page of writing.)

Tomás: No it's the same thing.

Liz: Oh, okay. Let me tell you one thing you do as a writer that is so fantastic. Do you know what the word *volume* means?

Tomás: Yeah.

Liz: What?

Tomás: Like in the radio. Or the way you speak, how loud you speak. Or how loud the radio is. Like the volume makes how loud it is. (I didn't expect Tomás to mention volume in this way, but when he said it, it made total sense that he would understand this word in relation to something in his everyday life rather than writing.)

Liz: Good. So if you have a little bit of sound and you turn it up, you have more volume. So it gets bigger. The same is true in writing. You know how with the radio if you have a lot of volume the sound fills up the air? In writing, teachers talk about volume, which means how much a student is writing. What happens is, sometimes in writing workshop, with some kids you look at their notebook and they have like . . .

Tomás: Short entries?

Liz: Yeah, like five lines and then a lot of blank space and on the next page is five lines and then maybe the next day they write four lines. And the thing is, by the time a week is up, they really haven't written that much.

Tomás: Yeah, like maybe a page.

Liz: Right. So one of your strengths is your volume. You're writing a lot. That's so important because it's hard to get better if you're not writing a lot. That is one of your biggest strengths. So, can you say back to me, what am I saying you're good at as a writer?

Tomás: I'm good at finishing a page and writing a lot of details. I almost never write just two lines and just go to another page and write two lines and go to the next page and write four lines. I wrote all the way to page forty-nine.

Liz: Yeah, you wrote a lot. Do you remember the teacher term I used?

Tomás: Ummm . . .

Liz: Volume.

Tomás: Oh, yeah.

Liz: So, if you ever hear a teacher say, "Oh, this student needs to work on volume," that wouldn't be you. You're writing a lot.

Liz: Okay. Are you done or are you going to keep working on this?

Tomás: I finished this one. Now I'm on this one. (He shows me the entry in Figure 10.2b.)

Liz: And what are your plans for this entry?

Tomás: Well I want to write about this one for at least today and tomorrow because I really like the topic. I might even choose it to publish.

Liz: What's this one about? "The day I caught my first fish . . ." Cool memory! . . . One thing you could work on is something I taught in a conference a little while ago, which is ending your sentences with periods. Even if you're doing play-by-play, you don't want to be like . . . this happened then this happened then this happened. . . . You want to pause after every sentence. And that means you put a period. And in fourth grade, although it's going to take a little effort at first, it's so important. When you say a sentence and it's over . . . you stop.

Tomás: So here I should take that *then* out and put a period?

Liz: You can if you want to, but this notebook is meant to show how you grow as a writer. It's not that I want you to go back and fix everything. It's just that, from now on, it's something you should start doing in your writing.

It's really important to start ending your sentences with periods. It helps the reader know when you finish a thought, but also it helps you as a writer. When you write about one idea, you stop and then before

I knew early on in the conference that I would probably help Tomás the most if we focused on ending sentences with periods. So, my research questions at this time were more for clarifying his intentions so that I could teach forward.

The language I use to describe why periods are important is very similar to the language I use in mini-lessons. When I find something that works, there's not much reason to change the way I say it.

I model by writing in the air, although I could have used a piece of paper as well.

Teaching forward

you go on to the next thing, you can ask yourself, "Hmmm. What else do I want to say about that?" For example, if I was writing about going to the beach, I might write, "We went to the beach and built sand castles and it was so much fun and then we were hungry so we had lunch and . . ." But when I use periods, I would say, "We built sand castles." Then I would say to myself, "Hmmm. What else do I want to say about the sand castles? Oh . . . (I pretend to write in the air) . . . We used our red buckets to make mounds with wet sand . . . *period*. After making five mounds, we made holes with our finger and pretended they were windows . . . *period*." So I want you to start doing the same thing. Write a thought and then . . . put a period.

Liz: So, now you're working on the time you got your first fish. And what part are you at now?

Tomás: At the part when I was playing with my cousins.

Liz: Is that before or after you caught the fish?

Tomás: Before.

Liz: Okay, so without me sitting here, write a little bit more. And what do you think I'm going to ask you to do?

Tomás: Two or three sentences with periods. Or question marks.

Liz: Exactly, whatever is going to end the thought. You're right that it doesn't have to be a period. It could be a question mark. Good point. Okay, I'll be back in a few minutes. (I take these few minutes to walk around and see how other students are doing.)

(When I return to Tomás, he has added to his entry, as shown in Figure 10.3.)

Liz: Okay, can I see?

Tomás: Want me to read it?

Liz: Sure.

(Tomás reads his entry out loud.)

Liz: Excellent! And you used those periods without me being there. Which makes me think you can do it tomorrow too. Can you say back to me what you just did as a writer?

Tomás: Put a period when I write a sentence.

Liz: Right. Keep trying to do that from now on, okay?

(I record notes from my conference with Tomás on my conference sheet. See Figure 10.4.)

As shown in the conference sheet in Figure 10.4, I used the "Maybe Next Time" column to record a possible teaching point for the next conference. Of course I would have liked for Tomás's use of periods to lead to more sentences that add description rather than sentences that continue to list events. But I've also come to value that teaching one small skill at a time is more realistic and creates a more solid foundation on which other skills can build.

FIGURE 10.3

> The day I cut my first fish h
>
> I was wacking up. I got up and
> to on some closse. went out
> said hi to my. I went to get
> my bike got on and went to
> my great Gramas' house. When
> I got there I saw my cosin
> wacking up. I went to them said
> good morning they said hi
> back to me they got dress and
> we played for a while. We played
> with the sinder block to through
> rocks in them. But then I toll them
> that I have to go home. I went
> to get my bike and went home.
>
> When I got ther I had to
> wash the dishes. When I was
> done I went to take a rest.

FIGURE 10.4

Name _Tomas_

Date	Working on...	Strength	Next Step	Maybe next time...
11/5	when caught first fish	volume	end sentences with periods	write about small moment

Jordan

Jordan, a fourth grader, was in the middle of writing a first draft for a personal narrative unit of study. Her teacher had already taken the students through the process of writing an outline and using the outline to guide the writing of a first draft. Figure 10.5 shows where Jordan was with her draft when we met for our conference.

FIGURE 10.5

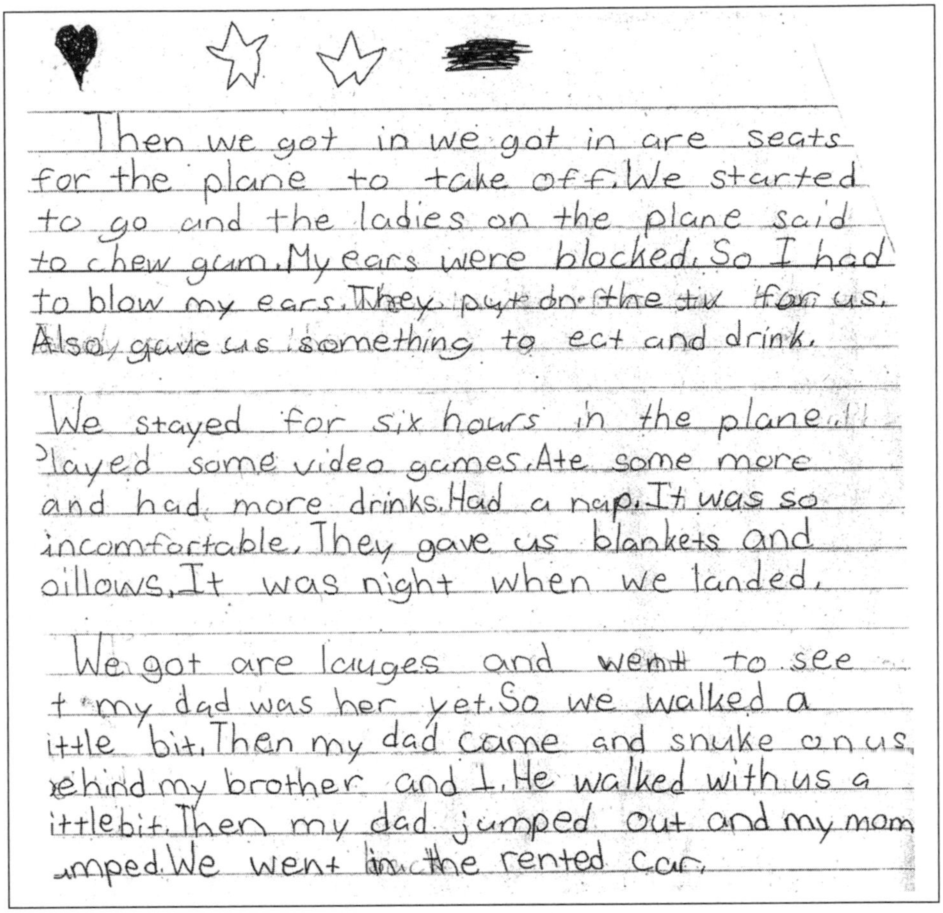

Then we got in we got in are seats for the plane to take off. We started to go and the ladies on the plane said to chew gum. My ears were blocked. So I had to blow my ears. They put on the tiv for us. Also gave us something to ect and drink.

We stayed for six hours in the plane. Played some video games. Ate some more and had more drinks. Had a nap. It was so incomfortable. They gave us blankets and pillows. It was night when we landed.

We got are lauges and went to see t my dad was her yet. So we walked a ittle bit. Then my dad came and snuke on us. behind my brother and I. He walked with us a ittlebit. Then my dad jumped out and my mom amped. We went in the rented car.

Liz: So Jordan, how has writing this draft been for you?

Jordan: I really liked it.

Liz: How come?

Jordan: Cause every time I write about a sentence it reminds me of when I did that thing.

Liz: Yeah, that's a nice way to put it. It is kind of like reliving the memory. That's so true. So, what you are working on now?

Jordan: Well I have this outline for my first draft and I'm on number five.

Liz: Let's see. Great planning. So, tell me a little bit about where you are in the writing process.

Jordan: Well, we did our outlines last week and then I think I'm supposed to be ready to edit soon because we have our writing celebration next week.

Liz: Very exciting. That will be great. Can I read your draft? (I read it for a minute.) You know, one thing you do really well, and maybe you hear this all the time, is that you write in complete sentences consistently, meaning all the time. And one reason that's good is because it means you're actually ready to write some more complicated sentences, which if you're doing run-ons—do you know what a run on is? (She shakes her head.) You go on and on and you never put a period.

Jordan: I've done that before somewhere here.

Liz: Well, you can still write a long sentence and it's doesn't mean it's a run-on sentence.

Jordan: Yeah, but I have this sentence that goes aaaaall the way like this and then stops right here.

Liz: But that's still kind of a sentence on its own. A run-on would go on and on and on and then maybe down here put a period.

Another thing I noticed is that you're starting to use dialogue. Like here when you have a person announcing something. Dialogue adds sound to writing and it helps bring the memory to life for me. It's something you actually might want to do more of.

Can you say back to me what are two things I just said you do well as a writer?

Jordan: Ummm, write sentences, complete sentences, and . . .

Liz: Something about sound.

Jordan: Oh yeah, dialogue. I wrote some dialogue.

Liz: Yes, those are two great things. . . . I'm going to write those two things in my conference sheet under "Strengths." (She watches as I write her strengths.)

You're working on this part of the outline, right? . . . Wow, that's a lot of numbers there. That's a lot of stuff to cover.

Jordan: Yeah, we did our outlines a couple of days ago. And I'm right here on number five.

Liz: So you're on the part when you got picked up at the airport?

Okay, actually . . . (while I reread her entries) I think today, because I think you're ready for it, I'm going to show you what has lately been one of my favorite words. Remember I said you were doing a really good job with complete sentences? And that you're ready to write more complex ones? A really good word that can help you do that, it's a simple word, is . . . *as*. So, instead of writing a single sentence, then a single sentence, then a single sentence . . . (I draw a visual on scrap paper) you can kind of join two actions with *as*. Sometimes it can start the sentence, like, "As the plane started to go up in the air, my ears popped." Or, "My ears popped as the plane started to go up in the air." You can put the *as* in the middle. See how it could join two things? Because I could have said, "The plane went up in the air. Then my ears popped." But what word did I use to join those two sentences, those two actions?

Jordan: *As*.

Liz: Yeah, *as*. So it doesn't mean every sentence now you use *as*, because that would be too much. Just once in a while.

Whenever I mention a student is writing in complete sentences, I always look for another strength to teach, because using periods is something they already *know* they do well. I just like to give them the "writing" reason why it's good.

This might have been a good time to have her say the Why back—*why* is it good to add dialogue?

I saw that she could develop each paragraph more (each paragraph represented a number on the outline). I thought about reworking the outline with her, which could have been an option. But I decided she was too far along, and she was going to publish in the next week. Since I had noticed she was ready to write longer sentences, I decided to teach forward into that instead.

I am giving the Why in several small parts. It might have been good to be even more explicit about how putting more information in one sentence can give a packed image to the reader.

Let's see. You are about to go to the part in your draft when you're in the airport right? So you could use *as* to join two actions. "I was doing this as . . ." Or you could join an action and a sound.

I'll let you write for a few minutes. Do you think if you write maybe three or four more sentences you can try the *as* thing?

Jordan: Okay.

Liz: Can you say back to me why I am teaching you about doing this thing with *as*?

Jordan: Ummm.

Liz: Want me to just tell you again?

Jordan: Yeah

Liz: Okay. You have good sentences. But they are all kind of the same length. (I draw the visual again.) You are ready to write more complex sentences. Because you don't want every sentence the same size. And one way you can write cool, longer sentences is to join two things, two different sentences with *as*.

So let's do one out loud. Could you give me an example of something in the airport?

I realized she wasn't quite ready, so this was one of those times I had her talk out an example before she wrote it.

Jordan: Ummm . . . "As we got off the airplane, I saw my dad."

Liz: Perfect! Yeah. In fact you used *as* the other way, which is great! Because you can start a sentence with *as* or you could put it in the middle . . . whatever you want. That's great!

Okay, just write for a few more minutes and see if you can put in one of those *as* sentences.

(Jordan works on her entry for a few minutes. Her addition is shown in Figure 10.6.)

Liz: (I read Jordan's added sentences.) Very nice! So, can you say what you did here in this sentence in terms of a craft skill we just worked on?

Jordan: I wrote a sentence with *as*.

Liz: Yes. And that's a great way to write a longer sentence. So, you can start doing this in any entry, okay? Great.

(The conference sheet showing the record of Jordan's strength and next step is shown in Figure 10.7.)

Most teachers would probably agree that having enough time to see all students as frequently as they wish is one of the greatest challenges of conferring,

FIGURE 10.6

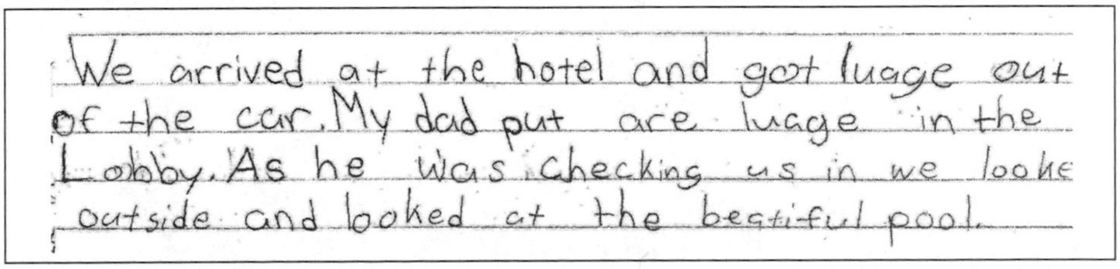

We arrived at the hotel and got luage out of the car. My dad put are luage in the Lobby. As he was checking us in we looke outside and looked at the beatiful pool.

FIGURE 10.7

		Conference Sheet		
		Name ___Jordan___		

Date	Working on...	Strength	Next Step	Maybe next time...
June 12	Draft California	Complete sentences. dialogue.	using AS to join two ideas.	

whether it is with reading or writing. Time is certainly one of the reasons why my conferring has developed the way it has. When I meet with students, efficiency and productivity is important. I just haven't had time to have lengthy conversations that may be wonderful, but aren't primarily focused on moving students' writing skills in some way in a short amount of time. Efficient conferences do not preclude students having a voice in the conference. There are also so many places in writing workshop that honor students' voices—their independence in topic choice, the sharing of work with each other, self-editing, peer conferring, and of course publications and celebrations. I still want the student's voice to be as strong as possible in the conference. After all, writing is still a personal and creative process even if it's also an academic subject. The more a child can help direct the conference, the better. But I also do my part in coming to every conference ready to teach.

The structure of a conference is not the only way to alleviate the challenge of time. In the following chapter I discuss the idea of group conferences, which is one way to see students more often. The one-to-one format, however, is the most conducive to teaching strengths and provides an individual focus that can't be replicated in a group setting. Only the individual conference allows for the teaching of individual strengths, which is an integral part to affecting students' perception of writing and themselves as writers.

11

Group Conferring and Other Management Techniques

Did you ever have a student who was always testing your management skills but was also the one who made you laugh the most? For me, that was Marvin. Marvin was in no way an angry child or trying to be disruptive. He just had, as they say, a serious case of ants in his pants. There were so many times when he would be talking and goofing around while I was teaching. When it started to escalate I would say, with all my first-year teacher expertise, "Marvin!" Every single time he would give this big-eyed, genuinely surprised look, then immediately put his hands together, look down at his lap and shout, "Sorry!" I would continue teaching, but inevitably his ants would get the better of him. Usually he would start with just a little movement in his chair, and it would gradually build until he was back to where he started. Then I would say, "Marvin!" again. He would look surprised, again, and snap back to his apologetic pose. My favorite memory of Marvin is of the time he somehow got hold of a science kit that was sitting on the ledge near him. I looked back from the chalkboard after writing a math problem, and there was Marvin with a magnifying glass up to his face looking straight at me. One eye was squinting and the other eye that was behind the glass was literally the size of a grapefruit. It was the funniest thing I'd seen all month.

Of course, most of the time, anything that interrupted instruction usually was not that funny. That first year I felt a tremendous gap between how much I was "supposed" to be teaching my students and how much I was actually accomplishing. Nowhere were my management skills tested more than during independent writing and reading time when I was trying to confer. Like many teachers, I had two main concerns:

1. Not having enough time
2. Students being off-task

These issues of time and students being off-task can span the whole school day. And every teacher has his or her own management system and way of dealing with unpredictable issues as they arise. Conferring requires an extra element of independence, where, in a sense, students are supposed to manage themselves. While there is no magic solution, this chapter offers some organizational and instructional techniques that can help with the management of conferring and independent writing.

Group Conferring

For several years, I thought that any kind of group work during independent writing would go against the philosophy of conferring and writing workshop in general. But, like many educators, I started realizing that the issue of not seeing children and their writing frequently enough was very real. This was not a reflection on the management of classrooms so much as on the reality of conferring. While being aware of the length of our mini-lessons can help, seeing and teaching one student at a time in any kind of quality way just can't be done that quickly. Classrooms that have the maximum number of students allowed or that have only forty-five minutes for writing workshop versus an hour are even more challenged by time.

I don't believe the term *group conferring* refers to any universal structure. But I purposefully chose this term over *guided writing*, which is similar in structure to guided reading, because I wanted to stay closer to the idea of a conference where there is explicit teaching about one thing rather than pulling groups together to "guide" them through their writing. Group conferring is still an evolving idea for me, and there are other forms of group support. But I thought it would be worthwhile to share my current thinking about how this kind of support could be brought into the classroom.

Research and Deciding

A group conference can still follow the research-decide-teach model. What differs is how the research and teaching are conducted. One option is to be aware of similar needs of students as you are conferring individually. Calkins, Hartman, and White point out in their book *One to One* (2005) that if they notice "four or five children have a hard time choosing topics, focusing their narratives, or using the word wall, instead of giving each child a variation of the same conference, the teacher needs to gather these children for a group conference" (32). This research and noticing of needs can also be done outside of class time by reading student notebooks, which allows teachers to get a bird's eye view of their students' writing as a whole. This is an advantage unto itself, just in terms of knowing your students and planning for lessons, but teachers can also use this as a time to look for any students who have common needs. Figuring out groups can be as simple as seeing a need in one student's writing and then, as you continue to read other students' notebooks, jotting down anyone else's name who fits in that category.

Because this kind of group support is skill centered, there has to be a specific reason to pull certain students together. The reasoning should be based on seeing common needs in certain students' writing, not based on seeing which students are at about the same overall writing ability, which might be the case for a guided writing group. Ideally, if a teacher asked me, "What made you choose those three students?" My answer would be something like, "They all need help putting quotations in the right place" or "All three of them need to work on writing beyond the end of the page." In a primary classroom, I might notice three or four students who all need to work on putting spaces between their words.

In order to best illustrate how a group conference might develop from the research to the teaching phase, the following section describes the three stages of a group conference I taught in a second-grade classroom. A group of teachers from the Tobin School and I conducted a two-month inquiry around the following topic: "How can we best support the different levels of writers in our classroom?" Ms. Duarte and Ms. Gann had some second graders who were writing several pages during independent writing and other students who were still struggling with some letter-sound relationships. Ms. Verdu, a teacher previously mentioned in Chapter 6, taught a combined class of first- and second-grade English language learners, and so naturally had an even wider range of students. With forty-five minutes for writing workshop, all three were feeling as if they weren't seeing students often enough and it was hard to plan mini-lessons that were applicable to everyone.

Although students can be pulled together for a group conference for a range of reasons, we decided to focus on skills that were hampering writing as opposed to looking for "cool teaching opportunities." This of course meant we were probably (but not necessarily) going to choose students for the group conferences who were writing below grade level. Teachers would still continue with one-to-one conferences, so we only looked for two or three groups in each classroom to work with over the next week.

Based on previous conferences, teachers had an idea of some common needs that would surface in their research. Ms. Gann and I noticed that there were several students who could use some support with using periods. Many students in the class were writing run-on sentences once in a while or beginning sentences with *And then*, but there were three students in particular who were barely using periods at all. Ms. Gann had already given several lessons addressing this issue, so we agreed this would be a good group to pull together for a group conference. Because the use of periods is such a common need in elementary writing, a mini-lesson in Chapter 7 and the conference with Tomás in Chapter 10 provide teachers with other ways to teach this skill.

Teaching a Group Conference

When I pulled this group of students together at a guided reading table, I explained to them how this was going to be similar to, but not exactly the same as, a one-to-one conference:

> *You know how in a conference we always teach you a strength and a next step? Well, we'll still keep doing that in regular conferences. But right now we're just going to work on one thing, which is ending sentences with periods. I know Ms. Gann did a lesson about periods last week, but today we're going to work on this—just the four of us.*

The next part was very similar to a conference or mini-lesson in that it followed the What-Why format of directly stating what was being taught and saying why it was good. Since I knew they had had a mini-lesson on this topic, I first asked them if they remembered why it was so important to end sentences with periods, and then expanded on the explanation where it was needed.

Next, I modeled the skill myself, similar to the way I would in a mini-lesson. All three students watched as I demonstrated writing a sentence, putting a period, and then pausing to think about what else I wanted to say before writing my next sentence. Before they tried it themselves, I asked each student to say back to me what we were working on and why it was important.

Until that point, the conference resembled a small mini-lesson with an audience of three. But with such a small number of students, I could maintain the accountability that exists in individual conferences by asking them each to say the teaching point back to me. Since Dante had an answer in mind, he went first. But each of the other students had to offer an answer as well. I encouraged them to use their own words. I was not looking for students to just repeat what the first student said.

Then it was the students' turn to try it in their own writing. I directed them back to their current entries and asked them to write one more sentence each, reminding them to just write one more thought . . . and then put a period. One student didn't get started right away, so I quickly looked at her entry and gave her a more personalized prompt.

What are you writing about? Your brother's birthday party? Great. Okay, so just write one more sentence about that. Go ahead.

As with the gradual release model that I would use in mini-lessons on this topic, I had them write two more sentences once they were done with the first one. After students had written several sentences, it was time to give more independence. I said the following to them:

All right, so now write a little bit more. I want you to show me you can end your sentences with periods on your own before you go back to your desks. I'll give you a few minutes and then see how you're doing.

Because the habit of writing without periods can be a strong one, I wanted to emphasize not just the use of this skill, but also their capability of continuing to write with periods on their own. The students continued writing, but without a set number of sentences to write. The conference at this point started to resemble the stage in guided reading when students read quietly to themselves. As they each wrote at their own pace, I checked in with one student at a time and either gave some positive feedback or supported them in some way if needed. Sitting at the guided reading table made it easy to move from student to student as they wrote their sentences.

Students finished their try-its at different times, which allowed me to give individual attention to each student before they went back to their desks. The positive feedback I gave emphasized their independence in addition to their ability to write sentences that end with periods. After a student had written three or four sentences on his or her own, I said something like the following:

Excellent. Look at that. (If other students weren't done yet, I might quietly read the sentences out loud, accenting a pause wherever they put a period.) That's great! And did I look over and say please put a period? Or did you do

it yourself? . . . Right, so now I know you can keep doing this on your own.
I'll try to check on how you're doing in a little bit, okay?

No matter what you teach in a group conference, you can quickly check back with those students toward the end of writing workshop. Whether a teacher does a formal or informal check-back, it only takes a minute or two.

Although students were not getting an individual conference, I knew it was still important to record the teaching point on each of their conference sheets. These students were not going to be meeting again the way students do in guided reading, so there was no point in keeping track of them as a group. After this conference, I wrote "Writing with periods" in the "Next Steps" column of their conference sheets. Because I didn't teach any strengths, I just left that column blank. Later on, I started using sticky labels to record group conferences. I wrote the teaching point on three blank labels from a sheet I kept in my binder and then stuck them on the conference sheet of each student in the group. Using the labels gave me a quick visual to indicate that the teaching had been from a group conference rather than an individual one.

As students move up in age, group conferences might be less about addressing issues of concern and focus more on craft skills. For example, when reading through the notebooks of a third-grade class, I noticed there were some students who were doing fine with volume and mechanics but were doing a lot more telling than showing. I decided I would pull these three students together and teach them about adding sound—specifically, writing sounds without *I heard*. I used a similar structure as with the second-grade group conference, including modeling examples. When it was time for students to try it themselves, I thought, "Why not use the try-it section in the notebook first?" Writing with sound wasn't a skill that could be used in every sentence, like using periods, but I did want students to try writing with sounds right after I taught it. Giving students a quick prompt for a try-it in a group conference allowed them to try the craft technique in isolation before adding the challenge of using it in a way that naturally fit with their entry.

When time was up for the try-it, each student in the group conference took a turn sharing what he or she wrote before they applied the skill to their current entries. It was wonderful for students to hear each other using the same skill but in their own unique way. Figures 11.1 and 11.2 are examples of their work. The example in Figure 11.2 is written by Jordan, whose conference I described in the previous chapter. You might recall I had taught her about using *as* to connect two ideas. Without any prompting from me, she used this additional craft technique during this group conference try-it. To me, this is a reminder that when craft instruction is small and specific, it can quickly become part of a student's skill set. Jordan was able to focus her attention on learning a new craft technique without forgetting what she had previously learned.

FIGURE 11.1

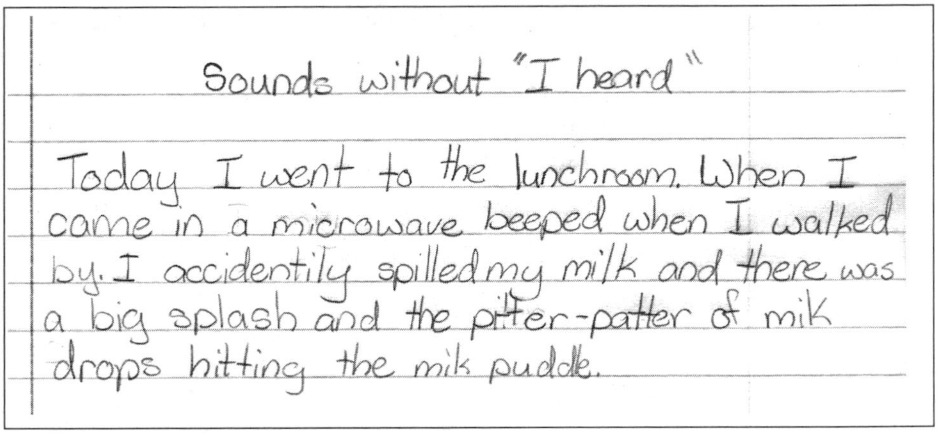

> ## Sounds without "I heard"
>
> Today I went to the lunchroom. When I came in a microwave beeped when I walked by. I accidently spilled my milk and there was a big splash and the pitter-patter of milk drops hitting the milk puddle.

FIGURE 11.2

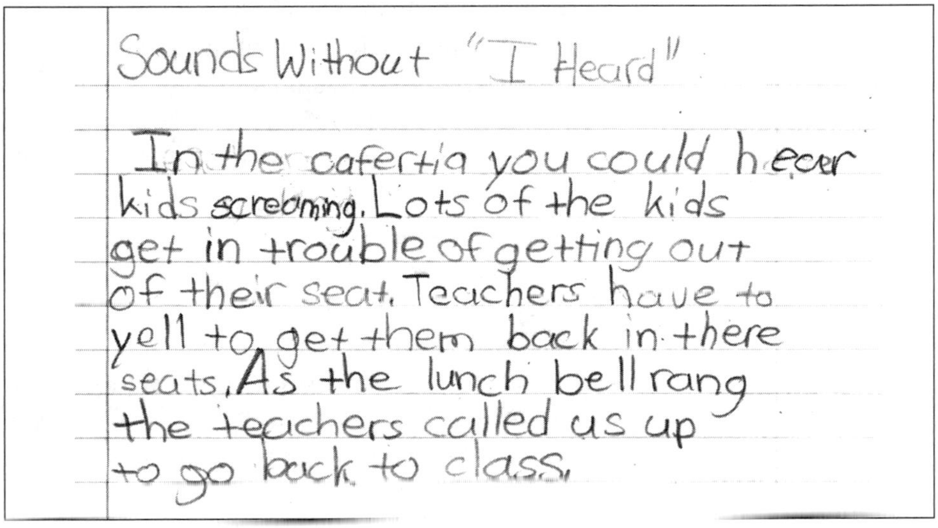

> ## Sounds Without "I Heard"
>
> In the cafertia you could heer kids screaming. Lots of the kids get in trouble of getting out of their seat. Teachers have to yell to get them back in there seats. As the lunch bell rang the teachers called us up to go back to class.

Scheduling Group Conferences

For any teachers interested in doing group conferences, I would recommend developing a schedule that will allow you to maintain one-to-one conferring. I'll admit it felt great to work with three students at once. It felt very productive. Conferring only with groups might mean you "see" more students in one week, but letting go of individual conferring would be a tremendous loss. It's really only in one-to-one conferences that you can offer tailor-made teaching. Trying to fit everyone into a group conference would also mean that you end up matching together people with the most common traits rather than really looking at what would help particular students the most. You would also lose the forum for teaching strengths. It's not that you couldn't infuse some positive comments about students' writing at the start of a group conference. You could. But the impact would not be nearly as powerful as when you are teaching strengths one on one.

There are other aspects of management besides group conferring that affect both the quality and quantity of independent writing and conferring time. The rest of this chapter looks at some possible ways to support the management of a writing workshop classroom, starting with the management of min-lessons. Mini-lessons generally begin writing workshop time, and students usually move into independent writing right after the mini-lesson. If you want to ensure that you'll be able to confer productively during that time, it's important to set a focused and productive tone beginning with the mini-lesson.

The Management of Mini-Lessons

The physical layout of a classroom can play a large part in the management of mini-lessons. Teaching the mini-lesson in a rug area or an area of small chairs shaped in a U brings students closer together and closer to the teacher. Pam Pitts, a fifth-grade teacher, didn't have enough chairs for a separate mini-lesson area, so she made a circle of "chairs" out of upside-down milk crates and chair pillows. One benefit of these "rug" areas, whether there is an actual rug or not, is that all students can feel your presence. Being within the teacher's immediate view can naturally make students feel more accountable for paying attention. Another benefit of a rug area is that students can be away from their desks during the lesson, which keeps them from being preoccupied by items in or on their desks. The actual physical transition of moving to the rug area is also a benefit. Giving students a chance to move gives the mini-lesson time its own visual space, and it can be somewhat preventative when the expectation is that students are about to sit and write for twenty to thirty minutes during independent writing time.

From what I have just said, you might think I would say that rug areas are critical, but that is not the case. If one can be created, then that's great. But if it's not possible, there are ways to mimic some of the aspects of a rug area. It may seem like a simple act, but I recommend giving students one minute before the lesson starts to get up and turn their chairs so that they are all facing the teacher. The most natural way for anyone to look at something for more than a few seconds is straight ahead. Very often, the reason students are looking in their desk or at their friends rather than at the teacher is because that is what's in front of them if they look straight ahead. Asking students to face me when their bodies are not facing me goes against the natural human tendency to be comfortable. When I have students turn their chairs, on the other hand, the most comfortable thing to look at is . . .me. Also, allowing students one or two minutes to stand up and turn their chairs gives them a chance to get up and move. They don't move across the room, but they do move. This transition and different arrangement, even if it's just a slight difference, visually and physically defines the beginning of a mini-lesson.

Introducing the idea of turning chairs or moving to a rug area as a transition is best taught during a management lesson. Compared to just telling students in the form of directions, any management mini-lesson makes room for teacher modeling and explanation of how this will help the flow of writing workshop, and gives students a chance to try out any new expectations.

An important overall expectation for all lessons is that students consistently look at the teacher during the lesson. Although every teacher might agree with this expectation in theory, I believe it happens less often than teachers realize. I'll admit that when I first started teaching, I didn't have the expectations that I do now that all students look at me throughout the entire lesson. I think somewhere deep down I felt that if I expected everyone to pay perfect attention the whole time, I would never be able to start teaching. Also, my focus when I first started teaching was more on what I was saying, not so much on whether or not every student was receiving my lesson. Of course, I've learned management tips such as the "stop in mid-sentence and look baffled that they are not looking at you" look. But I have also found that as the content of my lessons has gotten more specific, it has become easier to genuinely expect active listening from all students.

Believe me, I am not saying that some classrooms are not more challenging than others in terms of getting students' attention in general. There are also the occasional students who, whether they are having a bad day or hanging onto something that happened in the lunchroom, won't pay attention no matter what. My point is more about the fact that it is easier to expect full attention when you know that what you are teaching is clear and attainable.

Teaching Expectations in September

Even when students arrive in September already knowing what it means to have a writing conference, it's helpful if they learn exactly how conferring and writing workshop will look in your room. I typically spend at least one writing workshop period just teaching transitions. It's important to emphasize the word *teaching*. I do not just tell them my expectations about what to do before and after the mini-lesson, or how to get ready for the share at the end of independent writing. I model the expectations myself, explain why they are important, and have students try them out several times. When I teach these transition expectations in isolation, apart from any actual writing, everyone can meet them. Although being able to do these transitions may seem simple on the surface, I have conveyed the very clear message of, "You all know these transitions and can do them."

I have learned to include within most transitions a few minutes for students to talk softly—something I now make explicit to students. I could tell students that after the mini-lesson I expect them to go silently back to their desks (or turn their chairs around) and begin writing. But do I really expect this to happen all year long? One of my earliest lessons as a teacher was, "Mean what you say." If you say you're going to call home, call home. Otherwise you're not taking your own words seriously. And if *you're* not, why should the students? I also think this "mean what you say" rule applies to expectations we give to students. If I am going to say I expect total silence and mean it, then I am stating that even a few peeps would be unacceptable. I'm setting up a nearly impossible standard. This is especially true during those in-between times, however short, when I am not really teaching anything and students are not yet writing. If I am true to my word about students going silently back to their desks, then I would be reacting all the time. The other and more likely option would be to ignore any soft talking or small noises, because they really aren't that disruptive and it would be exhausting to respond to everything that isn't perfect silence. But that would mean I am willing to compromise for less than what I asked. So, one way to phrase expectations for transitions might sound like this:

> *After the mini-lesson is over, you have a few minutes before independent writing starts. You can talk softly, sharpen a pencil if you need to—just get comfortable. Maybe even talk quietly about what you think you might write. I'm giving you these minutes to talk quietly because the lesson is over and I know as a writer sometimes you just need a few minutes to get settled before you start writing. But when it's time for independent writing, it's time to write.*

This is a statement I can absolutely hold myself to and feel fair in holding students to as well. There is a kind of give-and-take mentality based on respect. Allowing them some time to talk softly acknowledges their experience of what it's like to be a student. But, in return, they need to respect the rules and expectations of independent writing. These comments about how expectations are set may seem trivial, but the details of language can make a difference: "Language has 'content,' but it also bears information about the speaker and how he or she views the listener and their assumed relationship" (Johnston 2004, 6). Understanding the writing experience from the student's point of view is something I can later draw upon if talking becomes a problem and I need to do a management mini-lesson on that topic. The tone would be one of surprise and disappointment:

> *Wait, I don't understand. I give you time to talk after the lesson. I do that because I know it would not be fair to just say "be silent." I give that to you. But when it's time for writing, it's time for writing. You can't talk and write about something else at the same time. It's kind of impossible. And I shouldn't have to spend time going around saying, "Get back to your writing. . . . C'mon get back to your writing." You know it's independent writing time.*

Whenever I teach this kind of management mini-lesson, the try-it consists of students practicing this transition. I have them talk (which is suddenly harder for them to do when it's part of a lesson) and then practice not talking while opening their notebooks when I say, "Okay, it's time for independent writing." They also suddenly think it's fun to do. Along with this practice comes the message that I know they know the rules. I make it clear that I had to give up a craft lesson in order to address this problem, so I hope I won't need to do it again.

On a side note, it also makes a difference when teachers talk softly during independent writing. This is true whether you are calling on your next conference, asking someone to stop talking, or offering some quick positive feedback. If teachers don't talk somewhat softly themselves, then they send the message, "Do as I say, not as I do." Whether you agree or disagree about whether teachers *should* be able to talk loudly during independent writing time, you're dealing with human nature. If the volume of one person is loud in a room, it sets a precedent for other voices.

Independence in Topic Choice

Many teachers of writing workshop know the benefits of teaching students how to come up with their own topics: they are more invested in what they write, and because a prompt was never given, students know they can't say "I'm done" as a way to stop writing. The expectation is that when students think they have finished an entry, they start a new one. They don't need the teacher to give them ideas in order to get started. This independence is essential to whole-class instruction as well as conferring. If we need time every day to give directions, prompts, or constantly offer ideas for students who are "stuck," we will have very little time for true instruction about the craft and mechanics of writing.

Adopting the idea that students don't need us to give them ideas of what to write about was a shift for me personally. Just about every writing assignment I can remember getting myself, from first grade up through high school, came from the teacher. So, during my first few years of teaching, I naturally gave prompts to my students, regardless of the genre we were studying. When I went to Teachers College and studied under Lucy Calkins, my entire view of how one could teach writing changed. I realized that students didn't need me to come up with ideas after all. I just needed to help them access their ideas.

Independence in topic choice is not something teachers should expect to happen naturally. The phrase "I don't know what to write about" can be a way for students to procrastinate, but it can also be a legitimate reason for not getting started. Sometimes the blank page, for adults as well as for children, can be intimidating or just plain overwhelming. It reminds me of the times when someone has said, "Tell me a joke." I have heard at least a hundred jokes in my lifetime thus far. Yet when someone says this, I draw a blank and can't remember any. Sometimes after a few seconds, I remember the same one or two that somehow surface during these times of pressure. There have been other times, however, when I've been out to dinner with a group of people, with little conversations happening all over the place, and suddenly one person says, "Oh! I have a good joke for you all. Okay, there are three guys all standing at the Pearly Gates, waiting to get in . . . ." And of course after this person finishes, I remember all the jokes I know that involve Saint Peter, the Pearly Gates, or angels. So I tell mine, and then there is suddenly a popcorning out of heaven jokes.

Similarly, we can't tell students to just write about anything they want and expect them to get right down to work with rich writing results. They, too, may come up with the same one or two stand-bys, which usually tend to be "My Birthday" or "My Trip to Six Flags." Students need strategies they can use independently to access those smaller, richer memories that may be lodged in their long-term memory, ones that are personal and can rarely surface from a whole-class prompt. I always spend the first few lessons of any unit of study teaching (or reviewing) strategies of how to come up with ideas in any particular genre. Like the initial joke in the dinner party example, these strategies can spark the memories that are not at the front of a student's mind. It's important that after we teach these strategy lessons, we set a clear expectation that students come up with topics on their own. A corresponding anchor chart that students can refer to can help them the next time they are stuck for an idea. This up-front investment in teaching—versus just telling—students how to be independent, complete with teacher modeling, makes a tremendous difference in how little or how much students will hang on to "I don't know what to write about."

Appendixes B, C, and D provide lessons that support student independence in writing memoir, nonfiction, and poetry.

Launching and Decorating Notebooks

One way to increase students' enthusiasm for writing is to give them time to decorate their notebooks in September. This can have a tremendous effect on the way students treat their writing notebooks and the way they view independent writing, whether they are in elementary school or high school. When it's just a standard black and white marble notebook, it is like any other notebook and the tone is very school-like. When students of any age are given time to make colorful decorations and bring photographs to put on the front, suddenly these notebooks become a reflection of their lives and who they are as individuals. Decorating notebooks is something that may not directly affect the management of independent writing, but it does impact it indirectly by encouraging students to feel more personally connected to their writing work. Indirect influences are important to consider. Not only are they preventative, but also they affect our other goal as teachers of writing, which is for students to have a positive association with writing.

Writing Spots

I highly recommend creating what I call "writing spots" in classrooms, which can double as reading spots during independent reading time. These spots are little individual nooks where students can settle in to write and can include pillows on the rug, beanbag chairs, and spots under large tables. You don't necessarily have to make lots of purchases to have good writing spots. I've created a writing spot by placing two chairs near the wall, one for students to sit on and one to put their feet on while they write. One year, I cleared out a small area on a guided reading table, put a small plant and pencil holder there, and called it "The Office." That's all it took to make this small spot desirable. Suddenly everyone wanted to sit in "The Office."

Writing spots are nice to have just for the fact that they give a few students a more ideal writing place each day, but they can also help with management. First, writing spots take advantage of the extra space in a classroom, which can cut down the number of students who are sitting next to—and potentially distracting—each other. Also, because the writing spots are desirable, they can be used as an incentive for students to get down to work in the first few minutes of independent writing. Students I work with know that before I start my first conference, I look around to see who is on task. I will tap someone on the shoulder and say quietly, "Do you want a writing spot?" to which they almost always nod their head. Some teachers include writing spots on a wheel almost like a work board so it's public information. Students know when it is their turn for a writing spot. In some ways, this makes the running of writing spots easier, but I have personally found I get more out of writing spots if students know I only give them to students who have started writing.

Intermission

Rather than having one uninterrupted session of independent writing during writing workshop, teachers can opt to break it into two sessions with what I call an "intermission." This small break can be a controlled, productive outlet for talking, which can sometimes prevent the build-up of conversation during the later part of independent writing. The intermission was another accommodation that came from thinking along preventative lines and from thinking about independent writing from the students' perspective. Even when I am at home writing, I can't go too long without having to do something—whether it is getting a drink of water or making a quick phone call. And that's when I am all by myself, sitting in a nicely cushioned chair. Those breaks make a big difference in keeping up my stamina over a long period of time, and sometimes students in a busy classroom benefit from breaks like this too.

During the intermission, which lasts about five minutes, students can talk in pairs about what they wrote or they can read each other's writing, both of which support the idea of a class being a community of writers. Some teachers are doubtful about students staying on task at this time, but given the chance, students like to talk with each other about their writing. I first tried this management strategy when I was working with a fifth-grade class that was having difficulty with stamina. After about ten minutes of independent writing, students started talking a lot, and the quality of writing went downhill. So, instead of expecting students to write for thirty-five minutes in a row, we had two sessions of fifteen minutes each, with an intermission between them. Even though the actual amount of time allotted for writing changed by only a few minutes, the break in the middle helped to keep up the quality of focused writing. Stamina is an important quality to build, of course, so having an intermission may not be appropriate for all grades at all times of the year. For some grades it might be used more in the beginning of the year or in response to students not being on task.

The only time I have students share out loud during the intermission is during a poetry unit of study. Poems are meant to be read out loud. Also, because they take less time to write than other genre, students tend to feel that they are "done" a lot sooner, even if independence expectations are in place. After hearing each other's poems during an intermission, students tend to go back to their writing with a renewed energy.

Where to Confer

Some teachers like to go to students' desks to confer, and others like having students come to a particular table in the room. There is no right place to hold conferences. Some people think conferring near other students will be disruptive. On the surface this might make sense, but students are usually not bothered by conferences next to them. And if they end up eavesdropping on a conference, it is almost always a good thing. One time I was conferring with a second grader, Nicholas, and the teaching point centered around using onomatopoeia. Nicholas explained that he was going to write the sound of a basketball going in the net but hesitated because it was not a real word in English. Based on this conversation, the concept of writing the real sound whether it's a real word or not became the teaching point (and became part of my list of

FIGURE 11.3

gathered craft). Nicholas completed the entry shown in Figure 11.3. Manuel, who was sitting nearby, overheard this conference. About ten minutes later I had a conference with Manuel, and he had written an entry about a car going "grrr." Without any prompting from me whatsoever, he had incorporated the teaching point from Nicholas's conference into his own writing. He admitted that he heard what I had taught and had decided to try it.

This is not to say teachers have to move around to have conferences. Some teachers just don't find it comfortable or they just like staying in one spot and having students come to them. My only recommendation would be to stay central. I've found that conferring at a table in the back corner of the room, although it may be where the best chair is, can cause other students not to feel as accountable for being on task. Other students will feel the teacher's presence if he or she moves two chairs to the central part of the room where he or she can look up every now and then and see everyone. It makes keeping an eye on other students much easier during a conference.

Like any aspect of teaching, managing a classroom is always a work in progress. The details of successful teaching practices sometimes don't make it into the spotlight when it comes to discussions about curriculum and instruction. I am still getting new ideas for how to manage materials and create enthusiasm for writing when I visit teachers' classrooms. I would encourage any teacher, and new teachers in particular, to seek out colleagues whose classrooms run well and find out the details of their practice.

Assessment

During one Thanksgiving vacation, I decided to go through several boxes of writing my parents had saved from when my sister and I were in elementary school. As I flipped through the many papers that were now mostly a dark yellow, laughing at the way that I too used to draw hands that looked like balls with little lines coming from all sides, I couldn't help but notice the different kinds of grades noted at the tops of my papers (see Figures 12.1a and 12.1b). I liked getting the star the best, of course, or any kind of sticker. But no matter what was at the top of the page, it was always an overall grade.

As expectations around the instruction of writing have changed, so has the assessment of writing. Instead of assigning an overall grade, many teachers now use rubrics that score different aspects of writing. Grading with rubrics helps teachers notice different aspects of writing, which then, ideally, impacts

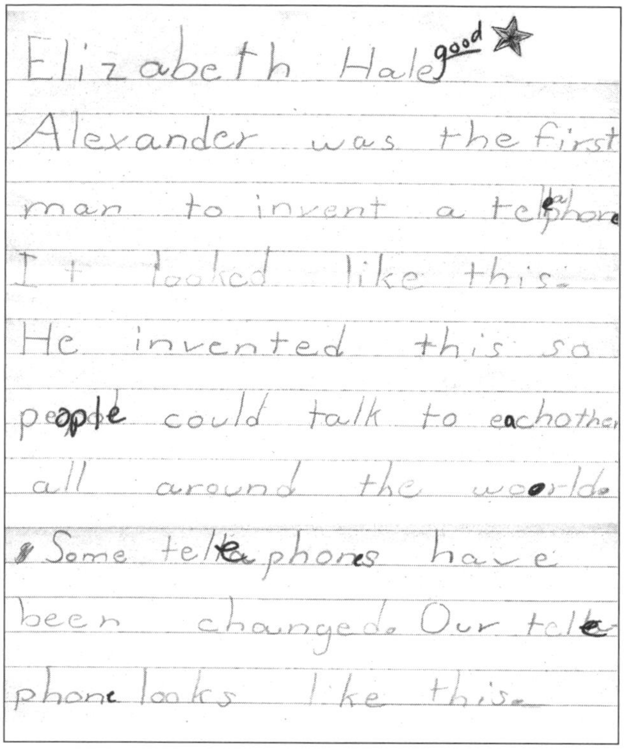

Elizabeth Hale *good* ⭐

Alexander was the first
man to invent a telephone.
I t looked like this:
He invented this so
people could talk to eachother
all around the woorld.
Some teltephones have
been changed. Our tele
phone looks like this.

FIGURE 12.1A

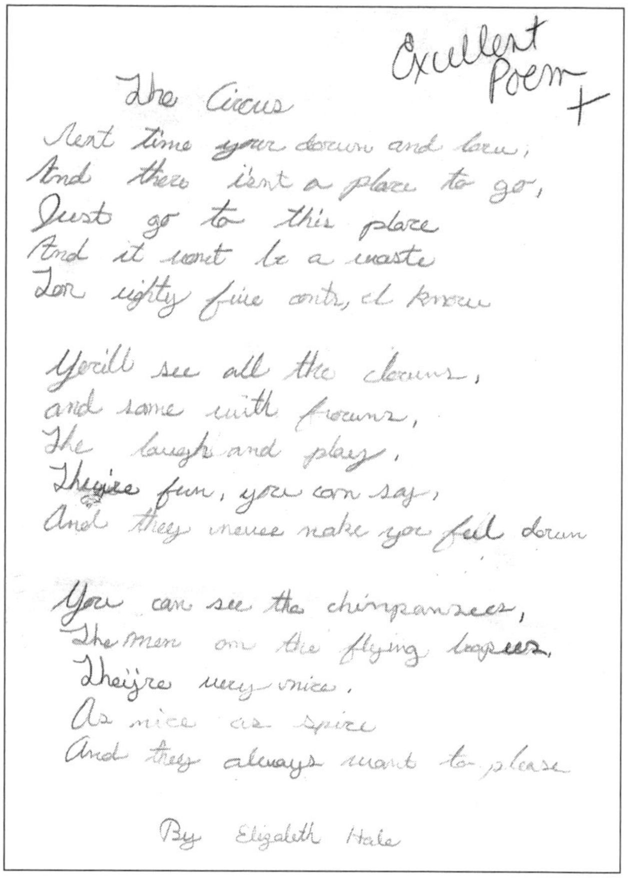

The Circus   *Excellent Poem +*

Next time your down and low,
And there isn't a place to go,
Just go to this place
And it wont be a waste
For eighty five cents, I know

Yo'ill see all the clowns,
and some with frowns,
They laugh and play,
They're fun, you can say,
And they never make you feel down

You can see the chimpanzees,
The men on the flying trapees,
They're very nice.
As nice as spice
And they always want to please

                    By Elizabeth Hale

FIGURE 12.1B

instruction. Grading students on several different criteria also honors the fact that students develop different aspects of writing at different paces.

Rubrics for writing assessment come in a variety of styles. The 6-Trait approach to teaching writing, developed by a group of educators in Oregon led by Vicki Spandel, has recently become a popular choice. Accompanying books, such as *Creating Writers* by Vicki Spandel (2005), help teachers better understand what the different traits mean and how they can support each trait in the classroom. Most standardized state tests have rubrics that show how scores are determined. In Massachusetts, for example, most fourth graders become very familiar with the rubric for the MCAS Long Composition, a standardized test that they have to take in the spring. I have also seen many different rubrics created by instructional leadership teams at the school level. Ideally, there is some consistency within a school about which style of rubric to use. The most important aspect of rubrics is not about the style that is chosen, but about how teachers can make their choice of rubric work best with their teaching so that it becomes an authentic form of assessment. Assessment is a vast topic, with many books written solely on this subject. This chapter does not attempt to cover all aspects of assessment but offers ideas of how teaching specific craft can support the development of authentic rubrics for classroom use.

Authentic assessment can mean different things to different teachers, so I should define what I mean when I use this term. The two main criteria that, in my opinion, make a rubric authentic are the following:

✿ Parts of the rubric reflect recent instruction
✿ The rubric communicates clear expectations to students

If a rubric reflects recent instruction, then the same rubric would not be used throughout the year. Creating a new rubric for each unit of study may not be what some teachers are used to, but if assessment is going to reflect instruction, then it really is essential. If writing workshop lessons came from a day-to-day manual, then a state or company-produced rubric would work as-is. Assessment would match instruction. The whole reason writing workshop is not a daily structured program is so teachers can base instruction on *their* students' needs. Premade rubrics can provide a very good starting place, but there is no other way to have rubrics that align with instruction except to have teachers involved in shaping them.

We don't use the same math test to assess different units in math. And we certainly don't use the same math test for third graders as we do for fourth graders. Shouldn't the same be true for writing? We may look at the same *aspects* of writing from grade to grade and unit to unit, but how can the same exact standard be used for different units of study or different grades? Where is the connection to instruction? And even if a class were to study the same genre at different times of the year, wouldn't they receive different lessons? If so, then each rubric should be slightly different, otherwise rubrics become not really an assessment of classroom learning but a periodic judging of work.

It's important to emphasize that I am primarily focusing on formative assessments that stay within the classroom and are part of the writing process. I am not referring to district or schoolwide data based on writing prompts, which *are* a periodic judging of work. In order to have comparative data, it's necessary to use the same rubric at different times of the year. Because this kind of rubric is used to assess an entire school or district on grade-level ability, it can't be personalized to classroom instruction. If classroom rubrics are going to be authentic, they inherently need to be different, even if only slightly, from those used for district or schoolwide data.

The Language of Rubrics

Assessing student writing with a new rubric for each unit of study doesn't mean teachers need to completely reinvent a rubric every time. The basic structure of the rubric can remain the same, as can some of the language. Books on writing assessment as well as any premade rubrics can be a great source for ideas about how to define each trait or aspect of writing. If teachers are using the 6-Trait writing approach, for example, those same six traits can provide a standard structure for each rubric. What can be changed is some of the language that describes each trait. There is always flexibility in this language, and most developers of rubrics support the personalizing of rubrics.

One reason teachers should adapt rubrics for their own classrooms is that it can help make the language more student-friendly when needed. When students receive copies of rubrics, they should be able to understand the criteria on which they are being assessed. I very often see rubrics with language that is very "writerly" but also general or nebulous. It's not that these more general expectations are not somewhat accurate of the overall goal, because of course we all want students' writing to "catch and hold the reader's attention" or "have striking words that linger in the reader's mind." We also want them to develop understanding of what it means for writing to have voice or sentence fluency and recognize it in read-alouds or other students' writing. But when it comes to producing a draft that will be scored with a rubric, it can be hard for students to rise to expectations when the expectations themselves are not that specific. The same is true for any goal. Imagine, for example, if a principal told teachers she was going to be doing a walk-through on the following criteria:

Classroom structures and materials support a literacy-rich environment

If it was my first year of teaching and I saw this criteria, I probably would not have had a very good idea of what was expected of me at all. In my first year, I was overwhelmed just with getting ready for the next day, so it would also have been very easy to forget about this expectation. It's not that I wouldn't agree a literacy-rich environment is important. But it's hard to give a lot of attention to an expectation when you don't really know what you can do to meet it. If I were given that expectation today, I would have a pretty good idea of what it might look like. Over the years I have learned the more specific criteria that make up this general goal, but it still doesn't guarantee that my understanding of a literacy-rich environment matches that of the principal who's giving the expectation.

It would be a very different story, however, if my principal, *along with* the above description, indicated more specifically what she meant:

Classroom Structures and Materials Support a Literacy-Rich Environment
Anchor charts are linked with recent instruction
Anchor charts are readable by all students in the classroom
Recent student work is posted

Literacy objectives for the day's lessons are posted

There is a writing center where students can get draft paper independently

When expectations are specific, it's more motivating to invest the energy needed to do well. With the more specific criteria, I know exactly what I could do in order to be successful. And if for some reason I wasn't motivated to be successful, expectations are a lot harder to ignore when they are specific. Notice that I also mentioned that these expectations would accompany and not replace the more general expectation. If I were that principal, I would still want to reinforce that these classroom criteria are what fall under "a literacy-rich environment."

In most rubrics, expectations about the more mechanical aspects of writing are quite clear and specific. Below are several descriptions that fall under the category of conventions or organization in various rubrics:

Correct subject-verb tense agreement is used

Written in a logical sequence

There is an inviting introduction

Ideas are organized into paragraphs

Spelling is mostly correct

Some of the above descriptors may be cumulative, grade-level expectations, and some might have been the focus of recent instruction. But they are all clear expectations. Although "an inviting introduction" may be a general term, the assumption is that lessons have been given on what that means for a particular genre. Regardless of whether students can master these types of expectations, they can, at the very least, understand these expectations.

Categories that have to do with craft and the descriptive aspect of writing, on the other hand, are not usually so concrete. Below are phrases that different rubrics use to describe word choice expectations.

Uses vivid, descriptive language

Words grab reader's attention

The writing is interesting to read

Striking words and phrases catch the readers' eye

The writer uses precise, fresh, original words

These phrases absolutely describe what we want students to do in their writing. For the sake of coming up with a score, these descriptions work fine. Most teachers don't find it difficult to assign a number based on these general descriptions. But they don't always mean that much to students because these goals are so general. When craft lessons teach students specific ways of being descriptive with word choice or writing with voice, then we are showing them

Table 12.1 Sample of Word Choice in a Rubric

WORD CHOICE	Words are powerful and engaging. Vocabulary used is not always average. Writing can include: • specific words such as brand names • variations of common words (especially for *said*)

ways to reach the more general expectations around voice and description that are on their rubrics. If a fourth-grade teacher taught lessons on using brand names and variations of words for *said*, then the category of word choice on a rubric could reflect this instruction (see Table 12.1).

Including topics of recent instruction in rubrics is not meant to replace the general descriptions of each trait or aspect of writing, because we always want students to keep the overall goal in mind. I would also want students to know they are being assessed on word choice in general, not solely on the use of brand names or variations of *said*. Students should understand that *any way* they use rich language will affect their score in word choice, whether they demonstrate something that was recently taught or not. The inclusion of specific craft just reminds students to take advantage of certain ways they recently learned to write with more engaging words.

A rubric's inclusion of instruction can also be cumulative. For example, if a fourth-grade teacher taught brand names in memoir, he or she might also include this craft technique under word choice in a rubric for a persuasive essay. One option would be to actually do a lesson on using brand names in relation to persuasive writing. Another option would be to just review it when students get a copy of the rubric.

Creating a Rubric

The best time to create a rubric is when students are about to write a first draft, about halfway through the writing process. This is the ideal time because it is after some writing instruction but before students start the final products on which they will be assessed. Creating a new rubric for each unit of study will be much easier if teachers keep a template of the overall traits to be assessed (either on paper or on a computer) along with descriptions of those traits. Ideally, the template also leaves blank space under each trait where recent instruction can be added or changed for each unit of study.

There are several different ways rubrics can be structured. Some rubrics offer explanations of what the aspects of writing look like at different levels. I personally prefer rubrics that present only the goals of each trait rather than a sliding scale of definitions. All I really want is for students to be aware of what to reach for, not what it would look like if they "somewhat" reached a goal, or "didn't really" reach a goal. I also find that as long as the goal for each trait is clear, it's really not that difficult to assign a number. Another reason to state only the desired goals on a rubric is that it lessens the number of words on the page. When a rubric is filled with words describing all the stages, it can be a little overwhelming for students. I do know some teachers who like having descriptions of what a trait or aspect of writing looks like at each stage. And if that makes teachers feel more comfortable in assessing writing, then of course that's important.

The tables that follow are several examples of how a rubric might look when it incorporates recent craft instruction. Table 12.2 is a fourth-grade rubric that uses 6-Trait writing as a guide. For the overall description, I used a

---

Table 12.2 Personal Narrative Rubric

		SCORE
IDEAS	*Ideas are developed and show previous planning.* Several revision entries helped to develop first draft Topic is focused enough to allow room for details	
ORGANIZATION	*The structure of the final draft helps move the reader through the text.* There is an inviting lead (besides "One day . . ." or "I remember when . . .") Draft is written in paragraphs There is a reflective conclusion or ending that gives closure	
VOICE	*The writer crafts the writing with an awareness of variety in tone and description. You can hear the person in their writing.* Writer sounds engaged in telling the story Writing can include: Different kinds of inside sentences (thoughts and feelings)	
WORD CHOICE	*Words are powerful and engaging. Vocabulary used is not always average.* Writing can include: Specific words instead of general words (proper nouns, brand names) Variations (for *said, looked,* and *walked*)	
SENTENCE FLUENCY	*Sentences vary in length and in structure.* Many sentences start with different words There are different-sized sentences: some short, some long	
CONVENTIONS	*Writer shows control of punctuation, spelling, and grammar.* Words are spelled correctly There is evidence of editing in the first draft Proper nouns have capitals Sentences end with proper punctuation	

combination of suggested language and my own wording. Some of the more specific expectations would be a result of recent instruction as well as grade-level and classroom expectations. It's important to point out that not every single trait will always reflect recent instruction. Although mini-lessons should represent a range of writing aspects, they may not always touch on all traits mentioned in a rubric.

Rather than using the 6-Trait or other established aspects of writing, another option is to create your own categories for rubrics. There have been many times in professional development sessions when teachers have spent a lot of time figuring out if students' wonderful descriptions and details should be reflected in the category of word choice or voice or ideas. This is natural, because some of the rubric language in these categories overlaps. This is reflective of the art of writing. When students write different-sized sentences, it affects sentence fluency, which in turn affects the voice of a piece: "*Voice* can be said, in its broadest sense, to encompass *word choice* and *sentence fluency* because it is closely connected to both" (Spandel 2004, 4). My recent thinking is that less overlapping might make expectations clearer to students. Table 12.3 is an example of how information similar to that in Table 12.2 might look with fewer categories.

Table 12.3 Alternative Personal Narrative Rubric

		SCORE
ORGANIZATION	*The final draft is clear and focused. There is a clear beginning and ending.* There is an inviting lead (besides "One day . . ." or "I remember when . . .") Draft is written in paragraphs There is a reflective conclusion or ending that gives closure	
DESCRIPTION	*The writer creates detailed images for the reader and has a variety of word choice. Topic is focused enough to allow room for details.* Writing can include: Different kinds of inside sentences (thoughts and feelings) Specific words instead of general words (proper nouns, brand names) Variations (for *said*, *looked*, and *walked*)	
SENTENCE FLUENCY	*The writer crafts the writing with an awareness of variety in tone. The writer is engaged in telling the story; you can hear his or her voice.* Writing can include: Different-sized sentences: some short, some long Sentences start with different words Sentences that use *as* to connect two ideas or actions	
MECHANICS	*Writer shows control of punctuation, spelling, and grammar.* All words are spelled correctly There is evidence of editing in the first draft Proper nouns have capitals Sentences end with proper punctuation	

Table 12.4 Sample of Illustration in a Rubric	
ILLUSTRATIONS	• Writing relates to the picture • Drawing is mostly filled up; not a lot of white space • There are small and big details in the picture

In other grades, teachers may want to emphasize different categories. If I were creating a first-grade rubric, for example, I would probably not choose to have voice as a category. I've certainly seen first-grade writing once in a while that sounds like the student and could be labeled as having voice. As Vicki Spandel points out, "Young students hear the traits long, long before those traits ever appear in their own writing" (2004, 12). We may support the recognition of voice in the early grades and create a foundation for writing with voice through talking and drawing, but it would not be a priority in terms of my instruction—certainly not to the point that I would want it to be a major category on an assessment. Instead, I might have a category that reflected the emphasis and instruction around drawing, which is an important part of primary writing (see Table 12.4).

Rubrics: Other Uses

In addition to being an assessment tool, rubrics can also be used as a planning tool at the start of a unit of study. Teachers can discuss which aspects of a genre they want students to develop. With a persuasive essay unit of study, what would our expectations be for voice? How would we word that? What does it mean for a persuasive essay to score high on sentence fluency? These questions would then ideally be followed with questions about next steps in instruction: How are we going to help students with this aspect of writing? What kinds of lessons could I teach?

Another way to use rubrics before students start their first drafts is to give them time to use the rubrics to assess samples of writing themselves. At the Thomas Kenny School, fourth-grade teacher Eli Jeremie and I have been saving copies of personal narrative essays from previous years for current students to score. When students receive a copy of a rubric, they have to discuss and score several anonymous essays in pairs. Students love it. They have spent their whole academic life receiving grade after grade. When they get to be on the other side, they really get into the task. Mr. Jeremie emphasizes that, along with this new power of assigning scores, they also have to be ready to explain their choices. They have to ask each other why: Why did you give this a 3 in organization? Why did you give this a 2 in word choice? After students talk in pairs, we have a class conversation about the scores they chose and the reasons behind them. This activity and discussion is helpful in familiarizing students with the expectations of the rubric, but also it is beneficial in quietly building up their own expectations of what they can do. When students critique their own writing, they can be distracted by the thought of having to rework their writing if they expose any weaknesses. By critiquing *someone else's* writing using the rubric, there are no consequences, so students can be free to be as generous or critical as the writing calls for.

I love watching students discuss essays with this kind of freedom. I recall one time when Mr. Jeremie asked some students why they gave an essay a 1 for organization. One boy held up the paper with a slight look of disgust. "What do you mean?" he said. "There's not even any paragraphs, man! The whole thing is just one big thing of writing." A girl across from him raised her hand, her face already showing annoyance with his opinion. "Yeah, but it still makes sense," she replied defensively, as if she had written it. "And there's a lead and also he put a last sentence. So it's not *that* bad."

This kind of discussion is not so unlike conversations teachers have when they talk about and score student writing using a rubric. Some focus more on what is missing and some focus more on what is there. This kind of dialogue, both for teachers and students, is helpful in developing an ability to see both strengths and weakness in student writing to determine a fair score. Conversations about scoring, however, should eventually lead to conversations about how these assessments can impact instruction. During professional development or in meetings to look at student work, the question that seems to get the most attention is, What number should we give it and why? Although it is important for teachers to feel comfortable discussing different aspects of writing and to discuss reasons behind suggested scores, the question that should get the most attention is, So what are we going to do about it?

This is where this book comes full circle, just as instruction and assessment should. Crafting writers starts with looking at our students' writing from all angles, and then based on those observations, moves on to planning specific teaching points, from craft techniques to mechanics to writers' strategies, that will help students develop their own unique repertoires for writing. If students need support in word choice, the next questions should be, How am I going to do that? What lessons can I plan that will help students increase the range of vocabulary they use in their writing? As you might guess by now, my suggestion would be that saying, "Teach more lessons on word choice" or "Teach lessons about exciting words" is a step in the right direction, but not a final answer. Ideally, what we offer in response to our assessments is one small, specific craft technique or writing strategy at a time that, lesson by lesson and conference by conference, will help students improve their ability to craft writing.

Final Thoughts

Crafting Writers looks at the art of writing before discussing the teaching of writing, but of course this is not reflective of what actually happens throughout a school year. We don't learn everything we can about writing at the beginning of the year and then for the rest of the year teach what we learned. There is a constant circular movement between what we notice about writing and what we teach. This happens on a larger, more public scale when teachers use rubrics to assess student writing, which may take place every few months when final drafts are turned in or when district prompts are administered. The circular movement of noticing and teaching happens at the classroom level when we notice patterns in our students' writing and respond in the next few days with whole-class lessons. This cycle of assessment and instruction—noticing and teaching—also occurs on a much smaller level during our conferences. One minute we are talking with students and noticing what they are doing in their writing, and only a few minutes later we are teaching them based on this information. The different-sized cycles of assessment and instruction that happen at different times are what allow us to get the most information about students in addition to providing more than one medium in which we can support students as writers.

Unlike assessment and instruction, the formal study of writing, whether it's through reading professional books such as this one or studying children's literature, is not an automatic part of the school day or even the school year. But when we tap into these resources, we can greatly increase the quality of assessment and instruction around writing. We don't need to formally study writing on a consistent basis. Teachers can spend just one or two grade-team meetings studying the writing of a particular genre, whether it's published writing or their students' writing, to support the next few months of instruction.

Getting to know some of the little secrets behind writing has helped me offer more specific teaching points in craft lessons and conferences, but my favorite part of gathering many specific craft techniques is being able to see these secrets in students' writing. Although it's wonderful when students produce final drafts with strong voice and vivid description that we can't wait to share with other teachers, those are not the moments that first come to mind when I think about the pleasures of teaching writing. What I remember most are the quieter moments in conferences with students like Jonathan, moments when I genuinely see strengths in students' writing and help them understand what they can do as writers. Those are the times that remind me of the incredible responsibility and privilege we have as teachers in the way we see our students and the way we influence how they see themselves.

Additional Mini-Lessons on Craft

Mini-Lesson: Inventive Spelling: Taking Risks with Words

The following mini-lesson is one I teach in the primary grades to support inventive spelling. Although it could be considered more a strategy lesson than a craft lesson, inventive spelling—and students' willingness to use it independently—directly affects word choice as well as volume. Students in the primary grades hear the phrase "Sound it out" all the time, both in reading and writing. I find that taking the time to model what I want students to do with unfamiliar words in addition to having them do a writing try-it helps give that extra push to students who may be reluctant to be independent when sounding out bigger words.

Because this lesson is taught in a first- or second-grade classroom, students usually come to a rug area for the lesson, where I use a whiteboard or chart paper to model.

Connection

These last few days I've noticed a lot of you using the word wall, which is great. But I've also noticed that when some of you want to spell a big word, like a third- or fourth-grade word, you keep asking me how to spell it.

Mini-Lesson

One thing we're going to work on today is sounding out words you're not sure how to spell, which is something you can do by yourself. We want you to take risks with bigger words. You could write sentences like, "We had a nice party," *(I usually say this sample sentence in a slight monotone voice)* and spell every single word right. But I'd rather you try to write, "I had such a special birthday celebration!" That's how you grow as a writer. Of course, if you know how to spell a word, we want you to spell it correctly. And we want you to use the word wall for words we've studied. But you're in second grade: you're not *supposed* to know how to spell *all* the words you want to write!

So, when you get to those bigger words you want to write, just keep saying the word to yourself and write the sounds you hear. You don't need us to sound it out for you. Pretend I don't know how to write the word *special*. That's definitely not a second-grade word. I would just keep saying it to myself and write what I hear. *On the chart paper I model writing the word* special *with inventive spelling while thinking out loud. Every few letters I pause and say the word to myself again. I model listening to what I hear, then writing a few more letters. My inventive spelling word usually ends up looking something like* speshul.

Now, that's not really how you spell *special*. But if you don't know how to spell a word, this is what we want you to do—write what you hear. Okay, now you're going to try this yourselves.

Writing Try-It *Students go to their desks, where they write in the try-it section in their notebooks or on a try-it piece of paper.*

Everyone turn to the try-it section. Okay, now write this at the top of your next blank page. *On the overhead I write the date and then "Writing by Myself."*

Now, I am going to give you some hard words—words you're definitely not supposed to know how to spell in second grade. And when I say that word, I just want you to say it to yourself and write what you hear. Are you ready? Okay. The first word is *building. Just about every time I do this lesson, all students can do this try-it. When I walk around the classroom, I comment on how they are sounding out to themselves rather than on the letters they choose. The words look different but always have at least some of the sounds. Another word that is good to start with is beautiful.*

Okay, this next word is a little harder. Are you sure you're ready? All right, the next one is *encyclopedia. Usually at this one, I get lots of surprised but excited looks and the "Whoa!"-smile combination. If there is time, I usually do one more. The figures show several examples. In this case, the third word is* delicious.

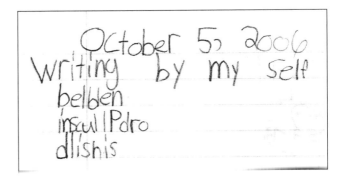

So today when you write a big word like *cousin* or *chocolate*, should you raise your hand and say, "Ms. Hale! Ms. Hale!"? *I imitate the desperate look that usually goes with this expression. Students usually laugh as they shake their heads and say, "No!" I am fishing for an answer, of course, but I do this with a purpose. I want to put a visual to what I am trying to steer them away from. This is somewhat similar to the "before" example in exaggerated writing as described in Chapter 7. By making a behavior concrete, you ensure that students are more likely to recognize it. This in turn allows them to make a choice not to do it.* That's right. You just sounded out other big words like *encyclopedia*. That's like a fifth-grade word! So you can definitely sound out any word to yourself.

Okay, it's time for independent writing. If anyone reaches for some bigger words today, we'll have some time to share at the end of the period.

Mini-Lesson: **Starting a Sentence with an *Ing* Phrase**

The following mechanics lesson introduces the concept of starting a sentence with an ing word. This lesson is most appropriate in the upper elementary or middle school grades when students are writing in complete sentences but could use support with different ways to write sentences. How I present lessons is influenced by previous instruction. For example, if I have already taught a lesson on using as to join two actions or descriptions, I would allude to this first and then tell students I am going to show them another way a writer can put two different actions in one sentence.

Connection   Many of you know how to use a comma in your writing for things like a series and with dialogue. But using commas can also help you add more information or details to your sentences, which I think you're ready to learn. Today I'm going to show you one way commas can help you add a descriptive detail to a sentence.

Mini-Lesson   Here are a few sentences that probably seem fine just the way they are. *The following sentences are already on the overhead. Each set of sentences below can be written ahead of time and then uncovered with a piece of paper as the lesson goes on.*

> Chrissy went running onto the beach. She was holding her oversized Snoopy towel.

The second sentence here adds more detail, but you don't always have to wait for that second sentence to add more description. Instead, you can sometimes start a sentence with the *ing* form of a verb. So, instead my sentence could look like this:

> Holding her oversized Snoopy towel, Chrissy went running onto the beach.

By starting with an *ing* word, I put two descriptions of what Chrissy is doing in one sentence. And the comma is what lets me do that. If I didn't have the comma there, then the reader would get confused.

When you are writing in your notebooks, of course, you don't need to go back, find two sentences you already wrote, and put them together this way. You could, but what I really want you to do is think about using *ing* sentences *as* you write. These kinds of sentences have two actions, so I notice that I use them a lot with people. What that means is that when you are about to write a sentence about someone doing something, look carefully in your mind and see if there is something else you can describe at the same time.

So, say I was writing about the time I picked up my friend Sarah at the airport and was about to write the following sentence: "I shouted to my friend Sarah." I could think back to that memory and look for something more to describe about myself. It could be something big, like a movement, or something smaller, like a facial expression. I could think back like this: "Hmmm. . . . Oh, yeah!" and then I would write the following sentence:

Waving my arms in the air, I shouted to my friend Sarah.

I showed two things I was doing in one sentence—waving my arms and shouting. You wouldn't write these *ing* sentences all the time, but once in a while this is a great way to add description to a sentence. It also helps with sentence variety, because it's one way to write a longer, more complex sentence.

Turn-and-Talk Try-It   Turn to the person next to you and tell them one way you can add a description to your sentences that I just showed you.

Writing Try-It   Okay, now it's your turn to try it. In the try-it section of your notebook, write the date and then write this at the top, "Starting sentences with *ing*." Then write a few sentences about the lunchroom, and see if you can write one or two sentences that start with an *ing* word. Okay, go ahead.

Several students share their try-its.

Okay, it's time for independent writing. See if today you can try one or two sentences that start with *ing*.

Mini-Lessons for Independence in Memoir Writing

Mini-Lesson: **Let a Story Spark a Memory**

Because this is usually the first lesson I do in a memoir unit of study, it doesn't sound like a lesson when it starts off. I like just sharing my writing and my story with a class before I get into the lesson.

Connection   *You can begin this lesson either by telling a memory of yours or by reading one that you wrote. I always read a memoir entry I wrote about the time my sister burned her knee at the beach, because I know students can relate to being at the ocean, getting hurt, or siblings. When I finish, I ask if my memory made anyone think of something that happened in their lives.*

Turn and talk to a person next to you and tell them what memory my story sparked for you.

Mini-Lesson   *Tell students that when they are stuck for an idea of what to write about during independent writing, they can use someone else's story to spark a memory. It could be a story they heard on the bus, a read-aloud from reading workshop, or a memory that someone shared yesterday. This strategy would then be listed on an anchor chart titled "Ways to Come Up with Topics for Memoir Entries."*

Try-It   So, tell the person next to you one strategy you can use now if you are stuck for a memory to write about today.

It is important to note that even though many students end up writing about the memory they talk about, I teach it as a strategy they can use from now on. This is not a lesson I tend to repeat. To further support student ownership, I always use the phrase "if you are stuck for an idea" when introducing independence strategies, regardless of the genre. Students need to know these lessons are not directions for just that day, but strategies they can use from then on.

Mini-Lesson: **Look Around the Room**

Connection   Today I am going to show you another way to come up with ideas for memoir entries so you can be independent writers.

Mini-Lesson   Another strategy you can use if you're not sure what to write about is to look around the room. Sometimes objects, whether they are big or very small, can spark a memory. *I model searching the room using this strategy. Then I share an object that sparked a memory. One time when I did this in a lesson, I pointed to the little, red, square fire alarm on the wall and told the class how it reminded me of the time in my first year of teaching when one of my students pulled the fire alarm and got so scared he hid in the closet. I emphasize the fact that the memory is not something I have thought of in a while but that looking at the small object made me remember that day.*

Try-It   Without talking, try doing this: Look around the room. See if you can find one thing, even something really small, that sparks a memory. Okay, now tell the person next to you if you found something that sparked a memory. *After they turn and talk, a few students can share. The best part of this strategy is that students come up with memories they might not have thought about otherwise, just by looking at a vent, a picture on an alphabet strip, or the keyboard on a computer. After a few students share, I say it's time for independent writing and remind them that if they are stuck, looking around the room is a strategy they can now use.*

- -

Mini-Lesson: What To Do When You Finish an Entry

Connection   These last few days I gave you some strategies for coming up with your own ideas. This is so you can be independent—you don't need me to tell you what to write about. Remember, you don't have to use these strategies—you can write about any memory. Because you've learned strategies for how to come up with topic ideas, you also don't need to tell me when you're done. So today we're going to go over what to do when you think you have finished an entry.

Mini-Lesson   When it's time for independent writing, the first thing you should do is reread a little bit of what you already wrote the day before. Then you have two choices. You can keep writing about the same memory or you can start a new entry. If you want to continue with the same memory, just write the date in the margin. *I model this on chart paper or an overhead.* If you decide to start a new entry, you can skip a few lines, write the date, and start writing. *I model this as well.*

Here is a poster to remind you of what to do when you finish an entry. *I have students read the poster with me.* You 1) Reread what you wrote; 2) Ask yourself: Can I add more?; 3) Start a new entry. You don't have to call me over and raise your hand and say, "Ms. Hale, I'm done!" I'll see your writing in our conferences. Instead, where should you look when you're done with an entry and you're not sure what to write about? Right, you use the poster.

Try-It   Turn to the person next to you and see if you can tell each other the three things you do when you think you have finished an entry.

Mini-Lesson: **Memory Sparker Poster**

Connection   I noticed yesterday several people looking at the poster when they finished an entry. Great job. You're definitely working like independent writers. Today I'm going to show you one more way to come up with ideas for a memoir entry.

Mini-Lesson   If you are stuck for what to write about, you can also use this memory sparker poster that has several possible beginnings on it, such as "I remember the first time I . . ." Sometimes just writing down the beginning of a sentence can make you think of something to write about. *I model using one of the beginnings for several different memories—just saying what the memory is about, not telling the whole story. It's important to note that these beginnings are not prompts. Not only is the use of the poster totally optional, but beginnings lead to many different memories for different people.*

Try-It   Now you try it. Pick one of the beginnings and see if it can make you think of a few memories. Turn to the person next to you and tell them what memory the poster sparked for you.

✿ ✿ ✿

The figures on the next page are examples of posters that support independence.

Posters for Independence

Ways to Get Ideas for Entries in Writing Workshop

📖 Let a story you heard spark a memory

👁 Look around the room

✿ Use the "Memory Sparker" poster

When You Finish an Entry

1. Reread what you wrote

2. Ask yourself: Can I add more?

3. Start a new entry

Memory Sparkers ✿

I'll never forget the time I . . .

I was so nervous when . . .

I remember the first time I . . .

Mini-Lessons for Independence in Nonfiction Writing

While there are many ways to write nonfiction, the following lessons relate to a unit of study that I call "Expert Nonfiction." Students write about topics they know a lot about rather than use outside research for information. Students will need to practice writing based on research during their middle school years and beyond. But very often when students dive into research writing in the elementary grades, they are caught between expectations that they write factual information but not copy facts from the text. Meanwhile, the reading of nonfiction text tends to suffer, because rather than focusing on all the rich comprehension skills for reading nonfiction, students tend to be busy picking out information to put into their writing. This is not to say students in the elementary grades should not write about topics they learn and read about in science and social studies, and knowing how to take notes from nonfiction text is certainly a skill students will eventually need. My point is to emphasize that writing without research first can create a foundation for nonfiction writing in general. I have found this unit incredibly valuable, because it allows students to develop their nonfiction writing skills *before* they have to balance it with research, whether that comes later in the year or in a later grade. Students also love it. I've done this unit of study with first grade up through fifth grade. Even though they may not know everything there is to know about more academic subjects such as sharks or the moon, they still know enough information about these kinds of topics to write about them. And when students understand that skills such as babysitting, shopping for shoes, and bike riding are also sets of knowledge they can share, they become much more invested in what they write. An added benefit of this unit of study is getting to know your students in ways that might otherwise not come up during regular class time.

I always make a point in any grade to model informational nonfiction rather than "how-to" entries. How-to pieces are a genre, and many primary teachers like how this genre supports the concept of sequence, but in the elementary grades it can be limiting in terms of helping students develop as writers. Unlike how-to writing, expert nonfiction is not as susceptible to sounding like directions with many sentences that begin with *And then*.

Mini-Lesson: Generating Ideas for Expert Entries

The first day of a unit can be a day to steep students in the upcoming genre. In this case, you could read several nonfiction books aloud (which then become future teaching tools for that genre), students could discuss what the term nonfiction means, and they could have time to browse nonfiction books in pairs before gathering as a class to share the topics they read about.

Connection   *Allude to books and topics you talked about the day before where the terms* expert *and* expertise *might have been discussed.*

Mini-Lesson   Remember the books we looked at yesterday? Those authors know a lot about their topics, and we are all experts on different things. So tomorrow, you're going to start writing about topics you know a lot about. But first, to help you get ideas for topics, you're going to brainstorm a list of things you are experts on. I'll show you what my expert list might look like.

At the top of an overhead I write, "I Know a lot about . . ." and then make a list while I think aloud. I make a point to tell students that I include topics that are common (such as teaching, driving, coffee) as well as topics that are more unique to me (swimming, Italy, making risotto). I list about ten to twelve topics.

Turn-and-Talk Try-It   Now it's your turn to think of things you are experts on. Tell the person next to you some of the things that you know a lot about.

Writing Try-It   Turn to the next blank page in your notebook. Write today's date and then at the top write, "I Know a Lot About: *They could also write "Expert Topic List"*. Then you can start writing down your expert list. Try to list at least eight or ten topics. Okay, go ahead.

On this day you can have an extended share. Students can also talk in pairs about what they know about some of the topics they listed. I usually wait for the next day before students actually write.

Mini-Lesson: **Expert Nonfiction Versus Memoir**

Although the following lesson is not about generating ideas, I do find that it sets an important foundation for students being able to write their expert nonfiction pieces independently.

Connection   *Allude to the writing that students did in a memoir unit (regardless of how long ago it was) and how that genre was a chance to share and revisit their unique memories.*

Mini-Lesson   Today you'll start writing about your expert topics. Writing nonfiction is different from the writing you did during the memoir unit. When people read nonfiction, they are not looking to hear someone's personal story—they want facts about a topic. They want information. So, when you start writing about your expert topics today, one word that's good to avoid is the word *I*, because we usually use words like *I* or *me* when we're telling our own story. For example, if I were writing a memoir about going swimming, I might say: "I remember one time I had a swim race last year. It was in Florida with an outdoor pool . . ." *I share this memory for about 30 or 40 seconds.*

But if someone was reading a nonfiction piece about swimming, they wouldn't want to hear my story—they want facts on swimming. So now I'm going to write about swimming on the overhead, but what word am I not going to use? Right, I'm not going to use the word *I*—or *me* or *mine. Especially in the younger grades, students will once in a while use I in their nonfiction pieces. As long as the entry does not become a memoir, it's usually fine.*

I model using live writing on the overhead. I'll usually write five or six sentences about swimming. When I'm done, I reread it out loud. If modeling this lesson in the primary grades, I might draw lots of picture facts rather than a scene that tells a story. For example, for the topic of swimming, I would make little pictures of goggles, a pool, a bathing suit, fins, and so on.

Try-It   Tell the person next to you the word you're going to try to not use too much as you write nonfiction today. Now see if you can tell the person next to you why you don't usually use the word *I* in nonfiction.

Mini-Lessons for Independence in Poetry Writing

The following lessons on poetry emphasize free verse, where students are not following formulas for writing poems. This is not to say there is not a place for the study and writing of structured poems such as haiku and diamantes. You could still have a unit of study on these more formulaic poems *in addition* to the unit described here.

One reason not to focus only on form poems is that there tends to be a lot of repetition throughout the grades. Lots of teachers end up teaching them. Another reason is when writing these kinds of poems, a student is not using language to the potential the genre of poetry offers. When teaching diamantes, for example, a teacher can expect that each student will probably come up with a nice product, but there is less decision-making on the students' part in terms of word choice, line breaks, and style. Teaching poetry within a workshop means we support students' independence, not to mention the fact that most contemporary published poetry is written in free verse. Letting go of having every single poem being predictably "nice" may be difficult for some teachers at first, but the pay-off is that you will help students create images and verse in their own words and uncover some amazing voices in the process.

Mini-Lesson: **Generating Ideas for Poems**

Teachers can spend the first day of this unit of study building enthusiasm for poetry through read-alouds, by having students look through poetry books in pairs or small groups, and by having class conversations that tap into students' background knowledge

Connection   Yesterday we had a great conversation about poetry and you had a chance to read and share poems from our classroom library.

Mini-Lesson   Tomorrow you're going to start writing your own poems. To get ready for that, we're going to make a list of things you could write poems about. You can write a poem about anything you'd like, but if you're stuck for ideas, it's good to have a list of possible topics.

One category of topics you can think about is nature. A lot of people write poems about nature. Even though we know the science behind things like ocean waves and rain, there is still something mysterious and beautiful about nature that seems to draw people to write poems about them.

After I explain this first category, I do the following:

1. *Write a few examples on the overhead*
2. *Have the class give me a few that I write down*
3. *Tell students they can start their lists. I encourage them to write down at least eight or ten topics*

Another category you can write poems about is everyday things. These are things you see or use every day, like a pencil, a driveway, or a shoe. I love these kinds of poems because it makes you look at the things you see all the time in a different way.

I then follow the same three steps listed above: write examples, take examples from the class, and have students write their own lists.

Try-It   Turn to the person next to you and share some of the topic ideas you came up with today. *A brief whole-class share can follow. I tend to have a longer share time because I don't want to merge this lesson with the following one, which needs their full attention and an entire class period. Ten minutes of this day can also be used for students to read more poems in pairs or decorate a poetry page in their writing notebook that marks the beginning of this new unit.*

Mini-Lesson: **Writing Free Verse Poems**

I tell students that for now, our poems are not going to rhyme. After this poetry unit, teachers can do a two- or three-week unit of rhyming poetry/rap lyrics. I explain to students that when you don't have to rhyme, you can put your energy into descriptions rather than figuring out what word rhymes with orange. Having a later unit of rhyming poetry validates the playful sound and students' enjoyment of rhyming.

Mini-Lesson   To try writing a free verse poem, where you don't have to follow a certain form or pattern, you're going to try something called freewrite. It just means you write whatever comes to your mind. You don't have to think about making complete sentences or paragraphs—you write whatever you see, whatever you feel. That's why a lot of time free verse poems don't have complete sentences but phrases. If you're writing about the beach you don't have to write, "The big waves are crashing on the sand." You can just write "big waves crashing." So, right now I am going to pick a topic on my poetry list. Hmmm. . . . I think I'll pick . . . coffee.

I go to the overhead and think about my topic for a few seconds. During the think-aloud for this poem I say things like, "Hmmm, okay, I'm thinking of what coffee looks like . . . hmmm what else, coffee is. . . . I'm thinking about it in my cup . . ."

The think-aloud in this lesson is very important. Students need to see that thinking and some effort are needed to go against the rules of the standard sentence. Once I finish, I reread the whole poem out loud.

<u>Coffee</u>

dark brown in
my cup
Every morning
waking me up
From the Earth
right to mugs

Steam rises as I close
my eyes
and smile

If you are not yet comfortable doing a freewrite in front of students off the top of your head, you can think ahead of time of some phrases you might write. Then when you write on the overhead, you think out loud as if they are just coming to you. However you choose to do it, modeling is essential to students understanding the concept of a freewrite. Students will not get it by explanation alone.

So remember, freewrite means you write whatever comes to your mind and you don't have to write in sentences.

Try-It   Turn to the person next to you and see if you can tell each other what it means to write a freewrite poem.

Forms for Researching Craft

Gathering Craft from Literature

Book _____ **Author** _____

Text	Page	Specific Craft	Why Is It Good?

Researching Student Writing

Student Name _____

Researching Strengths

Craft	Mechanics

Researching Next Steps

Craft	Mechanics

Conference Sheet

Name _____

Date	Working On	Strength	Next Step	Maybe Next Time . . .

F

Guided Practice in Researching Craft

Guided Practice #1

Imagine you are conferring with the student whose notebook entry is reproduced below. Look for possible strengths and possible next steps to teach this student. Think about all the specific craft skills presented in Chapters 4, 5, and 6. You can jot down your ideas and then compare them to what I noticed, shown on the back of this page.

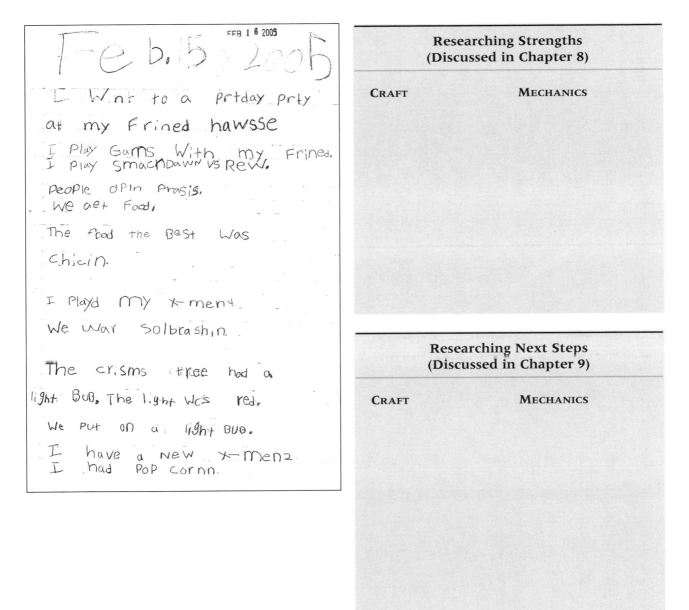

FEB 1 6 2005

Feb. 15, 2005

I Wnt to a prtday prty at my Frined hawsse

I Play Gams With my Frined.
I play smackdawn vs Rew.

People oPln Prasis.
We aet Food.

The food the Best Was

Chicin.

I Playd my x-meny.
We war Solbrashin.

The crisms tree had a
light BuB. The light Wes red.

We put on a light BuB.
I have a New x-men2
I had PoP cornn.

**Researching Strengths
(Discussed in Chapter 8)**

CRAFT	MECHANICS

**Researching Next Steps
(Discussed in Chapter 9)**

CRAFT	MECHANICS

For Comparison

Researching Strengths	
CRAFT	**MECHANICS**
Proper nouns: writes the specific name of the game	Inventive spelling: reaching for bigger words; could have written "We were having fun" but instead wrote "solbrashin" (celebrating)
Named specific kind of food	
Uses colors to describe	Uses periods at the end of sentences
	Fills up the page

Researching Next Steps	
CRAFT	**MECHANICS**
Including people's names	Writing to the end of the line
Using word wall (or other supports) for high-frequency words	Not writing capital letters in the middle of sentences
Staying with one memory at a time	
Inside sentences (feelings)	

If I were reading this sample of student writing during an actual conference, I would have the benefit of asking questions. For example, I would wonder if he was writing about two different parties, because he mentions both a birthday party and a Christmas tree. It could have been a December birthday, but this is the kind of information that can only be understood through conversation, further emphasizing that this kind of practice is meant to strengthen only one aspect of conferring, not to mimic what an actual conference is like.

Guided Practice #2

Similar to the process with the first guided practice, jot down strengths and possible next steps you notice in the following sample of student writing.

I had to stend on the top. It was horrible! Before, the first time I climbed, I felt accomplished that I touched the top, but Noo!! I had to go stend on top of I couldn't come down. As you climb your wearing a harness which the pull you as you climb with a rope (on a pulley) which is clipped to your harness, so if you slip up while climbing and fall you'll just dangle, your safe. So then you stend on the top. I was admirering the view, it's a great view! Then the counselor down below with the rope tells you to lean back and walk backward down. Some say —I think just to be funny— say, "Just lean back, like in the song! Lean back!" Some even did the movement with it. (Easier said then done!) So, I looked to the sky, prayed quick and asked him if he had a good grip on the rope, So after him reassuring me —more than twice— I lean back ever-so-slowly. It was fun. I did the moonwalk for a bit on the way down, then I tripped over a letter and I kept going more scared. It took forever to get down when I did I didn't see the ground and I sat on the ground with a kes-plop! Otherwise it was fun.

Next Mission: Kayaking. Before I go into that let me just say I fell in the lake. Luckily I had a life jacket or I would've been completely soaked right to the marrow.

Researching Strengths
(Discussed in Chapter 8)

CRAFT	MECHANICS

Researching Next Steps
(Discussed in Chapter 9)

CRAFT	MECHANICS

For Comparison

Researching Strengths		Researching Next Steps	
CRAFT	**MECHANICS**	**CRAFT**	**MECHANICS**
Uses different sized sentences	Uses comma (and phrases) to give a quick explanation to the reader	Mention people's names	Comma sometimes used where not needed
Begins a sentence with *As*	Use of commas throughout gives a variety of rhythms to sentences	Sense of smell	Being aware of using too many exclamation points
Gives reader an actual lyric when mentioning a song		Using *so . . . that* to further describe a feeling (being scared)	
Writes actual sound ("ker-plop")	Uses parentheses to give a quick explanation to the reader ("on a pulley")	Starting a sentence with an *ing* word	
Uses a range of "non-average" vocabulary • *accomplished* • *admiring* • *mission*	An advanced type of inside sentence: Uses dashes to set apart an aside ("I think just to be funny")		
Gives an ending thought at the end of the paragraph	Also uses parentheses for an aside ("Easier said than done")		
	Uses dashes to emphasis how to say something ("ever-so-slowly")		
	Use of paragraph spaces		

Because this writing shows a very good command of language as well as punctuation, there is a good chance this student would be somewhat verbal about her intentions for this piece or ideas about her writing. And if a student of this ability did not have much to offer in the way of talking about plans or next steps, then that could become my teaching point. Rather than look at the finer aspects of her writing, I might want to strengthen her ability to be reflective about her own writing. As I mentioned earlier, however, even when writing is "good," we can still come to the table with an eye ready to notice small craft steps that *might* become next steps.

APPENDIX

List of Specific Craft Presented in Chapters 4, 5, and 6

243

Chapter 4: Categories of Specific Craft

The Five Senses

Sense of Sound	Table 4.1	Page 36
Sense of Smell	Table 4.2	Page 38
Sense of Taste	Table 4.3	Page 38
Sense of Touch	Table 4.4	Page 39
Colors	Table 4.5	Page 40
Comparing	Table 4.6	Page 41
Specific Versus General	Table 4.7	Page 42
Describing the Background	Table 4.8	Page 43

Show Not Tell

Feelings	Table 4.9	Page 45
Thoughts and Feelings	Table 4.10	Page 45
Thoughts	Table 4.11	Page 46
Showing After Telling	Table 4.12	Page 47

Dialogue

Words Next to Dialogue	Table 4.13	Page 50
Dialogue Structures	Table 4.14	Page 52

Sentence Variety

Sentence Length and Sentence Beginnings	Table 4.15	Page 53
Combinations with *As*	Table 4.16	Page 55
Combinations with *While*	Table 4.17	Page 56
Combinations with *Until*	Table 4.18	Page 56

Word Choice

Variations of Common Verbs		Pages 58–59
Variations of Moods and Feelings		Page 60

Chapter 5: Crafting with Punctuation

Punctuation

Periods	Table 5.1	Page 67
Exclamation Points	Table 5.2	Page 67
Question Marks	Table 5.3	Page 68
Quotation Marks Around Dialogue	Table 5.4	Page 68
Quotation Marks Around Personal Names or Phrases	Table 5.5	Page 69
Quotation Marks to Show a Term Is Used Loosely	Table 5.6	Page 70

Crafting with Commas

Commas in a Series	Table 5.7	Page 71
Commas with Reverse Combinations	Table 5.8	Page 74
Commas with *Ing* Phrases	Table 5.9	Page 75
Different Places for *Ing* Phrases	Table 5.10	Page 76
Descriptive Phrases	Table 5.11	Page 77

Chapter 6: Primary Writing

Craft Techniques in Drawing	Table 6.1	Page 84
Shaping and Spelling Words	Table 6.2	Page 88
Using Capital Letters	Table 6.3	Page 88
Basic Craft Skills for Primary-Level Writers	Table 6.4	Page 90

References

Anderson, Carl. 2000. *How's It Going? A Practical Guide to Conferring with Student Writers*. Portsmouth, NH: Heinemann.

Anderson, Jeff. 2005. *Mechanically Inclined: Building Grammar, Usage, and Style into Writer's Workshop*. Portland, ME: Stenhouse.

Angelillo, Janet. 2002. *A Fresh Approach to Teaching Punctuation*. New York: Scholastic.

Beck, Isabel, Margaret G. McKeown, and Linda Kucan. 2002. *Bringing Words to Life: Robust Vocabulary Instruction*. New York: Guilford.

Calkins, Lucy. 1994. *The Art of Teaching Writing*. Portsmouth, NH: Heinemann.

———. 2001. *The Art of Teaching Reading*. New York: Longman.

Calkins, Lucy, and Mary Chiarella. 2006. "Memoir: Putting It All Together." In *Units of Study for Teaching Writing, Grades 3–5*. Portsmouth, NH: Heinemann.

Calkins, Lucy, Amanda Hartman, and Zoe White. 2005. *One to One: The Art of Conferring with Young Writers.* Portsmouth, NH: Heinemann.

Calkins, Lucy, Marjorie Martinelli, Ted Kesler, Cory Gillette, Medea McEvoy, Mary Chiarella, and M. Colleen Cruz. 2006. *Units of Study for Teaching Writing, Grades 3–5.* Portsmouth, NH: Heinemann.

Clark, Roy Peter. 2006. *Writing Tools: 50 Essential Strategies for Every Writer.* New York: Little, Brown.

Craven, Wes. 1999. *Music of the Heart.* Film. New York: Miramax.

Gray, Libba Moore. 1995. *My Mama Had a Dancing Heart.* New York: Orchard Books.

Horn, Martha, and Mary Ellen Giacobbe. 2007. *Talking, Drawing, Writing: Lessons for Our Youngest Writers.* Portland, ME: Stenhouse.

Johnston, Peter H. 2004. *Choice Words: How Our Language Affects Children's Learning.* Portland, ME: Stenhouse.

LaGravanese, Richard. 2007. *Freedom Writers.* Film. Los Angeles, CA: Paramount.

Menendez, Ramon. 1988. *Stand and Deliver.* Film. Burbank, CA: Warner Brothers.

Peters, Stephen G. 2006. *Do You Know Enough About Me To Teach Me?* Orangeburg, SC: The Peters Group Foundation.

Pinnell, Gay Su, and Patricia L. Scharer. 2003. *Teaching for Comprehension in Reading, Grades K–2: Strategies for Helping Children Read with Ease, Confidence, and Understanding.* New York: Scholastic.

Polacco, Patricia. 1992. *Chicken Sunday.* New York: Philomel.

Ray, Katie Wood. 1999. *Wondrous Words: Writers and Writing in the Elementary Classroom.* Urbana, IL: National Council of Teachers of English.

Rylant, Cynthia. 1996. *The Whales.* New York: Scholastic.

Spandel, Vicki. 2004. *Creating Young Writers: Using the Six Traits to Enrich Writing Process in Primary Grades.* 2nd ed. Boston, MA: Allyn and Bacon.

———. 2005. *Creating Writers Through 6-Trait Writing Assessment and Instruction.* 4th ed. Boston, MA: Allyn and Bacon.

Williams, Vera B. 1991. *Cherries and Cherry Pits.* New York: HarperCollins.

Index

Page numbers followed by an *f* or a *t* indicate figures or tables.